Bitter Winds

A Memoir of My Years in China's Gulag

Harry Wu
and
Carolyn Wakeman

A ROBERT L. BERNSTEIN BOOK

John Wiley & Sons Inc.
New York • Chichester • Brisbane • Toronto • Singapore

This text is printed on acid-free paper.

Published by John Wiley & Sons, Inc.

All rights reserved. Published simultaneously in Canada.

Library of Congress Cataloging-in-Publication Data:
Wu, Hongda Harry.
    Bitter winds : a memoir of my years in China's Gulag / Harry Wu and Carolyn Wakeman
        p. cm.
    ISBN 0-471-11425-1
    1. China—Politics and government—1949– 2. Wu, Hongda Harry. 3. Political prisoners—China—Biography. I. Wakeman, Carolyn. II. Title.
DS777.75.W787 1993
951.05'092—dc20
[B]   93-15799

Printed in the United States of America

10 9 8 7 6 5 4

For those who can never come to tell their own stories. My parents, my youngest brother, my campmates Ao, Lu, and Xing are among these millions.

Preface

A number of autobiographical accounts of post-Liberation China appeared in the 1980s, deepening our understanding of the political and social consequences of the Communist revolution by describing the personal lives of ordinary citizens after 1949. Yet the experience of China's prison camps remained largely undocumented, a forbidden area, its secrecy maintained by strict regulations but also by the reluctance of survivors to reveal their most painful and humiliating memories. Harry Wu determined to break that silence.

I first met Harry in 1986 at a Berkeley colloquium where I spoke about the dilemmas of those intellectuals in China who tried to serve the revolution. In response, he told me with some urgency about his nineteen years in the labor-reform camps, then a few days later he called to ask if I would work with him to write a book. At the time I had other commitments ahead, but when he approached me a second time in 1992, I agreed. By then I had read many versions of the revolutionary experience, and I wanted to add Harry's story of struggle and survival within the camps to the accumulating memoir literature.

When I began the project of co-authoring this prison memoir for publication as a special imprint for John Wiley & Sons, I inherited an array of drafts, journal entries, and newspaper clippings. Some appeared in Harry's own rough English, others had been dictated to English-speaking friends or written in Chinese for translation by non-native speakers. These preliminary versions, fragmentary but often vivid and affecting, contained troubling inconsistencies. They also left much of Harry's past undisclosed, tangled in a web of still unsorted memories.

During months of interviews, Harry tried to retrieve the events of thirty years, along with conversations, emotions, and processes of thought dating back to early childhood. I urged him to recall not just the moments of extreme duress that cry out for expression, but also the welter of less memorable experiences and relationships that reveal motivation and character while providing biographical and historical context. Sometimes he grew animated and leapt from his chair to demonstrate the technique of catching a frog with a string or excavating a cave house or trussing a prisoner. Sometimes he wept.

The resulting memoir testifies to the unbroken will of an individual who endured years of brutalizing treatment but refused to surrender to arbitrary and vindictive authority. Harry minimizes that achievement. "I am not a hero," he insists. "My past is no different from that of many thousands who have no way to tell their story." By exposing that shared past and recounting his disappearance into the labor-camp system so familiar within China but always concealed from foreign view, Harry has found one way to repay a debt to those he left behind.

The interweaving of oral history and biography can never be simple. At its most successful the union produces a narrative that combines the immediacy of personal experience with the stolidity of historical fact. That fusion has been my goal in *Bitter Winds*. I have tried throughout to reproduce the flavor and the rhythms of Harry's voice and to capture the earthiness of his peasant squadmates and the strident tones of his police guards. Much of the language is necessarily my own.

I wish to thank my editor, Emily Loose, my friends Todd Gitlin, Karen Paget, Sandra Sachs, Betsey Scheiner, Orville Schell, and Robert Tierney, and especially my children, Matthew and Sarah Wakeman, for their patience and wise counsel during the months I struggled with this book.

CAROLYN WAKEMAN

Berkeley, California
September 1993

Acknowledgments

Without two special American friends, this book would never have come to light. The first is John Creger, my first collaborator, who helped me in my first attempts to tell my story. He understands my experiences deeply and has helped me cast the devil out of my body. Carolyn Wakeman has given generously of her knowledge, writing skill, and sincerity.

Grateful thanks to my publisher, Robert Bernstein, an honorable man who fully realized the importance of my story and experience.

My thanks to the following, who have given their best for the book: Lin Jeffrey, Ramon Meyers of Hoover Institution, Ya Xian of United Daily News, Orville Schell, Yuan-Li Wu of Hoover Institution, George Hu, Lisa and Martin Husmann, and my book editor, Emily Loose.

I deeply appreciate the able assistance and support of Janet Moyer, which was critical in writing this book.

HARRY WU

Contents

Bitter Winds

1

Childhood's End

Shanghai in 1948, the final year of Nationalist rule, was a city of extremes. I was then a boy of eleven, small for my age, bookish, and keenly interested in baseball. The third of eight children, I lived in a comfortable three-story brick house on a tree-lined street in an affluent section of Shanghai's Western district. Each morning Father's pedicab driver dropped me at my Christian grammar school in the former French section of the city perhaps a mile from my house. The driver returned to the school's gates at noon carrying several stacked containers of delicious hot food prepared by our cook, which I ate in a separate classroom with a handful of similarly privileged students, apart from the noisy cafeteria where the other children jostled in line. After school I practiced calligraphy under my stepmother's guidance, then dashed outside to play with my friends until a servant called me for dinner.

I spent the years of early childhood almost totally insulated from the poverty, violence, and fear that gripped much of Shanghai. Rarely did I have occasion to leave my neighborhood, and I never knew that just half a kilometer from my home, carts routinely collected at dawn the bodies of those who had died from illness and starvation during the night. I remember a Sunday afternoon outing in 1948 when Father took me downtown to Wanjing Road to the largest department store to buy a base-ball glove. The pedicab driver parked just outside the entrance while we shopped, so I never mingled with the crowds on the streets, never noticed the hardship that must have been evident. After buying the glove my only thought was to rush home so that I could spend the rest of the day playing baseball with my friends.

I also remember the shock I felt when my younger sister ran home crying one morning after seeing a dead baby wrapped in rags abandoned on a street corner nearby. So effectively did Father protect us from the poverty and misery that I was not even conscious of the inflation that triggered bursts of panic buying throughout the city that year. My only memory of crowds mobbing Shanghai's rice shops comes from photographs I saw later in *Life* magazine, which Father subscribed to along with *Time* and *Fortune*.

The son of a small landlord in the prosperous and pictur-esque city of Wuxi, Father had been sent as a boy to a Christian middle school and later to St. John's University, the prestigious American missionary college in Shanghai that offered a West-ern-style liberal education taught in English. His degree in eco-nomics prepared him to enter the world of international com-merce, and he rose quickly after graduation to become the assistant manager of the Young Brothers' Bank, and later the owner of a knitting yarn factory. In those years I knew nothing about his work or his income, but I remember my pride when he bought a Westinghouse refrigerator and my excitement when he made a down payment on a Chevrolet in the summer of 1948. I never thought of my family as wealthy because some of my schoolmates lived in far greater luxury. It seemed normal to me to have three servants to help my stepmother with the house-work and the care of eight children.

Our life-style, typical of Shanghai's Westernized upper mid-dle class, reflected Father's education in two cultures. Rather than the stiff, carved rosewood armchairs and tables that fur-nished more traditional Chinese living rooms, he chose an ov-erstuffed sofa and a thick woolen carpet for our home, and he also bought a piano so that my elder sister and I could take lessons twice a week. Sometimes Father entertained his British banking friends, serving them foreign wines and brandies from the polished sideboard in our dining room. His favorite hobby was hunting, and he kept five shotguns in a locked wooden cabinet in the attic. He also raised a pair of pointer dogs that he took on trips to shoot birds in the nearby marshlands of Subei and goats in the wilds of Inner Mongolia.

Despite this cosmopolitan life-style, Father remained deeply traditional in his thinking. He loved art and collected scrolls by the most famous contemporary painters. I especially remember a pair of graceful, prancing horses by Xu Beihong that hung in the living room, as well as a life-size portrait of the mythic Yang Guifei emerging from her bath by Zhang Daqian and a cluster of flowers and butterflies by Qi Baishi. I also re-member the seriousness with which Father shed his Western suit and leather shoes for a traditional long silk gown during the Spring Festival holidays and again on the three occasions each year to honor my mother's memory. For those ceremonies Father would insist that we children also dress in long gowns.

To my knowledge Father never attended church, but he performed the traditional family rituals with great solemnity. Every year on April 5, the date for sweeping the ancestors' graves, the whole family assembled in the dining room while the servants placed a tantalizing array of meat, chicken, and vegetables at one end of the table. I always stared with a mixture of awe and fear at the display of cups, candles, and incense burners and at the small ivory stele engraved with Mother's name that accompanied the offerings to her departed spirit. Father would begin the ceremony by filling several cups with rice wine, lighting the candles and incense, and then kneeling down on a cushion to kowtow three times in our mother's mem-ory. We all performed these ritual gestures in turn, even our stepmother.

Mother passed away in 1942 when I was five, leaving Father alone to care for me, my elder sister and brother, and two younger sisters. I always assumed Mother died of illness, though no one ever spoke to me about the specific cause. Many years later an older cousin confided to me that her death had hap-pened mysteriously after a bitter quarrel with my father, and I felt shocked to learn that people suspected suicide. My father never spoke to me about her death, and I never learned the truth. I remember little about her, but I do recall my initial fear at gaining a stepmother a year after her death. We children assumed this new woman would be cruel to us and selfish, and we dreaded the lavish wedding Father planned at the Park Hotel, just beside the racecourse. He insisted on presenting us briefly to the guests at the reception. After the driver pedaled us home, we took refuge in the kitchen, fearing our fate.

To my surprise, our new stepmother came to find us immediately after the festivities. She appeared in the kitchen doorway still wearing her long silver gown and corsage of ivory carnations, then patted my brother and me on the head before drawing my youngest sister close and leading her upstairs to bed. I soon came to love this quiet, gracious woman, whose warmth and compassion contrasted to Father's aloofness and stern supervision.

Father placed great importance on education and planned to send all of his children to missionary schools. He enrolled my elder sister at the famous St. Mary's School for Girls in 1946, and then placed my brother and me at the St. Francis School in the fall of 1948. There we wore uniforms like those at a British public school, with navy blue jackets emblazoned with a crest on the pocket, short flannel pants, and knee-high socks. Our teachers were all priests and brothers in the Jesuit order, and one gave me the English name "Harry" during my first week at school.

I had always loved science, and I soon formed a deep attachment to an Italian priest who taught physics and ran the science laboratory. Father Capolito, a stooped man in his mid-sixties with a thick fringe of silver hair, had noticed me one day watching from the corridor while the older students worked in the lab. I remember the touch of his hand on my head as he drew me inside and showed me the specimen boxes containing his magnificent butterfly collection. When the weather grew warm in the spring, he borrowed a bicycle for me and started taking me on Sunday afternoon outings to the countryside to gather my own specimens. I became fascinated by beetles and soon learned to identify many different species by their shapes and the markings on their brittle shells. I also loved the special lunches Father Capolito packed of sliced ham with bread, butter, and jam, along with containers of milk and fruit.

During that spring of 1949, the bitter civil war between the

Communists and the Nationalists drew closer to Shanghai. After the Communist armies led by Mao Zedong had occupied the crucial northern cities of Baoding, Tianjin, and Beijing at the end of 1948, many government and business leaders in Shanghai purchased expensive air tickets to Hong Kong and prepared to flee with their gold and valuables. In front of us children, Father never mentioned these political events. He didn't want us to worry or to concern ourselves with anything except our school-work. One evening I overheard him tell my stepmother that he cared little about whether the government was capitalist or communist. People with knowledge and integrity would always be valued, he assured her, no matter who was in power.

Shaped by his own family's Confucian traditions, Father assumed that any solution to China's social and political problems had to begin with correct behavior. He remained adamantly aloof from politics, and I never heard him express an opinion about the outcome of the struggle. He did tell us once that he had refused the offer of a British banking friend to take my brother and me out to Hong Kong to escape the possible bloodshed and the reprisals that might accompany a Communist victory. The family would stay together, he declared. Our only responsibility as children was to study hard, learn self-discipline, and cultivate strict moral values. No matter what party was in power, we should be honest, stand on our own feet, and work hard for our country. Those were the principles Father lived by.

For several weeks in April and early May, we saw Father leave the house at night carrying a stick and flashlight. We knew he had organized a group of men to patrol the streets in an effort to protect our homes from possible looting and arson by marauding Nationalist soldiers who had deserted and were trying to escape to the south before the arrival of the People's Liberation Army. One afternoon I grew very excited watching as Father cleaned and oiled one of his shotguns, but he never again took it down from its rack. On May 24, he must have known something was about to happen because he sent all of us children to our bedrooms immediately after dinner. Sometime close to midnight, I heard loud footsteps pounding up the stairs to the third floor where I shared a bedroom with my elder brother. Father burst through our door with four men from the neighborhood, warning us to stay in bed and keep silent. My room had a balcony with a view of the street, and the men stood looking out from behind the heavy, floor-length curtains.

For awhile I tried to sleep, lulled by their low voices. Then someone called out, "They're coming, they're coming!" I jumped up and stood beside my father. In the dim light from the streetlamps, I could see Nationalist soldiers fleeing the city in disarray, some on foot and some in jeeps. Perhaps an hour passed before the People's Liberation Army soldiers appeared, marching smartly in columns two abreast toward the city center. Father seemed impressed by their discipline and relieved that the threat of violence had passed.

In the morning we learned from the radio that schools and offices would be closed for the day, but Father left early to find out what had happened at his bank. When he returned that evening, he seemed reassured. I heard him tell my stepmother that the streets were quiet, the situation was very good, a new era had begun. At that moment of optimism and growing confidence, I never guessed that the childhood I knew was soon to disappear.

For more than a year our family life continued largely unchanged. My parents insisted that we children be especially polite when the "aunties" from the new residents' committee office came to visit. And I remember Father turning in his hunting guns during the "campaign to suppress counterrevolutionaries" early in 1950, when all weapons in private hands were confiscated by the Public Security Bureau. Otherwise we carried on our daily routine as before.

Each night before dinner one servant would summon us children to the table while another carried out steaming platters of meat and vegetables and a tureen of soup from the kitchen. Only when we were sitting silently, our backs straight and hands folded, would a third servant call Father from his upstairs study. We always waited until he picked up his chopsticks before starting to eat. Then we waited even more eagerly for him to leave the table so that we could talk, argue, and grab the remaining food. After dinner we joined our parents in their private quarters for half an hour to talk and laugh together before finishing our schoolwork. I loved that part of the day. It was the only time I ever saw Father relax.

At school that year I learned to play soccer and swim, and I also began to study Roman Catholicism at Father Capolito's suggestion. What most attracted me to this foreign religion was the kindness, honesty, and serenity of the priests. Father Capolito treated his colleagues like brothers and me like a son. I joined his catechism class, and in 1950, after being baptized and then confirmed, I began to participate happily at my school in the activities of the Church.

During those same months the Communist Party worked hard to mobilize popular opinion in Shanghai against "foreign imperialists." President Truman's decision in March 1950 to send the United States Seventh Fleet to patrol the Taiwan strait appeared a deliberate provocation and a threat to China's hard-won independence. When in October 1950 war broke out in Korea, we students felt caught up in patriotic anger and indignation. We hated the United States, whom we called China's "number-one enemy," and we revered our "big brother," the Soviet Union.

From our political instructors we heard inspiring accounts of the Chinese army's heroic sacrifices on the Korean front, as well as reports about the Communist Party's achievements in distributing land to the peasants, reducing crime in the cities, and stabilizing the currency. We felt guilt and regret at the hardship suffered by the exploited classes in the old society, and we pledged to help the Communist Party build a bright new future. Had I been fifteen, I would surely have volunteered, as almost all the older boys in my school did, to serve on the Korean front, but I was two years too young.

In those years I had little affection for America. My only favorable impressions of Uncle Sam came from early childhood memories of World War II, when the United States and China were allies against Japan. I recall watching excitedly from a rooftop as American P-51s flew in formation over the Huangpu River, then peeled off to drop their bombs on Japanese installations during the occupation of Shanghai. I also remember several times receiving allotments of GI rations at my grammar school after the war ended in 1945. Once I tried to carry home twenty of those specially waterproofed cardboard ration boxes. Each contained a can of meat, a small spoon, some biscuits, butter and jam, and even two cigarettes. I imagined that American soldiers must be leading a wonderful life if they could eat such delicious food.

In that same fall of 1950, two new courses appeared in our school curriculum, one that taught us about Darwin's theory of evolution and another that taught the Marxist theory of social development. By then some of the foreign priests had already left. I remember one day just after dismissal when Father Capolito drew me into the lab. He took down two large wooden specimen boxes with sliding glass covers and said they were for me to keep. I felt so elated that I started to run home with my treasures, but Father Capolito called me back. "You must take good care of your collections," he said kindly, his hand on my head. I didn't realize the boxes were his parting gift. A few days later I asked Brother Xu, the Chinese teacher who abruptly began supervising the lab, what had happened to Father Capolito. "He needed to go back home and have a rest," came the gentle reply. It was months before I realized that Father Capolito would never come back to China.

In early 1952 all the students in my school attended an elaborate exhibit of photographs and documents that revealed the "crimes of the foreign imperialists who use religion against the Chinese people." The displays shocked me, and three left a lasting impression. One laid out an assortment of weapons— knives, pistols, even a grenade—supposedly discovered in the city's Christian churches, which allegedly proved the foreign missionaries were really imperialist agents and spies. Another was a collection of photographs of suffering Chinese children at missionary orphanages. I remember one picture of an American nun sitting down to eat a big meal of bread and milk while several starving Chinese children stood by looking on. Another picture showed the graveyard for Chinese children attached to a missionary orphanage. I didn't know then that many of those children had been deposited at the orphanages in advanced stages of illness and starvation and that the nuns had been unable to save them. But the display that shocked me the most was a collection of letters and photographs supposedly establishing intimate relationships between some foreign priests and Chinese women. The caption, written in large characters, read, "Wolves in religious clothing."

By early 1952 all of the foreign teachers at the St. Francis

School had returned home. The foreign principal had been replaced, some of the Chinese clerics had been arrested, and the rest had shed their black robes and crucifixes for secular dress. By then the school's name had been changed, and from then on I attended not St. Francis but the Time Primary School. A new principal arrived who had served with the Communist New Fourth Army, and a political instructor was assigned to each class to teach us Marxist-Leninist theory.

Also in 1952, as the antiforeign propaganda increased, Father's troubles began. The so-called Three-Antis movement, one of several political campaigns launched after 1949 to destroy any opposition to the Communist Party, was officially announced as an effort to eliminate the "triple evils" of corruption, bureaucratism, and waste. Actually the new campaign targeted the capitalist class, not just foreign missionaries and businessmen, but also their "running dogs," meaning any Chinese who had established close ties to the West.

One evening in the spring of 1952 Father didn't come home. We had no idea what had happened or where he had gone. Every night the servants set his regular place at the dinner table, and after we took our seats, our stepmother would nod to us to begin eating. She never touched her food, and we saw the worry that lined her eyes. By habit we never asked questions. Instead we lingered in her bedroom after dinner, talking quietly, avoiding quarrels, trying to offer some comfort.

A month passed before Father returned. One evening after dinner, he just walked into the living room, and he never mentioned his disappearance. We didn't realize until our stepmother told us a year later that he had been confined to a room at his bank and interrogated around the clock by Party activists about the bank director's alleged financial crimes. Unlike many who faced similar pressure, Father refused to provide false information and insisted that his boss had done nothing wrong. Finally Father was released, but the bank director, falsely accused of embezzling funds, spent the next five years in jail.

After Father's trouble in 1952, he received an official demotion and reassignment as a clerk at a smaller bank at a much lower salary. I knew my parents were struggling to pay the food and tuition costs for our large family. One by one Father sold his pedicab and gave up the driver. Then he dismissed the household servants. One day the piano disappeared, next the carpet, then the sofa and refrigerator. Workmen came to remove the downstairs telephone, leaving only the upstairs set. Sometimes we saw our stepmother leave the house with a package under her arm. We knew that she was selling jewelry and artworks to pay the household expenses.

In 1954 Party authorities, desperate to find competent management personnel after punishing so many "capitalists," wanted to promote Father again to assistant bank director, but he declined. Instead he announced his wish to retire from banking, and from then on taught English at a nearby middle school.

2

Shifting Winds

*I*n the summer of 1955, I prepared to leave home. My elder
sister had already graduated from St. John's University, married a classmate, and moved with him to Hong Kong in 1950
to join his family. My elder brother had completed a two-year
course in industrial engineering at the Qingdao Technology Institute and waited to receive a job assignment. In addition to
me and my two younger sisters, my parents had three new children at home to educate and support, and I knew my departure
would ease their financial burden. During my last term of middle school, I had considered my future carefully. Because I had
always earned top grades, I decided to apply to Qinghua University in Beijing, China's most prestigious institution for applied science, to study physics or chemistry. Then a series of
newspaper articles in the late spring urging young people to
serve their country by becoming geologists changed my mind.

In *People's Daily* I read an inspiring report written by the
Minister of Geology describing the important contributions geologists would make to China's future. Geology was a glorious
but difficult career, the article declared, requiring knowledge,
discipline, and dedication. Without geologists to discover China's deposits of minerals, oil, and coal, socialist construction
could not move forward. Without geologists to prepare land

surveys, the country's bridges, dams, and railways could not be built. "Geology workers are the advanced soldiers of our motherland's socialist construction," the article proclaimed, calling upon the most capable middle school graduates to apply to the Beijing Geology Institute.

The idea of a career in geology challenged and inspired me, and the next day I studied the brochure sent to my middle school by this new technical college. The Beijing Geology Institute had siphoned off the geology faculty from Qinghua University and other institutions, I learned, as part of the Communist Party's reorganization of higher education in 1952, when China adopted a Soviet rather than a Western model. The five-year program in engineering geology included two summers of field investigation. I grew excited at the thought of undertaking fieldwork in remote and difficult terrain and of acquiring a body of knowledge that would bring practical benefit to my motherland. When I filled out the national college entrance examination forms in July, I selected the Beijing Geology Institute as my first choice. The test results were announced in August, and I felt proud and happy to learn that I would qualify for any of the country's top tier of colleges. The Geology Institute accepted me immediately and asked me to arrive in Beijing on September 1.

During the last weeks of summer, my anticipation of the exciting future ahead mixed with sadness at separating from my home and family. I had been very busy during my final year of middle school, concentrating hard on my studies and preparing for the rigorous college entrance exams. I had replaced my older brother as captain of the baseball team, and in addition I had fallen in love. My girlfriend Meihua was a classmate of my younger sister's and had often been a visitor in our home. In the spring of 1954, my friendship with her had deepened. We took long walks and bicycle rides together and began to share our deepest thoughts. A year later, on the eve of my departure for Beijing, we exchanged necklaces as tokens of our love.

On the overnight train I sat amid a cluster of other enthusiastic young students bound for colleges in the nation's capital. We developed a happy camaraderie, and for much of the twenty-eight-hour journey, we talked and laughed together, singing revolutionary songs and sharing our patriotic ambitions and our romantic sense of adventure. I had never traveled before, and this was my first sight of peasants tilling terraced mountain slopes, my first glimpse of the poverty that gripped so much of the Chinese countryside. As I watched the landscape pass by outside the train window, I thought about the lessons of my political study classes. I felt a deep sense of compassion and ambition. My country, my people had suffered too much. I wanted to spend my life helping the Communist Party build a new future, a new nation, where people could lead lives of dignity, free of want and injustice. I wanted to help China grow strong, prosperous, and united.

That reverie began to fade soon after I reached Beijing. The first people I met at the Geology Institute were the political instructors responsible for organizing all fifteen hundred of us incoming students into military-style units headed by Youth League cadres. I found to my surprise that seven students in my class of thirty were already Party members, while sixteen were Youth League members. Only six others were "white and blank," meaning we lacked an advanced level of political awareness. At my middle school in Shanghai, "backward" students from "bourgeois" families had never been in such a minority.

Despite the warm greetings of Comrade Ma, the Youth League leader responsible for the ideological education of my class, I felt ill at ease in such a politicized setting. A cheerful young woman from a peasant family a few years older than I, Ma offered to help us with whatever we needed during the five years we would spend at the Geology Institute. She told us how fortunate we were that the Communist Party and the working people had made it possible for us to attend this university. We were to treasure our opportunity, we were to study hard, we were to live up to the trust of the people, we were to repay the Party's generosity and the blood and sweat of the working class, she urged. Even though I admired her commitment and sincerity and applauded the leadership of the Communist Party, I could not fully share Comrade Ma's convictions. I had worked hard in middle school to earn high grades and to perform well on the entrance exams, I thought. My own academic achievement had earned me admission to the Geology Institute, regardless of the sacrifice of the working people.

After her opening remarks, our Youth League leader began to prepare us for the "promote loyalty and honesty" movement that would occupy most of our time during that first week in Beijing. For the next two days we studied Party documents and listened to school officials explain how we should admire and respect the contributions of the working class and how we should remake ourselves into "newborn socialist people." On the third day Comrade Ma declared that it was time for us to demonstrate our own loyalty and honesty. We would each write an autobiographical essay describing the important events in our past lives. Next we would fill out forms identifying our relatives and our closest friends by name and providing their ages, addresses, and occupations. This information would help the Party with its work, she directed, so we should take care to be precise and thorough.

These first steps to becoming a university student made me slightly apprehensive because I realized that the information I offered would remain a permanent part of my personnel file in the college Party Committee's office. Mindful of Father's difficulties in 1952, I worried about how the specific details regarding my family connections could be used in the future. I knew the file could be consulted at any time, the information construed in any way. I also felt uncomfortable at having to make public so much personal information, including my relationship with Meihua. What right did the Communist Party have to inquire about my private life, I thought. But with Comrade Ma stressing the necessity of improving our "political stand" and ridding ourselves of "reactionary attitudes" from the past, I had no choice.

Even though I had no sensitive political connections to conceal, I worried about how to answer the all-important questions regarding my father's occupation. I realized that my responses would determine my "class background." Since Father had never spoken to us children about the amount of his income or the source of his earnings, I didn't know for sure whether he had ever owned property. If so, he would deserve the class label of "capitalist," the most reprehensible in the communist lexicon. So far as I knew he had no capital, and his earnings had always come exclusively from his salary, but I felt uncertain about how to list his occupation. Finally I stated his work as "schoolteacher" and former "senior clerk," the appropriate designation at that time for an assistant bank manager.

To my relief, the personal information I provided passed the scrutiny of the Youth League cadres without query at a class meeting the next morning, when two of my classmates had to account more fully for their backgrounds. One student faced sharp questions about an uncle suspected of being a landlord, while another had to answer charges that he had failed to report his father's ties to the Nationalist Party. I left for lunch believing I had no further problems. That afternoon Comrade Ma drew me aside. "So your father has served as a capitalist running dog?" she asked me. I flinched at her insulting tone, but finally she accepted my explanation of Father's employment and concluded that he was only an "agent of the capitalist class" and not a member of the capitalist class in his own right.

The practical significance of these class distinctions did not become apparent to me until I learned about the college's allocation of monthly student stipends to pay for meals and incidental expenses, like soap and toothpaste, envelopes and stamps. Asked to pay 12.50 *yuan* for the first month's meals, I used the spending money my parents had given me when I left home. Several days later I realized that most of the other students had received an allowance from the school of either 18 yuan or 15 yuan to cover both their food costs and their personal expenses. Students from the countryside, assumed to have the greatest financial need and accorded the highest political status, generally received the larger subsidy, while the sons and daughters of workers and soldiers received the lower amount. None of the seven in my class who had bourgeois or landlord backgrounds had received financial support.

I protested to Comrade Ma that my father was a schoolteacher with a low salary and five children at home to feed, and that he could not afford to pay for my meals. She assured me that I could apply for a stipend to begin the following month, then a few days later informed me that I would receive 7.50 yuan, half of the standard amount. I felt unfairly discriminated against and wanted to protest, but I kept silent. That was the first time I understood the hierarchy of privilege dictated by class background.

Once academic classes began, Comrade Ma reminded us

repeatedly that our most important objective as new students was to heighten our level of political awareness. We should make ourselves first "red" and then technologically "expert," we were told. I had hoped to prove my superiority in intellectual work, but it seemed that even the teachers did not fully endorse my enthusiasm for scientific learning. Some of them lectured tentatively and assigned work outside of class almost apologetically. I wondered whether the mass struggle movement launched in the spring of 1955, called the Elimination of Counterrevolutionaries campaign, had contributed to their caution. I had not paid much attention to the development of that campaign, but I knew from newspaper accounts that thousands had been interrogated, many arrested, and an untold number executed. Most of the targets had been released from detention and cleared of wrongdoing by summer's end when I reached Beijing, but fear lingered.

Comrade Ma often encouraged me to raise the level of my political awareness and become more politically active, but I always found a way gently to decline. I expressed my gratitude for her concern and promised to think about her suggestions, but I intended to focus my attention on my studies and sports activities. Also, I wanted to lead my own life and make my own choices.

I didn't realize how much I was setting myself apart from my classmates by staying away from political activities and also declining to join the singing, dancing, and drama clubs that drew the first-year students together. Such group events provided opportunities to get to know others socially and, with the Party's sanction, to enter into romances. Influenced by my father's aloofness from politics, I stayed away. Not only were my afternoons occupied with study, but I had founded a baseball team, and I also had Meihua. Twice a week we wrote letters to each other, always numbering the envelopes so that we would know if any went astray. I waited eagerly for mail deliveries and looked forward to the summer vacation we would spend together in Shanghai.

At the end of the year when final grades were posted, I received high marks, but I noted that Ma had failed to earn even passing grades in two courses. As a course representative I was responsible for her academic progress, just as she was responsible for my political progress. I had to speak to her about her failure. "I like you very much," I began, "but you always tell the rest of us that we must do well at our studies for the sake of the Party and the people. How is it that you yourself have not even earned passing grades in two subjects?" Ma asserted that study was less important for her than for me, but I sensed her embarrassment. Knowing how much of her time had to be spent on political activities, I offered to help her prepare for the makeup exams in mineralogy and crystallography. With extra study and coaching she passed, but she never forgot my reproach.

Back at home in Shanghai during the summer vacation of 1956, I saw Meihua nearly every day, relishing the time we spent together. That fall she would begin a teacher training course at a trade school run by the Ministry of Coal in Jinan, the capital of Shandong province. I could not afford a train ticket to meet her in Shanghai for the Spring Festival holiday in 1957 at the Lunar New Year, so we agreed that she would come to Beijing for the brief "sweeping of graves" vacation in April. Before we separated, we told our parents of our wish to marry after my graduation, and they gave their consent to our engagement. I returned to Beijing eager to work hard and optimistic about the life ahead.

In the autumn of 1956, shortly after returning to campus, I began to hear about the Party's new policy toward "intellectuals." Our political instructors spent less time lecturing us about the importance of the "class struggle" waged by workers and peasants against the bourgeoisie, and more time emphasizing the need for intellectuals to participate fully in the political life of the country. Students and teachers suddenly received special privileges, like a bus to transport us to the city center each day. A barbershop and a small restaurant opened on campus, and our focus shifted from political to academic learning.

This altered atmosphere brought changes in the Party's recruitment policies in 1956 as well. Students and faculty like me who were academically successful but not politically advanced suddenly found ourselves invited to apply for Party or Youth League membership. When Comrade Ma approached me one day to ask if I wished to join the Youth League, I thanked her for offering me such an opportunity but declined the honor, claiming that I didn't yet feel ready, that I needed more time to study and prepare myself for this important responsibility. What I didn't say was that I still felt reluctant to devote more hours to political study and organizational meetings, especially at a moment when the elevation of academic goals made political activities seem less significant than ever.

Midway through my second year of study, as the Spring Festival holiday approached in January 1957, another Youth League cadre asked me whether I felt ready to begin the process leading to membership. Encouraged by newspaper accounts of intellectuals who had recently joined the Party, I had already made the decision that at the next opportunity I would accept. With intellectual achievement increasingly valued by Party cadres, I wanted to join and thus declared that I would try to prove myself worthy of the Party's trust. The next day Comrade Ma offered me some study materials and asked me to sit down for a serious talk about my political "outlook."

"You come not from the working class but from the reactionary class," she began, her tone sympathetic, "so you will have to criticize seriously your family background. Only then can you become a newborn socialist person. You must begin with your father and describe how he has betrayed and exploited the working class. That way you can show that you want to become a true fighter for communism."

I hesitated. "I don't think my father should be considered a member of the capitalist class," I answered cautiously, "because I don't think he ever owned land or property."

"Whether your father owned property or simply served the capitalist class makes no difference," Comrade Ma stated, her voice growing stern. "To join the Youth League, you must admit that you have a reactionary class background and come from the exploiting class. That is the first step. Afterward you can draw a clear line to separate yourself from the contamination of your family. Only by criticizing your father will you show that you are qualified to join the revolutionary ranks."

"I want to think about it," I replied, suddenly cautious. "Perhaps I still have to study more." With that exchange, the matter of my Party membership ended.

In February of 1957, we began to study Chairman Mao's

call to "let a hundred flowers bloom and let a hundred schools of thought contend." The official encouragement of divergent opinions prompted cautious enthusiasm among us students. No longer would Party leaders require mechanical assent and obedience, I learned at a schoolwide assembly reporting on the Chairman's much-publicized speech about how to handle contradictions among the people. In fact, those cadres responsible for conveying official policies in the past would have to examine their own "work style." They would be required to confess any impulse toward "self-glorification" and would subject themselves to the criticism of the "masses." We students were to participate enthusiastically in this new Hundred Flowers campaign, we were told. We should boldly criticize the Party's work in order to help it correct mistakes and eliminate any previous "erroneous tendencies."

While at the Geology Institute everyone seemed to welcome this unprecedented relaxation of ideological control, editorials in *People's Daily* made it clear that few were responding to Chairman Mao's call for criticism. The political campaigns conducted over the first seven years of communist rule had made clear that expressing individual opinions had dire consequences. I could see that the newspaper articles used as study materials in our class meetings tried to counter people's fear that this sudden shift in policy might be a ruse to expose those who secretly opposed the Party, that the "early spring" would be followed by a "sudden freeze."

Throughout March and April, our school Party leaders continued to encourage criticism and candor. Gradually students and teachers alike grew more confident. As enthusiasm overwhelmed caution, a few in my class penned wall posters, stating their questions and opinions boldly on sheets of newsprint provided by the Party committee. Sometimes they took issue with the school's leaders or called for greater independence for the student union. Sometimes the students expressed their objection to the severity of the Elimination of Counterrevolutionaries campaign in 1955 or even dared to criticize the nation's blind reliance on the Soviet Union. I didn't participate in this increasingly spirited poster writing, but I felt excited that the opportunity for genuine debate had arrived.

In my class Comrade Ma urged everyone to speak freely

and hold nothing back. Now that the "transition to socialism" had been almost accomplished, she urged, the leaders needed our comments and our criticisms to improve the Party's work and help our country move forward. She assured us that no one would be punished for speaking out, that no one need fear the Party's disapproval. In response, a number of my classmates wrestled aloud with difficult questions about international relations and domestic policy. I joined in several of those discussions, even though much of the time my attention was distracted by thoughts of Meihua's approaching visit early in April and also by my selection for the all-Beijing intercollegiate baseball team. I was one of two chosen to represent the Geology Institute, and a busy schedule of practice games left me little time for political activities. I began to train seriously for the national baseball competition, slated to begin in August, and I also agreed to begin coaching the women's softball team.

Meihua arrived on April 3. For three days she stayed in the girl's dormitory, and we found several chances to walk alone on the campus and to hold each other and kiss. Her visit gave us a chance to begin talking about our future. Then she was gone. I waited ten days for her first letter, wondering about the unusual delay. She explained that she was very busy because her school would close earlier than expected, but that she had applied for a work assignment in Beijing, requesting a job near her fiancé. I wrote back immediately, urging her to try hard for that posting and promising that I would make a similar effort when I graduated in 1960 so that we could marry and settle down in Beijing. When she didn't reply immediately, I assumed the hectic final weeks of her teacher training program left her no time to write me a letter.

3

Counterrevolutionary Crimes

*D*uring the weeks that followed Meihua's visit, Comrade Ma became insistent that everyone in our class must speak out and contribute to the Party's efforts to "rectify" its previous errors. She announced in mid-April of 1957 a series of special meetings for us to air our views individually in the spirit of "blooming and contending" that the Hundred Flowers campaign promoted. Along with other Party leaders she assured us that this "rectification movement," unlike mass struggle campaigns in the recent past, would be conducted "as gently as a breeze or a mild rain." I still held back, out of habit, caution, and a continued instinctive reluctance to join political activities.

During the first of those special meetings, I managed to speak in general terms and avoid any specific statement of my own opinions. Before the second meeting I requested leave to attend a baseball match sixty miles away in Tianjin. But when I asked Comrade Ma on May 2 to excuse me from the third discussion because of an important baseball practice the following afternoon, she refused. "Tomorrow you must attend," she stated firmly without meeting my gaze. "Everyone must be present: everyone must work together to help the Party improve."

I took a seat in the classroom on May 3 at the appointed

time, startled that all eyes seemed to focus on me. Comrade Ma spoke a few words of greeting, her voice formal and cold: "Comrades and students, Wu Hongda never seems to have time to participate in our meetings, but today he has joined us. I suggest we begin by asking him to offer his opinions to help the Party." Everyone waited. Had I attended more meetings during the preceding weeks and followed more closely the direction of the debate, I would have known better how to couch my own remarks. That afternoon my thoughts were on the baseball practice, my guard was down, and I decided to respond candidly to the Party's request. Altogether I listed ten problems that I thought warranted consideration.

"First," I began, looking at Ma, "you start every meeting just like this by addressing two groups, making a distinction between 'comrades' and 'students.' I don't understand why you assign some people an inferior status when Chairman Mao has said that anyone who wants to participate in socialist construction is a comrade. When we leave the campus, even when we buy a mug in the cooperative store outside, we are always addressed as comrades. Inside the classroom it is different. You unfairly imply that some of us belong to a secondary rank when you differentiate in this way."

Next I criticized the severity of the political campaign against counterrevolutionaries in 1955. "I know little about the movement to eliminate counterrevolutionaries," I began, "but I do know that innocent people were hurt, like my elder brother. The Communist Party must take responsibility for its actions."

I had not learned of my brother's difficulties until October of 1955 when he stopped to spend one night with me in Beijing en route from his college in Qingdao to his first job assignment in Inner Mongolia. Crowded into the upper dormitory bunk beside me, he had seemed subdued and reluctant to talk. I could feel that he had changed. Having been a geology student for only one month, I spoke enthusiastically about my future, but my brother didn't respond. Then I asked why he was being assigned work in one of China's most remote and backward provinces. He answered sharply that he didn't mind hardship and that at least he had been given a job and allowed to retain his Youth League membership.

Not until the next morning when I accompanied him to the train station did he tell me that for the past five months he had been held in detention under "investigation." Just before his graduation in June, the Party cadres responsible for leading the attack to eliminate "hidden counterrevolutionaries" in his school had accused him of "illicit connections with foreigners" because of letters he occasionally received from our elder sister and from a former high school classmate who also lived in Hong Kong.

"They suspected me of being a spy," he said, "so they put me in a small classroom and hit me and asked me day and night what kind of relationship I had with my sister and my friend. If only I had a knife, even now I would try to kill them." Shocked to hear the degree of his anger, I tried to calm my brother. The ordeal was over, I urged, and he should try to forget the whole thing. But I never forgot, and when I began to list my criticisms of the Communist Party at the discussion meeting in 1957, I again heard the anger in my brother's voice.

As I spoke, I noticed that some people took notes and that Comrade Ma, as Youth League secretary, scribbled busily in her red notebook. I should have recognized this as a signal to be careful in my comments, but at that moment I had no thought that the climate of openness would change, and I rushed on to raise eight more points. I left the classroom feeling tired but satisfied that I had spoken truthfully and had discharged my duty to the Party.

By mid-May the early trickle of criticisms had become a torrent, prompting a directive from Party leaders on May 19 to suspend university classes citywide so that students and faculty could participate full-time in the rectification movement. At rallies and demonstrations on every campus, excited young people called for reducing the administrative authority of Party cadres within the universities and for moderating the influence of Soviet ideas about curriculum and teaching methods. One afternoon as I walked across the Qinghua campus to the athletic field for a baseball match, I saw clusters of students along the walkways, shouting and gesticulating. Posters flapped on the noticeboards and on the walls of several buildings, but I didn't have time to stop. Actually I had no interest in anything at that

moment but the playoff game. When we won, the Geology Institute's team became the all-Beijing champions for the second
straight year.

After the suspension of classes in May, our political instructors told us to spend every day studying documents and editorials in *People's Daily*, reading wall posters, and participating
in meetings. The discussions had grown so heated, the competition to offer criticisms so intense, that students even quarreled about available wall space on our campus and argued
about who had covered up another's poster. By then I had grown
alarmed about Meihua's silence.

Never had such a long time passed without an answer to
one of my letters, and I worried that after her return to Jinan
something might have happened to her, some illness or emotional problem. The days dragged by as I listened to reports
about the rectification movement over the loudspeaker in the
early morning, then sat in the auditorium in the afternoon for
more reports, often from Party officials sent from the propaganda ministry or the city government. Finally we all adjourned
to our classrooms in the evening for small group discussions
of the day's earlier reports. I found the discussions overwhelmingly tedious.

I ripped open the letter that finally arrived from Meihua
on May 24. Five weeks had passed. She was fine, she wrote, I
shouldn't worry about her, but the past was gone, and I should
forget everything that had happened between us. As I read those
lines, my world collapsed. Over and over I asked myself what
could have happened, what could have made her reach such a
decision with no warning. I could imagine no reason for Meihua's change of heart. Her words seemed so cold, so unexpected, that I feared some terrible problem, some emotional
distress so serious that she might even think of suicide.

Two days later, in a state of great anxiety, I knocked in the
evening at the door of my academic dean, a kindly old man
who had always treated me with respect. I showed him Meihua's
letter and pleaded that I be allowed to travel to Jinan to learn
what had happened to my girlfriend. I told him I feared Meihua's
distress might lead her to suicide. The dean listened, then approved a five-day leave. I knew that I should also request per-

mission from my department Party secretary, but I couldn't risk a refusal, so I rushed to the rail station early the next morning and purchased a ticket for the seventeen-hour trip to Jinan. At eight o'clock the following morning I arrived at the gate of Meihua's school.

Everyone in her dormitory seemed to be packing. The bunks were strewn with clothing, the floor scattered with papers. Meihua looked up at me with alarm. "How come you're here?" she asked. She seemed rushed, confused, preoccupied.

"What has happened?" I asked, holding out her letter. Embarrassed at my question in front of her schoolmates, she drew me outside.

"Everything's okay, nothing's happened," she replied hurriedly. "I got the job assignment in Beijing, and now I'm very busy. The school will close in two days, so just go back, you can't stay here."

"What made you write a letter like this?" I persisted.

"It's nothing, and anyway I can't talk about it now. Wait for me at the station after lunch. I'll come to see you off."

I napped fitfully on the wooden station bench until Meihua arrived. "You can see that nothing's wrong, so just go back to school," she urged. "I'll be leaving the day after tomorrow. After two weeks at home, I'll come to Beijing to meet you."

I made an impulsive decision to go to Shanghai to wait for her. "I can't return to school until I know what has happened," I replied, ignoring the fact that my travel leave would expire before I could return to my school. I boarded a train for Shanghai that evening and waited impatiently for Meihua. On the day I expected her to come, I telephoned her home twice, then visited her sister, but to no avail. The following afternoon she called me and explained calmly that she had stopped overnight to visit a classmate in Nanjing.

I couldn't understand her behavior. How could she delay when she knew I was waiting to see her? She assured me we would talk in the morning when she had rested, but again the following day when we met she avoided my questions. At one point she asked casually if I still kept the silver coin necklace, engraved with the words "I love you," that she had given me the previous summer when we parted. I drew it from my pocket and assured her that I always kept it close to my body. She took it from my hand, saying that it had grown tarnished and she would polish it for me.

Adding to my agitation when I returned home that evening was the fact that two notices from my school had arrived, a certified letter in the morning and a telegram in the afternoon, stating that my leave had expired and I should return at once to Beijing. My parents grew alarmed.

"Has anything happened to you?" my stepmother asked. "Did you receive permission to leave your school?" I tried to calm her fears by showing her the letter signed by my dean, but early the next morning yet another telegram arrived. This time the Youth League branch secretary ordered me in the sharpest words to return to participate in the movement.

"You must go back at once," my father insisted, "and in Beijing you must take extreme care. Keep quiet and say nothing. Something could happen that will ruin your entire life."

I telephoned Meihua and asked her to see me off at the station. Her face looked expressionless when we met, and again she brushed away my questions with the assurance that she would see me two weeks later in Beijing.

"Where is my necklace?" I asked when the train was about to leave.

"Oh, I forgot to bring it," she responded, unclasping from her neck the silver crucifix that had been my parting gift to her. "You can take this one. I'll keep yours until we meet again." She waved calmly as the train pulled away. For the entire journey I tried to discover some explanation for her evasiveness, some reason for her rejection. I arrived in Beijing exhausted and depressed.

"So, you've returned," Ma stated flatly the next morning, after finding me in the cafeteria. I had been away from the school for nine days. "You must report for a meeting tomorrow at two o'clock."

It was June 5, 1957. During that first day back, I learned that a counterattack against the Party's critics was under way in my college. *People's Daily* had already started to use the term "counterrevolutionary rightist" to refer to those whose independent opinions, previously welcomed and even required, were suddenly judged to oppose the "revolutionary line" and the socialist system. Apparently the volume and intensity of criticism, both in newspaper commentaries and on university campuses, had exceeded Chairman Mao's expectations. With the prestige and authority of the Party and its leaders at risk, an "antirightist" crackdown had begun. Already before I left for Shanghai, a few people had been "capped" as "bourgeois rightists" to isolate them as targets for criticism and censure, and to indicate the seriousness of their political crimes.

As soon as I took a seat in my classroom on June 6, Comrade Ma began to speak. I had never heard her tone so cold. "Today we discuss Wu Hongda," she declared. "First we ask him to explain his absence. It appears that he stayed away from Beijing for nine days without permission in order to avoid the rectification movement. Now that he has returned, he must be criticized. Second, we ask him to explain the poisonous ideas he spoke on May 3." With a shudder I realized that this criticism meeting was devoted entirely to me.

Comrade Kong, the Youth League member in charge of propaganda for the Party branch in our class, followed Comrade Ma's lead. "Why has Wu Hongda tried to escape from the rectification movement when everyone understands how important this campaign is to our country's political life?" he asked sternly. "I think the answer must be that he is afraid of making mistakes and wants to avoid criticism. I also think he is a liar. We all can see that he has deceived the Party and that he has not told the truth about his actions or his thoughts."

My explanation about Meihua's apparent distress, like my protest that I had received the dean's approval before leaving, had no impact. I had gone to Shanghai without permission from the Party branch, the six or seven activists in the room chorused. I had not responded to the certified letter and had returned to campus only under pressure, only after receiving two telegrams. I was to confess my true intentions in escaping just at the height of the political movement. "The rest of us welcomed Chairman Mao's teaching, and we have tried hard to help the Party correct itself, but we all remember what Wu Hongda said in May," accused one Youth League member. "Those were poisonous ideas. They show that Wu Hongda opposes the goals of socialism!"

The atmosphere in the classroom grew tense. I realized

that opinion had turned overwhelmingly against me. No one dared counter the denunciations of the six or seven students trusted by the leaders. The meeting ended promptly at five o'clock with Ma's "conclusion."

"Wu Hongda," she instructed, her voice tense, "you come from the bourgeois class, and you have many bourgeois ideas and actions to account for. You must be honest and make a serious self-criticism to the Party. In one week you must complete your thought summary in two parts, the first analyzing your escape and the second analyzing your poisonous ideas."

"Don't use the word 'escape'!" I interrupted.

Ma stood up from the table at the front of the room, her jaw rigid. "Now is not the time for you to talk," she shouted. I had never seen her face so hard. "Write your self-criticism and turn it in to the Party branch."

Not wanting to join my classmates heading toward the cafeteria, I walked around the campus for a few moments alone, trying to figure out what was happening. Why had my girlfriend left me? Why had I been singled out for criticism? Why had the attitude of my classmates turned hostile? Angry and upset, I decided that in my self-criticism I would accept responsibility for staying away longer than five days and that I would admit I should study Chairman Mao's teachings harder, but nothing more. I was stubborn, and I believed that I had done nothing wrong. I returned to my dormitory, wrote three pages, and handed them to Ma that evening.

Two days later she and Kong together returned my thought summary and declared it unsatisfactory. "In several places your account is not true," Ma asserted. "You did escape, and there is nothing wrong with your girlfriend as you claimed. She even has a job, so maybe your travel was all a trick. You have one week more to rewrite your self-criticism."

The schedule saved me. On June 30 the entire class of second-year students left for two months of required field research at the Geology Institute's branch station, about thirty miles southwest of Beijing near Zhoukoudian, the famed site of the discovery of Peking man. Five students in my class besides me had been criticized for wrong actions or wrong opinions. During the preparations to leave, my revised self-criticism was forgotten, and once we had left Beijing behind, we could temporarily ignore the political movement. The most serious political activists among my classmates kept a distance from me, not wanting to associate with anyone accused of opposing the socialist system, but in that remote setting, where we received no mail and even *People's Daily* arrived two days late, the rest of us gratefully left the tensions of the antirightist campaign behind.

Each day our class leaders sent us out in pairs to learn how to use the drilling equipment, measure the geological layers, or practice surveying techniques. Comrade Ma was my usual companion. Occasionally she reminded me to work hard on revising my self-criticism, but as we climbed through the hills her manner grew more sisterly. In fact, she seemed relieved to talk about the landscape, the villagers we met, the work we needed to complete. After the eight weeks of field training, she dismissed me along with the others so that I could return to Shanghai for two weeks of vacation.

At home I discussed my situation with my parents. Father had followed closely the growing furor of the antirightist movement in editorials and newspaper reports that denounced and threatened the Party's enemies. He believed that my political problems were serious and feared that I would suffer for my outspokenness. He told me not to be defiant, not to resist the Party's authority. "I know you are very tough, very stubborn, but this time you must also be very careful," he warned. My stepmother also sensed my danger. Weakened by a bout of tuberculosis and a series of painful dental extractions, she lay confined to bed. I could see how she worried about the family's economic burdens, and I felt sorry to add my problems to her other concerns.

At the end of August, I dreaded my return to Beijing. Meihua had not written me again, nor had she returned to Shanghai, and my two conversations with her sister shed no light on where she was or why she had ended our engagement. My heart felt heavy. Father offered to accompany me to the train station. After we had walked half a block, I asked him, on an impulse, to wait for me, and I dashed back home, calling out to him that I had forgotten something. Inside, I ran up the stairs and entered my parents' bedroom, amazed to hear my stepmother say quietly, "I knew you would come back." I stared at her gaunt face, her

sunken eyes, her pale skin. Overcome with emotion, I reached
out to clasp her thin shoulders in an awkward embrace. She
kissed my cheek, stroked my back, and whispered, "Don't worry
about me. Take care of yourself." We both sensed that this would
be our final parting.

The antirightist campaign reached its climax at the Geology
Institute in mid-September after the students and faculty members returned from the summer's field research. One by one
the Party leaders picked out those they intended to accuse. At
the end of September, Zhang Baofa, one of my classmates who
was the son of a landlord and a frequent critic of the Party
during the rectification movement, received a rightist "cap," or
label. One lunchtime I saw posters denouncing his "counterrevolutionary rightist crimes" spread across the signboard outside the cafeteria. That afternoon we all had to attend a serious
criticism meeting. Early in the proceedings Comrade Ma asked
me to speak out and offer my comments. I deferred, claiming
I could no longer recall Zhang's opinions, but later she returned
to me. By then all twenty-eight of my classmates had spoken,
and I too had to "show my attitude." I could not remember any
of Zhang's statements, I hedged, but according to what my classmates had alleged, I believed that his opinions were incorrect
and that he had opposed the Communist Party. Having achieved
a unanimous opinion, Comrade Ma dismissed the meeting.

A week later I learned that Liu, another student in my
grade, had been capped because some of his classmates had
reported to the Party branch that his personal diary contained
"reactionary" and antisocialist thoughts. After an investigation
he too was labeled a counterrevolutionary rightist. The next day
Ma and Kong asked me to turn over to them my own diary.
Angry and worried, I replied that my diary was personal, that
I had written nothing except thoughts about my personal relationships. They continued to pressure me. "If what you say is
true," Ma countered, "then show it to us. We won't blame you
for your personal feelings. We want to help you, and this is a
chance for you to prove yourself." In fact, I had never written
about anything remotely political in my diary, but I had often
given voice to my deepest feelings about Meihua. I vowed inwardly to resist and prevent the Party from intruding on the
one remaining private sphere of my life.

Finally Kong pounded the table. "Since you persist in refusing the Party's help, we no longer request but order you to turn over your diary." I had no choice. I could not defy the Party's command. Three days later they returned the diary to me without comment. Had they found any counterrevolutionary statements, I knew they would have retained my notebook as evidence. At that I grew very angry.

"You found nothing, as I told you, but you wouldn't believe me," I shouted. "You have violated the constitution and violated my human rights by forcing me to surrender what is only a personal diary."

Ma stood up. "Remember what you have said," she commanded me ominously. "Are you accusing the Communist Party of violating the constitution?"

"Not the Party, but you," I repeated. "You have violated my rights."

The moment passed, but the pressure on me increased when Ma ordered me to turn in the rewritten thought summary that I had never completed the previous June. Now I was to include every detail about the influences on my thought from childhood, including my family life, my middle school experience, and my class background, in order to explain my counterrevolutionary rightist actions and opinions. Hearing such a serious accusation so soon after the incident with the diary, I became truly frightened. I knew that if I were actually accused of counterrevolutionary actions, I could be sent to hard labor in the countryside or even to prison.

Ma's words early in October indicated another escalation of the charges against me, and her use of the word "rightist" outraged me. The Party might disagree with my views, I thought, but I had never done anything wrong or committed any crime. I certainly did not see myself as an enemy of the socialist system, and I didn't understand how they could brand me with the severest political label. I still sincerely wanted to work hard for my country, and it seemed preposterous to consider me an "enemy of the people." I did not realize then that within each university and each department, a quota of rightists had been set, and that it was the task of each Party Committee to select the designated number of people to label.

At lunchtime on October 20, a week after I had turned in

my thought summary, a crowd around the large bulletin board
outside the cafeteria pulled back as I approached. The students
stared at me awkwardly. No one spoke. Then I saw the banner,
written in large characters, proclaiming "Wu Hongda's Counterrevolutionary Crimes." Below this headline, six newspaper-
sized sheets of pale green paper itemized my offenses. My eyes
kept returning to the large red X crossing out my name, a designation usually reserved for criminals who had been executed.
Here the X signaled that I had been removed from the "ranks
of the people" and relegated to the political status of outcast
and enemy.

The poster had attracted unusual attention because as the
captain of the championship men's baseball team and the coach
of the women's team, I was well known at the Geology Institute.
I scanned the many accusations, including the charges that I
had escaped from the school without permission, that I had
expressed counterrevolutionary opinions, and that I had directly attacked the Party by claiming that it had not upheld the
constitution. What stung me most were two statements written
by fellow baseball teammates, who were my only friends at the
Geology Institute. "We now expose the counterrevolutionary
Wu Hongda," one declared, "for leading our team in a capitalist
direction." I had no idea what the accusation meant, but I had
built the team single-handedly, selecting and training the play-
ers. Those words chilled me. I stood in a daze until someone
tapped my arm to hand me a fork that had slipped unnoticed
from my grasp.

At the Geology Institute more than one hundred teachers
and four hundred students, out of a total student body of five
thousand, were capped as rightists in the fall of 1957. Twelve
other third-year students in the department of engineering geology besides myself were labeled. People seemed to have different reactions to the shame and fear attached to their status
as political enemies. Most simply bowed their heads and accepted their disgrace, but a few, like me, argued with the Party
leaders and protested that the accusations were unjust. Some
felt despair. One day in late October a fourth-year student managed to climb to the top of the huge chimney attached to the
boiler plant. The college security guards and the Party secretary
took turns with his classmates shouting through a megaphone,

trying to persuade him to come down. He said he would jump unless they agreed not to sentence him as a rightist. They refused. When the school firefighters began to climb up after him, he jumped to his death.

In January 1958 everyone knew that those labeled as rightists across the country would soon receive punishments for their crimes. To prevent incidents before the sentencing, the school authorities exercised tight control over all rightists on the campus. We students could still attend classes in the morning, escorted by a Party member, but during the afternoons and on weekends we were sequestered in a classroom to write summaries of our thoughts and receive political instruction.

As the Spring Festival vacation approached in early February 1958, a meeting for the 150 third-year students was announced. I saw Wang Jian, the cadre responsible for political education for the Department of Engineering Geology and Hydrology, seated on the platform. Beside him, the Party branch secretary called out one by one the names of twelve of the thirteen rightists in our grade and ordered us to a separate classroom, where perhaps ten Party members and one security guard stood by to supervise us. Not knowing what would happen next, we all felt great pressure. Then they sent us individually to yet another classroom where the deputy Party branch secretary sat at a table. In front of him lay a stack of papers.

When my turn came, the deputy secretary picked up the top sheet and began to read the accusations against me. "As a representative of the Communist Party, I hereby pronounce your punishment as a counterrevolutionary rightist. These are your crimes," and he read the list. I waited, knowing that to be judged guilty of the most serious rightist crimes warranted immediate arrest. "Your crime is not so serious," he continued, "but your attitude is very bad. Your punishment is to remain at the school under the supervision of the masses." He forced me to sign two copies of the sentence, then ordered me back to the large classroom where the Party branch secretary called us to come forward one by one. He read out our punishments in front of the assembled third-year students. Before he dismissed the meeting, he instructed the rightists to return to the small classroom. There the security guard separated us into two groups according to our punishments.

Zhang Baofa, the only one of us to receive the most serious sentence of immediate arrest, had already been taken away. One woman student received the mildest of the four sentences, no punishment other than the rightist label, and the Party secretary dismissed her to return to her dormitory. She seemed to tremble with relief and gratitude as she walked out the door. Five of the remaining eleven had received the second-level punishment of expulsion from the school to labor under the supervision of the working classes. The security guard took them away to their dormitories to pack their belongings before they were sent to the countryside where they would do physical labor. Six of us stayed behind.

The Party branch secretary announced the regulations governing the actions of rightists being supervised within the school. We had to write a thought summary every week, we had to be obedient, we had to sincerely reform ourselves, and we would not be allowed to leave the campus during the Spring Festival holiday. We would stay at the school and begin our reform.

Having to remain behind during the vacation made the six of us feel depressed and alone. Each morning after our classmates left for home, we sat in a room, reading newspapers and writing and rewriting our thought summaries. At noon we received instructions for our labor task. The first day the cadre in charge of our supervision, named Pan, told us to go out and catch rats to improve campus hygiene. When we protested that in winter rats were impossible to find, he gave us a quota of fifty flies each. This task he took very seriously, and he warned us that our situation would be very difficult if we did not fulfill our obligation to the Party. We quickly discovered that even flies were difficult to find in February, so at the end of the first afternoon I asked Pan whether maggots, which were fly larva, would satisfy the quota. He agreed.

While out hunting initially for flies, some of us had discovered a spot behind one of the latrines where the earth remained soft from the daily removal of night soil and where there were thousands of squirming maggots. The stench was very bad, but by scooping up some of that dirt, we could fulfill our quota in a few minutes. Carefully we each counted out fifty maggots, some days collecting fifty-five or fifty-six to show our earnestness at labor, then wrapped them in paper and went to sit for a couple of hours behind one of the classroom buildings. Sheltered from the wind, we could relax, chat together, and enjoy the pale winter sunshine.

My life changed after that. As a rightist, I remained under formal, continual surveillance, with Kong as my keeper. We both knew that if he discharged this responsibility satisfactorily, he could conclude his probationary period as a prospective Party member and take the formal Party oath. It would serve him well to guard me strictly. He followed me to the cafeteria, the dormitory, even the latrine. I could go to class or to the library in the evening only after informing him, and I could not leave the campus at any time. I ate alone, apart from my classmates, as no one would dare associate with an enemy of the Party. I sat in the back of my classroom, having lost the privilege to comment or ask questions. I attended no more class meetings and participated in no activities. Worst of all, I was expelled from the baseball team, and I could not play at all that spring. No one spoke to me. I became invisible.

In June 1958, all of the third-year students left for a second period of field study, this time to Shandong province. Even the rightists were allowed to go. For more than five months in the countryside, I encountered a different China. Never before had I lived among the peasants, who make up eighty percent of the population but inhabit a world unrecognizable to intellectuals raised in the cities. Walking from village to village, I never saw electricity or running water. I saw no one eat meat. I saw people covered with lice who had no way to bathe. I realized that these conditions, not the life I had known in Shanghai and Beijing, represented the norm for my countrymen. Living in the homes of the poorest peasants changed my thinking, and I understood for the first time that my previous attitudes had been selfish, that unthinkingly I had indeed opposed the goals of China's revolution. Outwardly I said nothing, but inwardly I acknowledged the validity of my counterrevolutionary label. In my mind I admitted my crime.

Back at school in December of 1958, I made a sincere apology to the Party and the people when next I was required to produce a self-criticism. I had been selfish, I wrote. I had been raised in a wealthy family, had led a comfortable life, and had concerned myself with study and sports, activities that were irrelevant to the needs of the masses. I realized my errors and hoped the Party would accept my apology. But even as I wrote, I knew that my change of attitude would not bring about a change in my status. My genuine contrition would have no practical consequence. Until the Communist Party decided to "reverse its verdict" and clear the thousands of people, mostly intellectuals, who had been accused as counterrevolutionary rightists, my own political disgrace would not be lifted.

With two years remaining of my five-year course of study at the Geology Institute, I tried to assess my options. As a rightist I would be treated as an enemy. I could no longer hope to be a geologist. I could not expect to live even as an ordinary worker. I would be forever an outcast, denied a job, unable to marry, excluded from social and political groups, always watched, distrusted, and spurned. I could no longer imagine a future in my own country. I decided to escape.

4

No Way Out

$\mathcal{T}$ he more I thought about the nature of the communist system, the more I saw a great wall rising in front of me. During my months of fieldwork in the Shandong countryside, I had watched peasants digging furrows several feet deep to plant their crops, spurred on by zealous cadres, some of whom sought advancement, some of whom believed that such methods would greatly increase the yield. Among the villagers some seemed to believe it possible suddenly to begin producing 10,000 *jin* of wheat rather than 500, on one *mou* of land, but most went along because they dared not oppose the Party's current line. This ill-fated attempt to increase agricultural production was just one of the follies of the Great Leap Forward, a movement that Chairman Mao had initiated early in 1958 in the deluded conviction that he could bring modernization to China in fifteen years. Instead he brought famine and economic collapse.

That autumn I was only twenty-one. I was energetic, ambitious, and technically skilled, but I could see no role for myself in my country's future, since everyone had to support the industrial and agricultural policies of the Great Leap Forward. To object that steel could not be produced by melting down farming tools and cooking implements in the "backyard furnaces" being constructed in the villages, factories, and schools was to oppose the revolution. As the antirightist movement had demonstrated, anyone who questioned the leadership of Chairman Mao was cast out and punished. I found China's situation tragic. The communist system had become totally irrational and self-defeating, yet it resisted and punished any effort to bring about change.

With all the rashness and overconfidence of youth, I decided that my only hope was to flee my country and leave it to its terrible fate. I guessed that other students who had been labeled as rightists would have reached similar conclusions, and I began subtly to inquire. By late 1958 I had found three who shared my determination to leave, all of whom I believed I could trust. We met furtively, hastily, knowing that we would be arrested, maybe killed, if our escape plans became known. We recognized the risks we faced, but we all agreed that remaining in our present circumstances was intolerable.

We devised a series of coded hand gestures so that we could communicate without detection. Our prearranged meeting spot was a particular tree on the campus; our appointed time was ten o'clock at night, just when the students returned from the classrooms and the library to prepare for bed. When one of us signaled by rubbing his nose during the day, the others knew to slip away to the tree that evening, usually to receive a brief message or pass on a map.

Step by step in the spring of 1959 we laid our plans. Everyone knew that the Hong Kong border, which had served as the principal escape route out of China in the early 1950s, had been closed down through vigorous surveillance. Our best chance was to use our skills at cross-country navigation and our expertise with compasses and maps to try and disappear across the remote mountains between China and Burma. We searched through the Geology Institute's library to find detailed regional maps of the terrain we would cross, along with charts intended for use by field geologists and surveying teams. Some we copied, some we ripped from books as we researched the best route across the rugged mountains of Yunnan province far to the southwest of Beijing.

In the midst of these preparations, we all were sent out in late July 1959 for a third field assignment, this time a two-month project to collect information for our senior theses. Everyone had a different destination. I would go to the Beijing Engineering Geology Bureau in the nearby Western Hills to assist the engineers in devising a plan to supply underground water to China's first nuclear power plant, soon to be constructed near Zhoukoudian with financial aid from the Soviet Union. I would first research how many wells were needed and how deep they should be sunk, then try to determine the best method of evaluating the quality and chemical composition of the water.

Before the four in our group left the campus for our separate projects, we agreed on a timetable for our escape. We expected to return to Beijing just before the National Day holiday on October 1, at which time we would request leave to return home and visit our families. In fact, we would meet in the Beijing train station and purchase tickets for the three-day journey to Kunming, the capital of Yunnan province. We planned to sit in separate cars on the same train, then regroup at the station after our arrival. By then we had done all we could to assure a successful escape. We had carefully chosen our route and had even managed to steal a number of blank letters of introduction, the kind used by geologists in the field to obtain rice, shelter, and other necessities from local village cadres. There was nothing left except to swear that if caught, we would never, even under torture, reveal our plan or the identity of the other participants.

Once again I enjoyed being away from the political tensions of the campus, and I found my research project challenging. But late one afternoon when I was playing basketball after work with the Bureau engineers, I noticed Wang, one of my group, standing outside the fence rubbing his nose to signal that he needed to talk. It was several weeks too early for him to return to Beijing, and I could not imagine what would bring him to the Bureau to look for me. Unable to interrupt the game, I rubbed my nose to signal that I would talk later. After dark I sneaked outside the gate. In rapid whispers Wang explained his predicament. He had fallen in love with an assistant engineer at the Hubei Geology Bureau in Wuhan, but her Party branch leader had discovered her relationship with a rightist. Her work unit had criticized her for associating with a counterrevolutionary, but still she continued to see him. When the relationship was exposed a second time, she faced a serious struggle meeting at which Wang knew her fellow workers would accuse and threaten her for lying to the Party and disobeying its instructions.

Seeing no way to avoid involvement and not wanting to disrupt our escape plans for October 1, Wang had decided to use the 300 yuan advanced to him for expenses at the start of his field assignment and flee to Beijing to find me. He urged me to leave with him and contribute my advance money to buy train tickets to Yunnan for the two of us the next day. I listened to his plan but decided the risk was too great now that he was a fugitive from his work unit and sought by the Public Security Bureau. Moreover, we had no way to include our other two comrades. I urged Wang to turn himself in to the Geology Institute authorities, hand over the state's money, admit his mistake, write a self-criticism, and ask for forgiveness. Becoming involved with a local woman and taking public funds to flee from the supervision of the masses were serious political errors for a rightist, but perhaps not actual crimes, I told him. We would have to postpone our escape plans, but we would try again. He seemed to agree, and I sneaked him into the engineers' dormitory to sleep that night, assured that he would leave to face the school authorities before dawn the next morning. He was gone when I awoke.

Two weeks later, with my fieldwork completed, I returned somewhat apprehensively to the campus. I learned immediately that Wang had been arrested, but no one would talk about the case. I had no way to find out whether he had revealed our escape plans under interrogation. If he had confessed, I would be arrested next. Abandoning all thought of trying to leave the country, I applied to visit my family for the three-day holiday as if nothing had happened. I could think of no alternative but to board the train to Shanghai and hope that Wang had remained silent.

The day before my expected departure for home, Comrade Ma appeared in my dormitory. "A political meeting has been scheduled at the Bureau just after National Day to evaluate your final thought summary," she announced, her eyes expressionless. "Your permission to travel to Shanghai has been denied."

Thirty engineers waited for me in the Party Committee's

meeting room at the Geology Bureau on October 3, 1959. Chief Engineer Ning declared that the meeting had been called to assist me in reforming my thoughts. His words sounded ominous, but I noticed with relief that he did not use the label "counterrevolutionary rightist" when he referred to me. He ordered me to make a report, but I had no idea what he expected me to say. All I could think of was to recite my familiar list of self-accusations—my level of political thought was too low, I had a bourgeois background, I hadn't studied Chairman Mao's works hard enough.

"Have you ever done anything to harm the working people?" Ning demanded.

Avoiding his question, I continued speaking about my many mistakes. To my relief Ning called a break in the meeting, and for a few minutes we sat alone at the table. I had always known him to be a fair and kind man, but I was amazed when he poured me a cup of tea. Party cadres do not extend courtesies to rightists. Ning seemed to wait for me to speak. "We have spent two months working together," I began, "and you know me to be a straightforward person. Please tell me what the problem is."

Ning drew out a bank withdrawal slip for fifty yuan bearing my signature. Stamped on the top line was the date, September 10, the day after Wang had slept in the dormitory. Ning said that one of the engineers had that morning discovered his account missing fifty yuan. I realized immediately that Wang must have forged my name to withdraw money for his escape and failed somehow in the attempt, but I couldn't reveal those facts to Ning. If I claimed that I knew nothing about the bank account, that the signature was not mine, the authorities would investigate further. If I told the truth and said that Wang had slept in the dormitory the previous night, they would ask what he was doing there. I could see no alternative but to confess my guilt and declare myself a thief.

I felt miserable, but I told Ning that I had taken the money to buy tickets to visit my family. Fortunately I had in my pocket the money my stepmother had just sent me to pay for a ticket home to Shanghai, so I pulled out fifty yuan and asked Ning for forgiveness. He put his hand on my back to comfort me and said that sometimes people make mistakes. Then he left the room, assuring me that he would dismiss the struggle meeting

and that I shouldn't worry. A few minutes later he walked me
to the gate, shook my hand, and urged me to do nothing again
that would jeopardize my future. Never had I met a Party member like this, I thought, as I walked toward the bus stop.

Shaken by Ning's kindness and my own fraudulent response, I walked several miles back to the Geology Institute
from the central bus station in Beijing, needing time to consider
my next step. I decided the only way to deal with the school
authorities, who would demand a report of the struggle meeting,
was to confess. That evening I told Kong I had stolen fifty yuan
from an engineer at the Bureau. He screamed that I was not
only a rightist but a thief, then ordered me confined to the dorm
while he went off to report my latest outrage. Knowing that
Wang might already have confessed and that the authorities
might just be waiting to accumulate evidence before arresting
me, I dreaded the possible outcome of my statement. For several
weeks I wrote my self-criticism again and again, never satisfying
the Party leaders at my school and constantly worried that at
any moment I would be picked up by the police.

Sometime in November of 1959, I felt a strange mix of
despondency and daring. Upset and confused, unable to see any
prospects for the future, I lost interest in writing up the results
of my research project. I stopped caring about my political situation. As the Spring Festival holiday approached in early 1960,
I felt the sense of desolation ever more acutely. The Lunar New
Year was the most important time to unite with family and
friends, but I would not have that privilege. I began recklessly
to leave the campus at night, without permission, to roam the
city on my bicycle. At Taoranting Park, far to the south of the
Geology Institute, I discovered a pavilion where young people
danced and drank tea in the evenings. I had always hated dancing, but I sat mesmerized by the sight of others my age laughing
and enjoying themselves. This vicarious pleasure gave me some
respite from the emptiness of my life at school. For a few hours
as I watched the dancers, my loneliness and misery would recede. I can sit here for a moment in the same room with these
carefree dancers, I would muse bitterly, but when I leave, I
enter an utterly different world.

One night a couple spinning wildly on the dance floor stumbled and fell almost at my feet. Everyone laughed, and the boy

fled in embarrassment. I helped the young woman stand up, then offered her my tea. I had noticed her often before, whirling like a butterfly. She was graceful and pretty, and I asked if she would like to walk outside to clear her dizziness in the cold air.

I learned that her name was Li and that she was a nurse at the Number Four People's Hospital. When she asked in return about my work, I fell silent, and when she said she wanted to see me again, I decided to leave. Already it was midnight, I was a rightist under surveillance, I slept in a dormitory room with eleven other students, and my campus was half an hour's bike ride away. Then suddenly I didn't care. I told her that I was a college student and a rightist, that I came to the park just to make myself feel alive, and that I could never be her friend. Sensing my pain, she dismissed my caution. That night we became boyfriend and girlfriend in secret.

After that I lied repeatedly to Kong about my whereabouts on Saturday evenings, then cycled off to meet Li. He reported my breaches of discipline to the school's security authorities and I listened to their criticism many times, but I continued to sneak away to meet her in the park. Not wanting Li to be hurt by my political situation, I always guided our conversations in other directions. The less she knew, the less she could be held accountable if I should someday be arrested. My efforts at protection triggered Li's suspicions. She often accused me of having another girlfriend or even a wife, since I refused to take her to my college or introduce her to my classmates. Then one day she called the college switchboard to learn the number of the telephone in my dormitory. She wanted to find out if I really lived there. Kong answered the ring, then stormed over to find me.

To receive a phone call was a special privilege, certainly not permitted to a rightist. Kong demanded to know why a girl would be calling me, then ordered me to report to the Party office and confess. Struggle meeting after struggle meeting followed in March and April of 1960. Kong, Ma, and the other cadres responsible for my surveillance criticized and threatened me. They hated the fact that I had resisted their discipline and defied their control. That spring I had begun to think ahead to the completion of my five years as a student at the Geology Institute. I hoped that a transfer away from the campus would give me the chance to begin anew in different surroundings. Like all those soon to graduate, I checked my mailbox often, knowing that even rightist students were assigned jobs and waiting for notification. That letter would determine not only my employment, but where I would live, my destiny.

With all jobs decided by the school personnel office, my expectations remained low. Those among my classmates with exemplary political records would receive posts at the Geology Bureau and assignments as assistant teachers or low-level administrative staff at the Institute. They had earned the Party's approval and would reap the reward of jobs in Beijing, thereby escaping the hardships of life in the countryside or the small provincial cities.

My history of counterrevolutionary mistakes would deny me the privilege of working in a college or a government office. But I expected that the school authorities would find some practical use for my training, especially after a faculty committee gave my senior thesis on the water supply for the plant the highest mark and a special commendation. I thought I might be sent to a remote industrial facility to do mineral testing or perhaps to a field station in the far northwest to collect soil samples. My living conditions would hardly be easy, but at least I could have a fresh start, apply my technical knowledge, and contribute to the development of my country. Little did I realize the folly of such plans.

On April 27, Kong sought me out in the cafeteria. With graduation nearing he rarely accompanied me anymore, so I grew wary when he asked politely whether I had finished eating and could follow him outside for a talk. The sky was gray with clouds as Kong clasped his hands behind his back and led me slowly around the expanse of hardened mud that served as a playing field. He spoke predictably, almost casually, about the necessity of reforming my thoughts. All the while I watched the overcast sky and wondered about the reason for this idle talk. I feared that the authorities had somehow learned about the escape plans made the previous fall. After an hour Kong looked at his watch. It was almost nine o'clock when he announced that we had to attend a meeting.

Over the past two years I had been summoned often to group criticism sessions. Out of habit I took a seat in the back row of the classroom, hoping that this morning would bring merely a repetition of previous proceedings. Then I looked up. On the blackboard, beneath the colored portrait of Chairman Mao, the chalked characters "Meeting to Criticize Rightist Wu Hongda" stared back at me. My stomach tightened. Then Wang Jian strode to the front of the room. Normally Kong and his fellows from the Youth League branch office chaired these criticism meetings themselves. Some people sat stiffly, while others turned awkwardly to look at me. Wang's opening words broke the silence: "Today we meet to criticize the rightist Wu Hongda." A chorus of allegations sprang from the audience.

"Wu Hongda still refuses to reform himself!"

"He opposes the Party, he must be expelled!"

"Down with Wu Hongda, he must now show us his true face!"

For perhaps twenty minutes the accusations continued. I stared straight ahead until Wang Jian signaled for me to stand. "According to the request of the masses and with the full authority of the school," he intoned, "I now denounce, separate, and expel the rightist Wu Hongda, who has consistently refused to mold himself into a good socialist student and has chosen to remain an enemy of the revolution."

Precisely at that moment a uniformed Public Security officer appeared at the doorway. "Representing the people's government of Beijing," he declared as he stepped to the front desk, "I sentence the counterrevolutionary rightist Wu Hongda to reeducation through labor." He motioned me forward and pulled a piece of paper from his jacket pocket. My eyes fixed on the blood-red badge beside his lapel. How could this be happening, I wondered.

"Sign here," the officer commanded, pointing to the bottom of the form. His hand seemed purposely to cover the body of the document, preventing me from seeing the charges for my arrest.

"I wish to see the accusation against me," I replied, guessing that my year-old plan to escape had been discovered.

"Just sign your name," he repeated.

"It is my right," I asserted, suddenly feeling bold, "to be informed of my crimes."

"The people's government has placed you under arrest,"

he countered impatiently. "Whether you sign or not doesn't matter."

I knew that signing the warrant meant agreeing with the decision for my arrest, and I tried to stall, hoping that someone in the room would support my request to know the charges against me. Anger and fear rose in my throat. No one spoke. With no other choice, I bent to scrawl my name. I knew that anyone arrested for trying, even just planning, to escape was usually shot.

The officer grabbed my arm to lead me across the playing field toward my dormitory room to collect some clothes and bedding. My cheeks burned in shame when I saw my former teammates practicing for a baseball game. "Please let go of me," I asked. "I won't run away. There's no place for me to run." The officer released his grip. He even seemed to reassure me.

"Don't worry too much. We all have to change our thoughts. Maybe after three months or six, you'll come back and be given a job. Work hard at reforming yourself, and you'll return a new socialist person."

I had a more immediate worry. The only concrete evidence of our escape plans lay in my dormitory room. Under the sheets of newspaper that served as a liner for my desk drawer, I had hidden a map of the Burmese border taken from the library. The school's security personnel would certainly collect all of my belongings after I left. If they found the map, my life would be worthless.

We walked into my building, North Dormitory Number Five, then up three flights of concrete steps to my room. Six double bunks flanked the walls and six desks clustered in the middle, each with two drawers. Leaning against the bunks, two security cadres watched us enter. Their eyes never left me. Fortunately the far corner of my top bunk lay outside their line of sight.

Acting as if frantic to collect my possessions, I slid out my lower drawer and reached over to dump its contents onto my bunk. A bottle of blue ink spilled across the quilt, and I threw up my hands in dismay. I had formulated a plan. "No need to hurry," one of the cadres said. "Take your time." By then I had found the map. I perched on the bunk and twisted my body toward the wall, slipping the folded page into my pocket.

Jumping down, I told the Public Security officer I had washed a length of cotton cloth and left it hanging in the basement to dry. "Take only what you need for tonight," he ordered. "The rest will be sent later." Ignoring his words, I darted past him into the corridor. I was agile and strong after my years of athletic training, and I flew down the stairs, hearing his footsteps not far behind me. Just inside the door to the basement, I pulled open the heavy furnace door and stuffed the map inside. By the time the angry officer reached my side, I was calmly folding the cloth beside the drying line. My heart pounded, but I said quietly, "You see? I wanted to have it made into trousers, and I was afraid if I left it here, it would disappear."

I finished tying a few belongings inside my quilt, and the angry officer guided me to a waiting school jeep. At the district police station, a duty officer took my fingerprints and removed my keys and watch, my shoelaces and belt, even my library card.

"This can't be happening," I thought to myself again. "There must be some way out."

Outside they motioned me back to the jeep, where I sat alone for perhaps two hours. I thought about trying to escape, but many police walked around inside the Public Security compound. Finally the driver appeared, then a guard leading a second prisoner, who climbed in beside me on the hard rear seat. He looked dirty and disheveled. I felt insulted to be thrust alongside a common criminal, no doubt a vagrant from the countryside picked up for stealing food from a Beijing market during this time of famine. We rode in silence for more than an hour. I could see nothing outside the olive green canvas roof. The screech of brakes signaled our arrival at the Beiyuan Detention Center, which I soon learned was a holding facility for prisoners awaiting relocation to the labor camps.

Inside the first gate a sentry inspected the documents of arrest. A ten-foot-high brick wall stretched as far as I could see across the flat, green expanse of the North China plain. I stared at the second gate. When a duty prisoner motioned me forward, I hoisted my bedroll awkwardly to one shoulder, grabbing my beltless pants with my free hand. Then I waited, squatting awkwardly just inside the yard, seemingly forgotten.

5

Inside the Gates

*I*nside the detention center I watched more than a thousand inmates sitting cross-legged in circles of thirty on the hard-packed ground of the prison yard. Two political instructors paced behind each group, alternately reading aloud from the newspaper. At around four o'clock buckets of food arrived. Still no one acknowledged my existence. A couple of hours passed before a duty prisoner led me across the prison yard toward what I guessed, from its domed roof and huge chimney, to be an abandoned brick kiln. It took a few moments for my eyes to adjust to the dim light inside. Then I could see perhaps forty quilts folded along two *kang*s, the traditional brick sleeping platforms with heating ducts below that are used throughout North China. The kangs lined the opposite walls of a narrow room. Besides the doorway opening, a small window cut through the thick kiln wall provided the only source of daylight. I deposited my bedroll at a designated spot on the kang, placed my mug and towel on the shelf above, and tried to imagine how I could live in such surroundings, sandwiched into a sleeping space that looked about two feet wide.

I knew that as a new prisoner I might at any moment be summoned for interrogation. I needed to determine the probable reason for my arrest so that I could devise an explanation.

I had to plan my strategy quickly. I didn't wish to be caught off guard, but my mind refused to cooperate. The events of the day rushed back at me. I saw the face of the officer with the arrest warrant and the bloodlike red insignia on his badge, then the spreading blue ink on my quilt and the heavy metal grate of the dormitory furnace. I couldn't focus my thoughts.

The duty prisoner told me to join one of the squads in the yard for political instruction. I had missed the second of the two daily prison meals, he added, but I had no thought of food. Outside I sat down cross-legged, copying the posture of the other prisoners with their eyes cast downward, their hands on their knees. I hoped not to attract anyone's notice. By then it must have been well past four o'clock. Thinking hard about the accusations I might soon face, I retained nothing from the squad leader's droning words about the necessity of reforming our thoughts through labor. I sat there for perhaps an hour, then moved inside for more study on the kang. One of the duty prisoners instructed me about camp regulations, and at nine-thirty the order came to sleep. After a latrine call, all the prisoners filed into the kiln, stretched out side by side on the kang with their feet toward the wall, and fell asleep. My mind raced. I didn't know what would happen to me next. With men crammed on both sides of me, I could find no position that felt comfortable. Once I tried to sit up, but the guard barked a reprimand. Overhead dangled two light bulbs, casting a gloomy circle across the curved, coal-blackened ceiling.

Around midnight a duty prisoner called my name from the doorway. I tried to still my growing panic as I followed him outside and into a small, bare room. A police captain sat behind a single table. "Squat down," he barked without looking up. He shone the desk lamp onto my face. "State your name, age, occupation, and the nature of your crime."

"I am a counterrevolutionary rightist," I answered quickly. "In the Hundred Flowers campaign I attacked the Communist Party. I still have a lot of poisonous ideas."

"We know all that. What else? What else?" shouted my interrogator. "Don't you understand the Party's policy? Leniency to those who confess, harshness to those who resist reform." He stood up, walked around me, then kicked open a second door. I saw a body hanging from the rafters, then another

sprawled on the wet floor. I couldn't see their faces or tell if
they were unconscious or dead. "This is what happens to those
who resist the Party's authority," he snapped. "You're a young
student. I'll give you another chance. Tomorrow night come
back and confess fully." Terribly shaken by the glimpse of those
who had apparently resisted reform, I returned to my slot on
the kang. I had no idea what I would say at the next session. I
knew only that if my answers sounded false or incomplete,
I too would be hanging from the interrogation room ceiling. I
didn't sleep at all that night.

At five-thirty the next morning a duty prisoner shouted the
order to get up, and we filed outside in groups of five. I quickly
learned the morning drill: Dip one hand into a small wooden
bucket that served about ten people, splash your face with dirty
water, return to your quilt, and sit cross-legged at attention to
receive reeducation from *People's Daily*. Not until ten o'clock
did a cart arrive from the kitchen. The duty prisoner thrust at
us two small steamed buns that were darker in color than any
wotou I had ever seen. I couldn't guess what they were made
of. Then he poured a ladleful of thin soup with a few floating
leaves of some kind into the enamel basin I had brought from
school. I bit into one wotou. It tasted bitter and the texture was
very coarse, probably from the addition of chaff to the crudely
ground sorghum flour. I couldn't eat and passed my buns to the
prisoner squatting beside me, who was called Big Mouth Xing.
He stuffed them into his mouth, mumbling a few words of
thanks.

At ten-thirty we filed outside to sit cross-legged in rows on
the ground for a special teamwide meeting. From a mud platform at the center of the yard, the head study class leader named
Shi surveyed the fifteen hundred assembled men. Also a prisoner, he had earned the authorities' trust and now wielded considerable power over his fellow inmates.

"May First and the celebration of International Labor Day
are coming," he announced. "In preparation the Beiyuan Detention Center will pay particular attention to hygiene." I knew
that hospitals and schools, offices and shops, always arranged
special sanitary measures on the eve of a major holiday, but I
had never imagined what took place in a prison.

"Strip down," came the order. "Begin!" To my horror, all

around me prisoners undressed to their undershorts, then began searching their partners' bodies for lice. I couldn't disobey, so I pulled off my shirt and trousers, appalled at this mass effort at delousing. Then in my most polite voice I told Xing, who was assigned to be my partner, that I had never seen a louse and that he should attend to his own hygiene.

Xing chortled loudly. "What? Someone who's never seen a louse!"

"You there!" the study leader shrieked suddenly, his body tense, his finger pointing rigidly. "What do you think you're doing?"

My jaw clenched. I realized that Shi was pointing at me. Shame flushed my cheeks. He must have heard Xing guffaw and noticed us sitting idly. Shi's lips snarled as he stepped down from the platform and marched angrily toward us.

I could see how Big Mouth Xing had gotten his name. The corners of his mouth seemed to stretch all the way to his ears. He looked about my age, slightly taller, lean and muscular. When the duty prisoner had assigned us to work together that morning, Xing had merely looked at me and yawned.

Even during my weeks of geology fieldwork in the countryside the previous year, I had never been in such close physical contact with a peasant. I shuddered inwardly to note Xing's yellowed teeth and the dark gaps where several molars had fallen out. His ears looked black with dirt, bits of sleep crusted the corners of his small eyes, and a strand of dry mucus clung to the edge of one nostril. I could not imagine grooming this body for lice.

When Shi reached us, Xing muttered, "We're getting started, we're getting started. Don't blame me."

I turned to the study class leader and politely offered an apology. "This is my responsibility. Sorry, but I don't actually know what a louse looks like."

Shi threw back his head and howled. "Unbelievable!" He exchanged glances with Xing, then narrowed his eyes and pointed toward the stone platform in the middle of the yardful of prisoners. "Get up there," he shouted. I hesitated. Without my clothes in public, I felt ashamed. "Get up!" he screamed angrily.

I mounted the platform, afraid and embarrassed, and

bowed my head. More than a thousand prisoners stared up at me.

"Here is someone who claims he has never seen a louse!" study class leader Shi declared to the undressed prisoners. They craned their necks curiously. "He's just arrived, but there's no doubt he comes from a capitalist family! Maybe someone can help him learn."

A short round-faced prisoner, who limped slightly from a deformity that made one leg shorter than the other, jumped to the platform grinning. Between his thumb and forefinger he held a louse, belly up, just beneath my nose. Its white legs waved helplessly above its flat body. Everyone laughed. Study class leader Shi dismissed me with a contemptuous gesture. "This louse is only his first lesson. It's just the start of his reform!" He turned to me with disgust. "You obviously have a long, long way to go."

I returned to my spot in the yard and vaguely heard Xing mutter an apology. In my mind the study leader's words reverberated: "a long, long way to go . . ."

That afternoon sitting inside the kiln during study class, I tried to think clearly about the next interrogation. I had to decide whether to admit my role in the aborted escape plans as a sign of contrition or hope that the order for my arrest had been issued on some other grounds. I knew that being caught in a lie would provoke the harshest punishment. Then for a moment my luck changed.

Outside the kiln window, opposite my place on the kang, I saw my geology classmate Wang, rubbing his nose, using our old signal. I couldn't imagine how he had found me. Cross-legged with my hands on my knees, I didn't dare to move. According to prison regulations, even shifting your legs required permission. My body tensed. I had received no news about Wang since his arrest, and I could not afford to lose this chance to find out whether he had confessed. I waited for the duty prisoner to turn his back, then quickly rubbed my nose in reply.

I took several breaths before raising my hand to request permission from the duty prisoner to use the latrine. "Later," came the curt reply.

"I can't hold it, I have to go now," I insisted.

"Are you trying to make trouble?" His voice rose.

Desperate to leave, I touched Big Mouth Xing's leg with my knee, silently asking for his support. "Let him go," Xing muttered. "If he shits here, it will smell."

Xing stood up when the duty prisoner nodded. Inmates were not permitted even to visit the latrine unaccompanied. We walked together across the yard, but Xing stopped at the open doorway to avoid the stench. Inside I saw Wang squatting over the cement trough. He stared straight ahead and whispered, "I don't know you, I don't know anything about the fifty yuan, I don't know anything about the escape." Then he was gone.

Those few words saved me. Suddenly I felt grateful for the morning's louse lesson. If Wang had not seen me standing almost naked on the platform, he would never have known of my arrival, and I could have made a serious error by confessing the plan to escape.

At midnight as I lay sleepless and uncomfortable, the duty prisoner again called my name and led me outside to the small office. "Have you thought it over?" asked the police captain behind the table. His tone sounded even more cold and menacing than the night before.

"I must explain one more thing," I replied nervously. "I also took fifty yuan."

The captain pounded the desk and swore, "Fuck your mother! What do you mean you 'took' money? You still want to save your face! You stole it, you stinking intellectual! Get out of here."

My whole body trembled, but I felt that I had passed a crucial test. I had stood up to my captors' intimidation and provided a credible confession. The authorities had not, after all, discovered my secret plan.

For the next several days prisoners continued to arrive at the detention center each night. I could see that most of the new arrivals were not political prisoners like me but villagers picked up for theft or vagrancy, like so much human trash, presumably as part of the Beijing police effort to cleanse the city's streets in preparation for the national holiday on May 1. Because of overcrowding some of the earlier arrivals were being transferred out to clear space in the kiln for detainees needing to be processed. Big Mouth Xing was one who received notice that he would be sent to labor in the nearby Xindian Brick Factory.

The afternoon before Xing's departure we squatted outside chewing the second of our daily rations of wotou. Curious about my new friend, I asked why he never removed his heavy black padded greatcoat. Except during the sanitary measures of the previous week, I had never seen him take it off. He ate and slept in his coat, wearing it even under the midday sun. His small eyes bulged at my question.

"I could never lose this coat," he answered sharply.

"Why does it mean so much to you?" I persisted. The coat didn't appear to me to be worth much money.

Xing's voice grew low and gravelly. "You intellectuals know nothing about these things." He flapped the coat's broad, thick lapels. "At night I find a corner, cover myself up, and sleep on the street. Without this coat I would freeze." He paused, unaccustomed to long explanations. I knew that Xing had no education and could write only the three characters in his name.

"Without this coat I wouldn't eat!" His words began to tumble forth. "A chicken brings twenty-five yuan right now on the street. I can jump on a train, get off near a village, pull a handful of grain out of my pocket, and sprinkle it on the ground. When a chicken bends its neck to eat, I grab it from behind, twist its neck, and shove it under my coat. People in the city will pay a lot for a chicken right now. I don't eat like an emperor, but I don't go hungry."

Xing's eyes narrowed proudly, and he folded his arms. The scarcity of food in Beijing had brought him a source of livelihood. His coat was the means of his survival.

Xing wanted to talk. In the simplest words he explained how difficult it had been to travel from his village in the southern part of Hebei province to Beijing where he hoped to find food. By the time he left home, many of the peasants in his village had grown too weak to undertake such a journey. He had delayed his departure to care for his mother, who was so frail and ill from starvation that she could hardly speak. One night she told him that her time had come. She wanted her son to leave the village and save himself. The next morning she died. At the edge of her quilt, Xing found five pieces of dried yam that she had refused to eat, her final gift to her son. He slid the yam chips into his overcoat pocket and set out immediately. Lacking the strength to bury his mother, he covered her face and just left her lying on their kang. He often had nightmares, he added in a low voice, that the starving village dogs had found her body.

Xing made his way to Baoding, a provincial city on the rail line about ninety miles south of Beijing. Sometimes he walked, sometimes he sneaked aboard a train, stealing whatever he could to survive. When the police caught him on a train to Beijing they beat him, but then he ran away. The next time he was less fortunate. A few days after reaching the capital, he was arrested for petty theft and sent to the Beiyuan Detention Center for labor reform.

Xing's description of conditions in his village shocked me. In Beijing I had never heard about the severity of the famine in the countryside only half a day's train ride from the capital. I began to realize the consequences of the recently failed harvests. Xing's story made me glimpse the suffering caused by the methods of deep planting I had seen in Shandong province, and by the exaggeration of yield statistics as local cadres tried to respond to inflated demands from Party leaders. Never before had I realized the results of the Great Leap Forward.

About two weeks after Xing left Beiyuan for the brick factory, our squad leader picked me to read aloud from the newspaper in the afternoon study class. I knew the privilege of reading was a sign of increasing trust. A hard rain fell. I sat cross-legged on my quilt, watching the yard turn to mud outside. From among the pile of newspapers tossed on the kang, I pulled out a sheet dated April 27, the exact date of my arrest. My thoughts flew back for a moment to the Geology Institute. Almost a month had passed. I gazed at the weathered, illiterate faces around me and wondered how many of my classmates had already been assigned jobs.

I was reading aloud absentmindedly when two security guards appeared in the doorway. I could feel their scrutiny. "You, Wu Hongda," one interrupted. "Stop reading and come here. Follow us." They led me to the security office where a police captain ordered me to report immediately to the Beiyuan Chemical Factory. A guard led me across the prison yard through a low wire fence that enclosed the production facility adjacent to the detention center. "From now on you will labor here," said the guard as we entered a low brick building that served as a laboratory.

Three workers labeling dusty vials of chemicals looked up when I entered the room, gave their names, and explained my duties. Two, I learned, were pharmacists who had been branded as "historical counterrevolutionaries," meaning their "crimes" had preceded the establishment of the People's Republic in 1949. Most likely they had worked in some capacity for the Nationalist government. The third was a lecturer in chemistry from Beijing University and a rightist like me.

Each day, they told me, I would carry materials for testing back and forth between the laboratory and the chemical factory workshop. I felt a surge of gratitude. However menial, the job would relieve me of the deadening routine of political study morning, afternoon, and evening. As a prison laborer I would be able to walk around, and my living conditions would improve. I would sleep in a different part of the brick kiln on a crude, double-decker wooden pallet bed. Rather than two meals a day, I would get three with a larger allotment of grain. And most importantly, my job would require me to walk about the factory compound alone, a rare freedom in a setting of constant surveillance.

By then I had come to understand that in China's prison system, labor is simultaneously considered an obligation, a punishment, and a reward. You have to admit your crimes, demonstrate the willingness to reform your thoughts, and show you have accepted discipline before you earn the privilege of work. During the month of initial detention, I had to prove my obedience. After that I could be assigned to labor to proceed with my reform.

During the first two and a half weeks I was not allowed to write letters to my family. My only contact with the outside world was a note and small package that arrived from Li, the beautiful dancing butterfly who had persuaded the Geology Institute's security office to tell her my whereabouts. I unwrapped her package, remembering the seven or eight times I had met her in the park. Inside were a towel and toothbrush, some pencils and envelopes, some soap and hard candies. Her note said only, "Reform yourself hard. I will keep hoping." I left a note for her with the guard, thanking her but urging her not to try to contact me. I never heard from her again.

Soon after I moved to the labor-reform barracks for prisoners assigned to the chemical factory, the captain in charge approved my request to write my parents and inform them of my arrest. I knew how frightened my stepmother would have been at my silence, as she had written to me regularly after I left home for Beijing in 1955. But I also knew her frailty. Fearing the effect my letter would have, I chose every word carefully and assured her that I was being treated well. I posted the letter on May 15, 1960, and waited for a response. No return letter arrived. I tried to imagine the reason for my family's silence. I wondered if they had decided to cut off contact with me out of caution now that I was a criminal, or if they refused to write as a sign of disapproval. As the days passed, this question troubled me more and more.

Then one afternoon early in June, the duty prisoner found me in the chemical factory and told me to stop work. I followed him to the visiting room and saw my older brother sitting stiffly on a bench, his face stern. I had not seen him since 1955 when he boarded the train for Inner Mongolia. Not knowing why he had come, I asked about the family. "They're okay," he said curtly, "but you have done many wrong things to hurt not just the family, but the Party and the country. Now you have to take the consequences for what you have done. You have only yourself to blame for your situation, and the whole family has denounced you. We have cut off relations with you. You must study Mao Zedong thought very hard, reform yourself diligently, and become a new socialist person." He handed me a package that contained a new pair of cotton shoes and a rolled-up towel with some candies inside.

I felt shocked to hear from my brother's mouth the same words I heard repeatedly from the police. With a guard listening, I couldn't tell my brother to stop talking like that, so I tried to interrupt him with other questions.

"How's our father, how's our mother?" I asked, but he only ignored me. That made me angry.

"Answer my questions," I said.

"You should feel ashamed even to ask about our parents," he shouted back.

The guard interrupted to prevent an argument and echoed my brother's accusations. "Wu Hongda, pay attention. You need to be educated by your brother." I felt my fury rising.

My brother broke the silence. "You should just die here like this," he said. At those words I threw the pair of shoes at him, just missing his shoulder.

"I don't want anything from you," I shouted as I turned toward the door to end the encounter.

"You must accept the criticism of your family," warned the guard. "Be careful," he added. "And take the shoes."

I picked them up and walked back to the laboratory, stunned by my brother's harshness. I had no way then to understand his bitterness. He never told me that he was en route back to Inner Mongolia from Shanghai after attending our stepmother's funeral. Nor did I know that she had committed suicide by taking an overdose of sleeping pills on May 17, the day she received my letter. Only in 1979 would I learn that my brother had received a telegram telling him to hurry and come home and that he had stopped in Beijing to find me, planning to travel together back to Shanghai. At the Geology Institute he had learned of my arrest six weeks earlier and had gone on alone. Father had asked him to visit me in the camp on his way back when he passed through Beijing and had warned him not to tell me that our mother was gone. Father wanted to spare me that pain. But in my brother's eyes, I was responsible for our stepmother's death.

Besides the problem of my family's rejection, what preoccupied me after my brother's visit was hunger. Prisoners in the camps become obsessed with food, and during a year of famine when even workers who loyally serve the Party are starving, those sent off to labor reform can barely subsist on their daily rations. Even after I started receiving three servings a day, I felt continually hungry. My regular route back and forth from the laboratory to the factory took me past the security guards' private vegetable garden. Several times a day I would stare at the cabbages and cucumbers, warning myself not to take risks, but one night when I was hungrier than I had ever felt, the smell of cucumbers overwhelmed my caution. For the first time in my life, I stole. I bent over and snatched a small cucumber from the vine. The skin crunched as I chewed it. I swallowed quickly, savoring the moisture and the peppery flavor. Four or five more times in the next two weeks I visited the police garden.

Hungry prisoners possess a keen sense of smell. As I returned to the laboratory with a load of chemicals one night, my stomach rumbled and out came a cucumber belch, just as I passed one of the duty prisoners. His nose began to twitch. Then he grabbed my arm and dragged me to the security office where an angry-faced guard demanded, "What have you been up to?" I knew I should lie, but I had been in the camps less than two months, and I had not yet become skilled at making up explanations.

"What have you been up to?" the guard repeated.

"N-nothing . . ." I stammered.

"You've been stealing vegetables," barked the guard.

"I just . . . I just . . ."

"Okay." He cut me off sharply and waved me out of the office.

Informed the next day of the police captain's decision that I could not be trusted to move around the camp alone, I was reassigned to the storehouse. There my task was to remove and then return the various chemicals used in the factory and to record in a log all incoming and outgoing substances. I missed the freedom to walk outside, but still I considered myself lucky. At least I was not back in a situation of constant supervision.

By July I had grown used to the daily schedule for prison labor. We assembled outside our barracks each morning at eight o'clock for roll call, then marched to the factory. In the factory yard we were fed, and at nine o'clock we began two hours of group study. At eleven the duty prisoners gathered us together for lunch. At noon we resumed work, stopping only once for rest and a meal until we finished our shift at midnight. Then the guards gathered us again, gave instructions about our reform, and returned us to our barracks for a final roll call. We slept from one o'clock to eight when the routine began again. Seven days a week.

One day in mid-August several prisoners, obviously distraught, came to my storage area and pleaded for me to provide them with some alcohol, which they knew was stocked among the supplies. They always liked to drink, they said, and they needed alcohol. They were suffering, and I was their brother.

They wanted to ask me a favor. I had to help them out. Immediately I refused. Not only did I want to protect my job, but I knew that drinking methanol, the only kind of alcohol in the storehouse, could be fatal. These were peasants who either didn't know its lethal effects or who were so desperate that they didn't care. I felt sorry for them. However miserable I felt, I thought, at least I had no such addictions. A few days later two of the prisoners approached me again, pressing me to give in. Again I refused and told them that industrial alcohol was poisonous. "You don't drink, so you don't know," they urged. "This alcohol can serve as a substitute."

I had forgotten those incidents when a few days later a police captain entered the storage area, glowering at me. "You will now confess what you have done!" he shouted. "You have given out chemicals privately without registering them in the log."

I replied firmly that I always recorded outgoing chemicals and that I had never given any chemicals to unauthorized persons. "I'm warning you," he answered, raising his voice even louder. "The Party's policy is leniency to those who confess, severe punishment to those who resist!"

His accusation frightened me, but I insisted on my innocence. Later I learned that one of the prisoners who had approached me had become near-sighted, another had lost his vision completely, symptoms of methanol poisoning. The police guard came again to ask whether I had controlled all industrial alcohol strictly and dismissed my protestations of innocence. If alcohol had disappeared from the storeroom, he claimed, then I had been lax in my duty, and I would be held responsible.

Again considered unreliable, I was transferred to the main factory workshop where I labored with the other prisoners under the supervision of the team captain. This third assignment required me to stand at a workbench all day drying a white mash of wet chemicals into powder. I had no idea what the substance was. They told me it was called "G-salt." In order to dry it, I needed to control the heat under six enameled iron plates, adding or removing lumps of coal in a bricked-in grate beneath to keep the temperature constant at 325 degrees centigrade. I had to test the temperature continually. At 330 degrees the powder would turn a yellowish ivory color, but if it reached 350 degrees it would turn red and be rendered useless.

At the start of my assignment I worked very carefully. Useless powder, I understood, meant punishment. But one day, tired and hungry, I dozed off for a few moments as I tended the grate. When I jerked awake, all the powder on one of the plates had turned rust red. I had ruined 9.9 kilograms.

"Get out of here!" shouted the security guard in charge. Humiliated, I turned to go, but before I could leave, he slapped me across the face and kicked me several times. That powder costs 10,000 yuan per kilogram, he screamed. My error had cost 99,000 yuan.

I walked away, limping slightly. The physical pain was not so great, but I had received an ugly wound to my pride. This was the first time anyone had struck me in prison. Only recently, I thought, I was a top student and a champion athlete. People looked up to me. Now any policeman could slap me like a dog whenever he liked, and I could do nothing. I felt angry and afraid.

After this incident the prison authorities decided I was not fit to work with chemicals, and during the first week of September they ordered me back through the fence from the factory to the detention center.

6

Learning from the Peasants

On the morning of my transfer back to the detention center in September 1960, I spotted Big Mouth Xing, as I was heading toward the brick kiln on my way to study group. Four months had passed since his transfer, and I had not expected to meet him again. I felt strangely happy to see this rough peasant, but something about him had changed. He seemed much thinner than before.

"Where's your overcoat?" I asked as we met at the entrance to the kiln. He didn't answer at once, and I repeated the question, adding with a smile, "Have you given up stealing chickens?" I wondered what had happened to him after he left in May.

"I couldn't make it on the outside," he replied.

He seemed to be ignoring my question. I thought he was remembering his efforts to survive on the streets after leaving his village. Then Xing became animated. He seemed to speak to himself, throwing his gnarled hands in the air.

"Nobody can! Every day in the city they searched us. Daytime, nighttime, anytime. There's no place to hide anymore. No food. Even in Beijing, in the stores and markets, there's no food, not even to buy. No cake or biscuits or meat. Nothing. And," he lowered his voice solemnly, "all the chickens are gone. I couldn't find one anywhere. Couldn't find any food. I was so hungry I traded my overcoat on the street for two small steamed buns and ate them right there."

I assumed that Xing had spent the past several months at the Xindian Labor Reform Brick Factory, until he told me he had escaped. He slipped through police security, expecting to find more food living by his wits in the city than he could get in the labor camp. But in Beijing he found no food at all. The worsening famine had made survival on the streets impossible. Finally feeling desperate just to survive, Xing walked up to a police kiosk and turned himself in. With no identification papers, he knew he would be arrested. Back he came in September to the detention center.

"What about your clothes?" I asked, looking curiously at his new coat, a dirty, worn People's Liberation Army jacket. The khaki green showed brighter in the spots where the insignia had been torn off. "Where did you get that?"

"Stole it."

"How can you do that?" I asked disapprovingly.

"What do you mean?" Xing replied, puzzled. "This is a small thing, not important, not a big deal at all." He turned away without a trace of concern. I still couldn't accept his indifference to moral standards, but I knew my own thinking was hardening as I too learned about survival. My disapproval was giving way to respect. Xing did what he had to in order to stay alive.

"Damn . . . Sonuvabitch . . ." Xing would mutter under his breath every morning as he stared disgustedly at the two shrunken black buns the duty prisoner dropped into his bowl. "Every day two meals. Every meal two black buns. Every bun two-and-a-half ounces. Half wheat chaff, half sorghum. One bowl of watery soup and one piece of salted turnip." Driven by hunger, Xing became more aggressive. When someone on the kang neglected for a moment to pay attention to his food . . . *ffftttt*. His bun disappeared into Xing's huge mouth. The prisoner might yell, jump on Xing, even beat him. But the guards would not care if a prisoner lost a wotou, and certainly Xing did not care. He felt his own hunger acutely and didn't bother about scruples. He couldn't understand my hesitation. "Nobody here will take care of you," he warned me. "You have to take care of yourself."

I was twenty-three, a college graduate raised in an affluent, urban family, and a political criminal. Xing Jingping, three years younger than I, was a peasant from a starving village, a thief with no education and no political viewpoint. The gulf between us was vast, yet I grew to admire him as the most capable and influential teacher of my life.

Xing was bold, and sometimes this got him into trouble. On national holidays the government granted prisoners the favor of one meal of good food. On October 1, 1960, National Day, everyone in the detention center received two plump buns made of actual wheat flour. Those buns had a delicious, sweet flavor when compared to our regular wotou, which were dark in color and rough in texture, made from a bitter mixture of sorghum and chaff. Everyone also got a ladleful of vegetable soup, not just water with a few floating weeds, but a broth made with bean sauce and pieces of pork fat with the skin left on. Every portion, about three ounces, contained four or five pieces of pork fat. I held my bowl in both hands, savoring the pungent smell and the rich taste.

For this meal our squad of fifteen was divided into three sections. My group ate first, and the others sat waiting hungrily for the duty prisoners to bring more buckets of food from the kitchen. Xing sat beside me, his bowl empty, his eyes roving round and round. Clearly he liked this meal very much, and he wanted more. He was just waiting for an opportunity. Noticing his eyes, I caught his arm. "Hey, everyone gets only one portion," I said. "Your heart, my heart, everyone's heart is made of the same meat. Don't be so harsh and unfeeling."

Xing shook off my hand. His voice was like a growl. "So who do you think you're taking care of? Even if I can stay alive today, I don't know about tomorrow. I can't even look after myself. How can I think about other people?"

Suddenly Xing's tall, thin body froze. His eyes fixed on something happening at the door. He stared at the two study class leaders, who enjoyed special privileges because of their closeness to the guards. According to regulations, they should receive no more food than ordinary prisoners. The same quota supposedly applied to all, but in fact the security personnel would often look aside so they could take an extra bun.

Two duty prisoners had just come through the door with full food buckets. The study leaders stopped them and started picking through the holiday soup, choosing extra pieces of meat for themselves. Everyone noticed, and in seconds the whole room seethed with the prisoners' rage. I felt hot with anger. Those buckets were for the whole group. The study leaders were prisoners also. Not only did they intimidate and humiliate us in the study class, but right in front of us they were stealing our food.

I nodded my head angrily in their direction, but Xing had already leaned forward. Suddenly he shot up from the kang and made straight for the soup bucket. The two study leaders had their backs toward us when Xing charged, butting his head between them. He plunged his face into the soup and began lapping like a dog. The study leaders began furiously beating him, but Xing ignored their blows and kicks. The bucket tipped over, and soup spilled across the dirt floor. Xing, on all fours, put his face to the mud and licked up every piece of pork fat. The study leader named Ling picked up the empty bucket and clubbed him, splitting his head open. Xing stood up, bean sauce, blood, and mud smeared across his face. He didn't shout or cry. He just stood there, blood trickling from his head.

"Maybe it wasn't worth it," Xing said when I saw him next after his release from seven days in solitary confinement. I had no idea what conditions he had endured, but I could see how much thinner he looked after subsisting for a week on starvation rations. "I really got some good pork meat and vegetables. But I lost it all in these seven days." He pointed to the wound on his head. "You see here? I won't forget." What he meant by that I wasn't sure. He would not forget the lesson that he shouldn't steal food, or he would take revenge on Ling?

In the weeks after National Day, the crowding in the kiln became unbearable. The Beiyuan Detention Center had been intended to hold fifteen hundred prisoners, but after the Beijing police scoured the streets to remove the city's undesirables before the holiday, the facility overflowed. The kangs were clogged with bodies. No longer did we have two feet of space, but we lay on our sides, pressed tightly together. Twice each night the duty prisoner gave orders for everyone to turn over, and we

shifted to the other side in one collective movement because
the kang was too crowded for us to move independently. I became impatient for assignment to a labor camp.

Personnel from the different labor-reform facilities
throughout the Beijing district visited the detention center during October, responding to orders from the Public Security Bureau to ease the holding center's crowding. "Hey!" Xing called
to a captain from Qinghe Farm as the prisoners stood lined up
in the yard for scrutiny one morning. "Hey, how about me? Do
you want a good worker?" He threw his shoulders back and
pushed his chest forward.

"Who are you?" the captain shouted in his face, angered
by Xing's boldness. "What do you think you're doing?"

"I'm a peasant. I can do any job, carry any load. I work
hard, and I don't care what I eat. Let me go!"

"Okay," the captain agreed. "Step out."

"I'm leaving," said Xing. "See you later." He looked happy
as he raised his hand to me in farewell and headed off toward
the kiln to tie up his quilt. The transfer would mean more food
for him.

When the police captain walked by me, he paused. I didn't
dare call out boldly the way Xing had.

"What's your name?"

"Wu Hongda," I answered quietly, my eyes fixed on the
ground.

"How old are you?"

"Twenty-three."

"What is your crime?"

"I'm a rightist."

"Where did you come from?"

"I'm a college student."

The captain moved on. I walked slowly back to the kiln.
Xing already had his things rolled up in his quilt. Seeing my
dejected look, he perched on the kang and spoke sharply. "In
this world no one else cares anything about you. I don't know
how many books you have read, but all that reading is useless.
None of it will help you here. You have to take care of yourself."
Then his voice softened. "You have to take care of yourself. It
doesn't matter how smart you are. Sonuvabitch, in this place

the strongest one is the best one." Many times Xing's words would come back to me.

That night I saw more newly arrived prisoners being assigned to tents pitched around the yard. The kiln was full beyond its capacity. Often there was no wash water at all, no way even with dirty water to rinse our faces.

Xing was lucky, I thought. He was free. It might be a bitter, limited freedom, but anything seemed preferable to the miserable, still deteriorating conditions at the detention center.

Rain fell steadily in mid-October. The tents leaked, and the yard turned to mud. I remembered the rainy season in Shanghai when I was a boy. Then I would peel off my clothes, pull on my swimsuit, and run gleefully through a downpour. Now the rain made me heavyhearted, and with Xing gone I was lonely. Never before had I dreaded the autumn rains, but this year they made me think of the approaching winter. I wondered how I could survive the cold with so little food. Already by late September the prison diet had begun to take its toll, and I had felt myself growing weak. By late October, my ribs looked like a washboard.

Then another fear set in. After three or maybe six months you will come back and get a job, the policeman had claimed on the day of my arrest. Six months had already passed, and I had no reason to hope for release. Why had my brother denounced me? My stepmother must have received my letter. My parents must have been notified by the Public Security Bureau. I had written to them once each month during my labor at the chemical factory, but they had not replied. After I returned to the detention center in September, I was not permitted to write. My sister had sent a brief note and a small package of food in August, but she had said only that I should reform myself well. I couldn't dismiss my worry about my family. Were they all right? Had something happened? Irrational fears intruded on my thoughts. Did my stepmother still love me? Had I brought shame or trouble to my family?

Finally I realized that I could not worry about my family anymore. I couldn't afford to worry about anything except myself. I was losing weight fast. Somehow I had to get more food. I had to preserve my health. Nothing else mattered.

Xing, I realized, was actually far more intelligent than I. He instinctively possessed a shrewdness and understanding that I couldn't hope to match. He had managed to escape from Xindian, come back to Beiyuan, and leave again for Qinghe Farm, always adapting to necessity. He was the one who was truly educated, not I. He had graduated and gotten a job, while I remained, waiting.

When study leader Ling asked me one day to become the class record keeper, I jumped at the chance. All newcomers had to confess their crimes in front of the group. My job was to write down everything they said. For this service, Ling authorized the duty prisoner to give me half a bun extra at every meal.

Unlike most of my fellow prisoners, Ling was a Party member. He had been sent to East Berlin to study astrophysics and had fallen in love with a German girl. The couple had escaped together to West Berlin, but later Ling regretted his decision to defect. He felt guilty for abandoning his country after the government had supported his research, and he returned to East Berlin and asked the Chinese Consulate for help. He gratefully accepted an air ticket back to China, but upon landing in Beijing, he was escorted directly to Beiyuan, labeled as a "thought reactionary."

Ling's voice broke into my thoughts one afternoon in late October when study class had ended. "Pay attention. Tomorrow there is another chance to leave," he whispered. "It may be the last chance. The Yanqing Steel Factory cadres will come to choose some workers." I had no idea why Ling was helping me. It was unthinkable for a study leader to single out an ordinary prisoner and offer advice.

That night I lay awake wondering what to do. I knew that any prisoners not yet weakened from hunger would want to be chosen for the steel factory. "I must get out of here," I told myself. "This may be my last chance." To make myself look more like a worker, I decided that for the inspection I would remove my glasses. At that point I knew I had started thinking like a prisoner. I was indeed remolding myself. To survive within the camps, I would have to work the system.

The next morning the Beiyuan guards lined up all the eligible prisoners in rows of a hundred. Then five or six security cadres from the Yanqing Steel Factory took charge.

"Move!" one shouted, and a line of prisoners marched past. The recruiters looked them over. "Move!" they shouted again as another line marched past. "Run!" they shouted next. Everyone broke into a run to demonstrate his fitness and strength. Some stumbled, weakened from hunger.

"Take him away!" they ordered when a prisoner fell down.

"Run!" I told myself when my line moved forward. "Don't fall, run, run, keep going." I talked to myself as though I were a racehorse. I pretended I was running around the bases. "First . . . second . . . faster. Keep going!" But this was not a baseball field. I was running for my life. I summoned all my energy and desperately willed myself on.

Prisoners who managed to finish the required laps formed a separate line at the far end of the yard. The steel factory cadres walked around us, patting our chests, feeling our shoulders, neglecting only to open our mouths and examine our teeth. Sometimes they would stop to fire questions at a prisoner. Finally they came to me.

I was still breathing hard, my heart pounding, but I dropped my shoulders, raised my washboard chest and looked straight ahead. I had lost perhaps twenty pounds, but I had not forgotten how to discipline my body.

The first cadre, whose name was Yang, had a blotched face, stained teeth, and lips darkened from tobacco. A heavy padded coat with a fur collar hung from his shoulders. His head tilted lightly to the left as he spoke, and he pointed with fingers yellowed from heavy smoking.

"What do you do?"

"I'm a student."

"What's your crime?"

This time I answered directly, without shame, "I'm a rightist."

"Captain," I called as he turned away. "Captain, I'm a strong worker."

"You finished the run?" He seemed not to have noticed, though my chest still heaved.

"Yes, I was an athlete at school."

"Athlete? So what does that mean?"

"It means I'm strong, I can labor." I spoke forcefully, but

he looked at me from the sides of his eyes, saying nothing and passing by.

Then the second cadre approached to make a final choice. Just before he reached me, I broke regulations and stepped out of line. I had to do something to get out of the detention center. I had to make the second cut.

"Captain," I started again, my tone even more serious. The second recruiter pushed me in the chest, back toward the line of prisoners.

"He already passed you. We don't need you. Why did you step out? Get back."

"What's going on?" called Yang, turning back.

"I can do this job. I want to work." I addressed both of them firmly and took a chance, stepping forward again.

"You don't look like much of a worker," said Yang. I reached up and pulled off my glasses.

"Look again," I called boldly. "Don't let my glasses fool you. I'm strong. I'll work hard!"

"Okay, okay." Lines of vexation, mixed with slight enjoyment at my discomfort, showed on Yang's forehead. He waved his hand for me to stay where I was, then turned and moved down the row.

I felt as if I had hit a home run, as if my foot had touched home plate. My whole body trembled in relief.

7

Beyond the Wall

$\mathcal{T}$ hree days later I sat huddled for warmth in a group of thirty prisoners on an open truck bed bumping across the mountains north of Beijing, beyond the Great Wall. Snow started falling as we left the detention center in midafternoon. It was October 25, 1960. Cold and very hungry, I pulled up the collar of my heavy, padded overcoat. At each corner of the truck bed, a security guard stood watch to prevent escape attempts. We were not permitted to stand or stretch. The occasional thud of a rifle butt striking a prisoner who had raised his head or ventured a word with his neighbor broke the silence of the journey.

I hugged my knees, kept my head down, and began to think intently. My optimism about being transferred had turned to dread. For weeks I had longed for a labor camp assignment because of the promise of work and extra food, but the harshness of the guards on the truck told me my expectations of better treatment were probably mistaken. I still could not believe that my words or actions at the Geology Institute warranted this kind of punishment. I also could not imagine what would finally happen to me. I had received no sentence, nor would I ever face trial. Reeducation through labor was an administrative, not a judicial, penalty. It could be applied and extended without reference to a legal code.

For half a year I had survived on little food. Each day at the detention center had brought study classes and struggle meetings, with only brief periods to walk in the fresh air. How long would I remain a prisoner? Was I really a criminal? I began to wonder whether I truly was in the wrong. Perhaps my ideas had brought harm to the majority of the Chinese people. Perhaps I really had opposed my motherland when I criticized the Communist Party. I stared out across the dark sky and the falling snow and wondered where I was headed and what would become of me. Though I had largely forgotten my Catholic faith, at this moment of adversity I instinctively prayed to God to forgive and protect me.

"Climb down! Get out of here!" shouted one of the police guards. By the time the truck reached the Yanqing Steel Factory, many of the prisoners felt stiff from the cold. When they didn't move immediately, the guards kicked them off the truck bed. They rolled like stones. Half jumping, half rolling, I hit the frozen dirt on my feet. My knees wouldn't bend, and I collapsed as a shock of pain traveled up my legs.

We limped in a ragged group toward a far corner of the factory yard. A prisoner approached us, astonished at the sight of newcomers. "Why have you come here?" he asked. "All production has stopped. We are waiting to move somewhere else. And now more come?" He walked away, shaking his head in disbelief.

As I tried to absorb the meaning of his words, the cold and my hunger confused my thoughts. "I want to labor, I believe I can labor. Besides, a human being has to do something. I need food. If I work, maybe they will give me more food. But that prisoner says all work has stopped here. Does that mean no food?"

The Yanqing Steel Company, I would soon learn, was administered by the Beijing Public Security Bureau. Incorporating not only a steel factory but a brickworks and two small iron mines about five miles apart, it operated as a state-owned production facility using prison labor. Its prison name and number were unknown to local residents. By the time I arrived, the production facility had been abandoned. The economic failures of the Great Leap Forward meant that in North China electricity could be supplied only to Beijing and to certain important industries and universities. Without electricity, the steel factory had no need for iron, and thus the mines also lay idle. The entire compound was part of the industrial sector that the government had declared temporarily "dismounted from the horse."

Why had we come? The Beijing Public Security Bureau had apparently ordered all of the labor camps under its jurisdiction to accept some of the overflow of newly arrested prisoners from the city. No preparations had been made for our arrival, no additional shelter or provisions had been made available. In camps whose production had been "dismounted" from the economy, there was no work to be done. There was also a severe shortage of food.

We arrived at the steel factory at around six o'clock, and we simply squatted on the snow-dusted ground. We had eaten nothing since leaving the detention center that afternoon. Finally some trucks appeared again at the gate to the yard, and the security guards climbed down to call out a list of names. One of them was mine. I wondered where on earth I would be taken next.

Night had fallen and, still without food, I felt the cold ever more sharply as I huddled in the truck with the other prisoners. In the darkness we wound up a narrow, rutted mountain road and then descended steeply into a rocky gorge. When we reached a wooden gate, two policemen stepped out into the cold from a small guardhouse. The snow flurries had stopped, and a few stars hung high above the rugged rock walls. The only other light came from dim floodlamps above the doors of buildings stepped into the mountainside. We stood in the bitter wind while the guards counted us, called our names, and transferred our files. Still no food.

"You sleep up there," shouted a guard against the wind, pointing up the hill to the farthest cluster of buildings. "It's ten o'clock, too late to do anything more tonight. We'll see to everything tomorrow." The trucks backed around and rumbled away. The only remaining guard pulled up his collar against the wind and hurried away to his own quarters as we headed for the barracks.

At the end of October north of the Great Wall, the wind

slices through the mountains. I felt bitterly cold, but I stood for a few moments looking up at the sky, amazed at our freedom. There were no guards and no walls. We had been given no regulations. I realized that escape must be all but impossible from this desolate canyon.

We climbed up the path to examine our lodgings, hoping to get warm. Each building measured about fifteen feet by fifty feet. A crude wall divided the structure into two rooms. The windows, crosshatched with vertical and horizontal slats, had once been covered with paper. The doors blew freely in the wind. It was obvious that no one had lived here for a long time.

My squad chose the rear section of one building because it seemed the most sheltered. Kangs faced each other on opposite walls beneath the windows. The night was too black for us even to consider searching for wood to start the small stoves beneath the kangs that could warm the brick platform. Gusts of wind rustled the remaining shreds of window paper.

I moved quickly to be the first to occupy the far corner and stay as much out of the wind as possible. Xing's words came back to me. You have to take care of yourself; don't be concerned about others. My energy drained away. I sat with my back to the corner, my arms clasping my quilt tightly around my shoulders. All night I hovered near sleep and waited for morning, whatever it would bring.

Just after sunrise a guard's voice yelled, "Come out, come out!" I had never seen such a barren landscape. Steep rock cliffs rose on all sides. The row of barracks had been cut into the rock near the top of a small cleft at the base of an almost vertical mountain. On the opposite side of the cleft at about the same height, I could see the mouth of the Yingmen Iron Mine. A railroad track, rusty with disuse, led from the mine entrance to an ore-loading station.

A footpath led from the guardhouse below past the barracks and around the cleft of the mountain to the mine entrance about 400 yards away. Along the path stood several sheds. The guard pointed out the prison kitchen, the repair and maintenance shops, the security office, the confinement cells, and a separate police kitchen and police living quarters. Treeless and vast, the rocky mountain slopes made prison walls unnecessary. The rough dirt road we had traveled the previous night provided the only access to the outside world.

A guard appeared on the path with an older duty prisoner carrying a bucket and ladle. Each new arrival got two ladles of thin corn gruel. "How's it going?" the guard asked as we rapidly swallowed the porridge.

"We're too cold," someone complained.

"How can we sleep in the wind?" another asked.

"It's always cold in North China in the winter," replied the guard indifferently. "You'll get used to it." And he started down the hill.

Again I heard Xing's words. "We need paper for the windows," I called out.

"Wait. I'll see what I can find," the guard called over his shoulder. He returned at around ten o'clock, carrying some newspapers but without any wheat paste. If he had brought any, we would have eaten it.

"What about tacks?" someone asked.

"There aren't any tacks," the guard answered.

"Then what should we do?" we asked together.

The guard shrugged his shoulders and smiled helplessly. "I don't know."

"We're cold. We need something to burn under the kang," I persisted.

"Go out and look for weeds and grasses."

We set out to search the desolate hillsides for fuel, but we were too hungry and cold to look energetically. I could see the effort was futile, so I returned to the barracks and wrapped up in my quilt. Keep yourself warm, I thought. Don't get too cold. Save energy. Don't move around. Sleep, just like a bear in winter.

That afternoon a security director from the factory appeared in our barracks. "What's the problem?" he asked with no trace of sympathy. The guard who had brought the newspapers conveyed our request. "I approve two pounds of wheat flour from the storehouse," he answered, writing the order quickly in a small notebook.

A guard accompanied the duty prisoner who carried up a small bucket of wheat paste that had been cooked in the prison

kitchen. He watched carefully as we set to work, but I managed
to swallow a few handfuls when he was watching someone else.
Even before we had finished gluing the paper to the window
slats, I could see that the newsprint was too thin to be very
effective. It blocked only a little of the wind.

In these primitive surroundings two hundred of us began
to eke out an existence. The guards bothered to count us only
in the evening. They didn't seem to worry about our escaping.
We didn't have enough energy, and there was no place to go.

That first afternoon I lay on the kang reading the *People's
Daily* that had just been plastered on the window. An editorial
commemorated the tenth anniversary of the Chinese Volunteer
Army's departure for North Korea to defend the motherland
against the American imperialists. I thought about how in 1950
I had been a patriotic boy of thirteen. Every day my teachers,
the newspaper, and the radio had reported the latest victories.
We knew how many planes had been shot down, how many
tanks destroyed, how many South Korean and American soldiers killed. I remembered how fiercely I loved my country and
how passionately I wished I were old enough to join the struggle
and fight on the battlefield. A decade had passed. Famine
gripped the country, and factories lay idle. I had been pronounced an enemy of the motherland I once hoped to serve. I
no longer knew what I believed in.

That evening we had our first meal of solid food since leaving the detention center. The duty prisoner handed us two wotou made of corn chaff mixed with very rough sorghum. The
buns were cold and rock hard. We got no vegetables, and no
one even hoped for oil or meat.

After a week of this diet, my bowels stopped moving. Most
of the other prisoners had the same problem. The sorghum had
hardened in our intestines, causing sharp pain. The weakness
caused by our hunger compounded our distress. The only way
to move the bowels was to reach inside the rectum and pull out
the hardened sorghum lumps.

One morning I noticed the police cook carrying a basket
of cabbage down the path from the mine. Pulling out the sorghum balls had begun to cause bleeding from my rectum, and
the pain was sharp. I knew I needed vegetables in my diet to
relieve the distress. That night while the other prisoners slept,

I sneaked from the barracks and in the darkness followed the path around the end of the cleft to the mine entrance. I could smell the musty scent of cabbage as I drew closer, but then I saw a rusty iron lock across the gate. I returned empty-handed and greatly disappointed but nonetheless pleased with my new boldness. I was beginning to understand how to stay alive.

A month had passed when one morning a guard called the prisoners to stand in lines outside the barracks. Without explanation, he paced back and forth, choosing several men from each squad. He motioned with his hand for me to step out. "Follow me," he said to the ten of us as he headed toward the mine.

With production halted, the mine served as a root cellar to store the huge heads of cabbage that provided a mainstay of the prison guards' diet. Every week to prevent spoilage, the cabbages had to be turned, the outside leaves removed, and the rotting heads separated from the others in the pile. The guards had decided to assign this job to a select group of prisoners.

We followed the young police captain into the mine where stacks of cabbages lay against one wall. He positioned himself between us and the entrance, and we began rotating the heads and pulling off spoiled leaves. Not half an hour had passed when I saw one of my workmates tear out the tender inner leaves from a large cabbage head and quickly stuff them into his mouth. Another prisoner did the same, then a third. In spite of my hunger, I hesitated. Like most Chinese, I had never considered raw cabbage edible. Then I realized I had to seize any chance for extra food. I tore out a cabbage center, and a wonderful flavor, fresh and sharp, filled my mouth. I could feel the cabbage settle satisfyingly in my stomach.

The mine passage where we worked was only five feet wide and just tall enough for us to stand. It had been roughly dug, and the walls provided many dark crevices that could conceal us from the sight of the guard. As I worked, I noticed that several of the cabbages I turned were surprisingly light. They looked normal on the outside, but their tender inner leaves rested in my fellow prisoners' stomachs.

"Have you finished?" the guard called after a couple of hours. I had just pulled out the center from my fifth head, and I chewed and swallowed hard. "That's it for today," he called, stopping to count us. One prisoner remained behind in the mine, still gobbling a last cabbage. "Only nine! Where's the other person?" the guard shouted angrily, pushing past us to discover the tenth prisoner with a mouthful of vegetable. "Get out!" he yelled as we marched in a line back toward the entrance.

From the barracks across the cleft, our fellow prisoners watched curiously, wondering what special work we had been assigned. The guard walked over to the guilty prisoner and started shouting, then slapping and kicking him. As he fell, three more cabbage centers dropped out from the folds of his overcoat.

The guard yelled with greater fury, beginning to understand. "What have you been doing?" He ordered all of us to take off our coats, and cabbage hearts plopped to the ground. As many as four or five tumbled from some prisoners' clothing. I was the only one who had not carried any out. I calculated roughly that a hundred cabbages had been damaged. "Get out of here!" he commanded, slapping at the worst offenders and waving us toward the barracks.

I turned, but he shouted at me to come back. I feared he would strike me, but instead he ordered, "Pick them up, pick them up!" I realized that in his eyes, I alone was reliable, and he wanted my help. He led me down the path to the police buildings, the cabbage centers stacked in my arms. To my surprise, we passed by the security office, then the police kitchen. The guard stopped at the door to his own room. "Leave them here," he ordered, waving me back up the hill. As I turned to go, I saw him carry the tender cabbages inside and realized with a shock that the guards would also steal when given a chance to supplement their meager food supply.

Early in January 1961, death came among us for the first time. Even though we had been living for more than two months in such harsh conditions, I felt surprised. The two prisoners who died had been among the first to fall sick. One had contracted tuberculosis, and the other succumbed after many days of continuous diarrhea. I began to understand the side effects of prolonged malnutrition.

The next time the cabbages needed to be culled, I was the

only one from the first group sent again to the mine. The captain announced menacingly that any prisoner caught stealing would spend seven days in solitary confinement. I warned myself to be careful. I would eat as much as I could inside the tunnel, but I wouldn't try to carry any cabbages back. I understood the advantage of maintaining the guard's trust. This was the way to survive.

After that I was called to cull the cabbages once a week. I no longer thought of eating the cabbage centers as stealing. I was simply taking care of myself, and I began to suffer less distress from the sorghum balls.

One evening after the captain notified me that we would be going to the mine the next morning, one of my squad members named Heng approached me on the kang. "Hey, brother," he called. I knew that he had been the leader of a Beijing street gang. He had already formed a group of hoodlums inside the camp, and they called each other "brother" and spoke a street lingo I barely understood. Other squad members had warned me that Heng's gang had been calling me a running dog. "He fingers his brothers for the police," they said. "He makes them drop their cabbages, then eats by himself while his brothers suffer."

Heng drew his face close to mine and spoke quietly, his eyes hard. "In this situation we need to help each other out. Do you know what I mean? Don't eat all those cabbages yourself. Think about your brothers."

I understood his meaning. He was telling me to bring some cabbages back.

"Sorry, that's impossible," I replied. Stealing to feed myself was one thing, but I had no intention of taking that risk for someone else.

The next afternoon I came back from the mine without any cabbages. Heng stopped beside me as I sat on the kang. "Bring some back the next time or watch out!" he hissed.

To back up Heng's threat, two of his gang members grabbed me behind the barracks the next day, knocked me down, and kicked me. I had never been attacked by hoodlums, and I had no idea how to defend myself. No one helped me.

My only recourse were the security guards, and I reported

the incident, showing my bruises. The captain was unimpressed, saying only, "If it happens again, let me know." I thought of Xing's words and wished he were there beside me.

After my next trip to the mine, I again returned empty-handed. Heng's gang knew I had reported to the captain, and they gave me a second, more brutal lesson. The next morning the intimidation continued when one of them grabbed my wotou.

That evening one of my squad members, a short, thin prisoner named Shen, approached me. "What's the problem?" he asked.

"They tell me to steal cabbages for them, but I don't want to and I don't dare," I answered. "What should I do?"

Unlike the gang members, Shen had a middle school education. He had already been in the camps for many months. "Let me tell you," he said, quoting a proverb. "Sing a different song in different mountains; speak a different language in a different region."

Squatting beside me, he whispered, "I've been here two years, and at the beginning I had the same trouble. They always tried to get me to steal for them, and they grabbed my food and beat me. But one day I fought back. I chose the head of the gang and used a spade. I gave him a bad gash on his shoulder. After that no one bothered me. In the camps there is only one rule. The fierce one fears the relentless one, and the relentless one fears the foolhardy one. If I am the foolhardy one, I am at the top."

"I understand," I said slowly, wondering if I had already forgotten all the moral principles that once had guided my life. To survive in the camps, I needed new skills and different attitudes. I realized that my "reeducation" had reached another stage.

The next time I left for the mine, two gang members approached me. "Heng wants us to tell you that your hands had better not be empty when you come back." I nodded my head, as if in agreement.

That day I hid one cabbage center under my coat. By then the guard trusted me and often didn't bother to check my clothing. As I stood in a line outside the entrance while the others were searched, I could see Heng watching from across the cleft.

Our barracks was the highest on the hillside, and he stood by the door, looking across toward me, waiting. Okay, I thought, and on the walk back I picked up a stone, one that just fit my hand.

Heng grabbed my arm at the barracks door as I was about to walk past him. "Step inside," I said. He followed me, not suspecting anything, and I turned, raised my arm and brought the stone sharply down on his head. Blood flowed from a gash three inches long as he fell down. I jumped up to my corner space on the kang, brandishing the bloody stone, and shouted, "I've had enough of your threats!" Everyone stared in shocked silence. Breathing hard, I pulled out the single cabbage center and threw it to my friend Shen, the small prisoner. No one came near me. I had suddenly become powerful, and from that moment on the other prisoners looked on me with a new respect.

Shen stood up and said, "Easy, easy, everyone, easy," calming the situation. No one in the barracks made a move. Two of the gang members tended to their injured leader.

Heng and his gang had frightened me, stolen my food, and beaten me, but now I had seen their blood. I had learned how to steal, how to protect myself, and finally how to fight. And I had managed to keep my special job tending the cabbages. My disapproval of Xing's street values seemed part of another life. I had a new ethic of survival. In those surroundings I could not afford compassion or generosity or decency. No one would help me but myself.

8

The Running Dog

$\mathcal{T}$ hree months after my group of two hundred prisoners arrived at the defunct Yingmen Iron Mine, on January 27, 1961, orders came from Beijing to close completely that branch of the Yanqing Steel Factory. After hearing the announcement, I waited outside the barracks for the afternoon meal, stamping my feet against the North China cold. I had done nothing except sit in political study classes and cull cabbages since late October. My mind had grown as numb as my toes.

The security captain called us to attention. We would be transferred immediately, he announced, to the Xihongsan Mine branch labor camp, which was several miles closer to the steel factory than Yingmen. Now that all production had stopped, the Public Security Bureau wanted to collect Yanqing's five hundred prisoners at one site in order to increase efficiency in distributing supplies. Standing in line for roll call, I wondered whether the change would improve our living conditions or increase our food rations. I also counted the names. Only one hundred ninety-five prisoners waited to climb onto the trucks. Five of us were left on Yingmen's rocky hillside.

At a glance I could see that the Xihongsan barracks had been built, like those at Yingmen, with prison labor at the start of the Great Leap Forward in 1958. After the duty prisoner assigned me to a squad, I carried my bedroll up to my new quarters. They offered no improvement. One of the larger stone dwellings built against the mountainside, my barracks had six rooms, each with a kang occupied by twelve prisoners. Wattle covered the inside walls, newspaper covered the two small windows along one side, but nothing covered the tamped mud floor.

I recognized my new security captain instantly. Captain Yang was the recruiter who had chosen me from the lineup at the Beiyuan Detention Center when I had thrust myself forward in October, wanting to follow Big Mouth Xing's example and try my luck at a labor reform camp. At that time I hadn't imagined being assigned to an abandoned iron mine north of the Great Wall in the depths of winter.

When we met again, Captain Yang looked at me with narrowed eyes. "You're here? How's it going?" With a wave of his hand, he ordered me to wait in the barracks until he called for me. I had no idea what he wanted or why I should be singled out.

Early in the evening the duty prisoner summoned me to the security office. From behind his desk Captain Yang watched my face intently as he asked me a series of questions. "Where are you from? Do you have a family? What did you do before coming to the camp? Why were you arrested? A rightist? What did you say in 1957? Were you a good student?" He nodded mechanically after each reply. I tried to think why he bothered to inquire about my background. All of his questions could have been answered by consulting my file. He seemed to be testing me, weighing my responses. Finally he dismissed me, saying, "I'll have work for you tomorrow."

At Xihongsan prisoners had no regular labor assignments, just temporary work duty repairing the buildings or the mountain road, sometimes constructing a wall or a pigsty. To fill the prisoners' idle time, the guards scheduled study classes after each meal, from eleven o'clock to three and again from six o'clock to nine. On the first morning a duty prisoner called me from the study session to report to the security office.

The room smelled of tobacco smoke and unwashed clothing. One weekend each month, I learned, Captain Yang received leave to visit his wife and two children in Beijing. Otherwise this was his home. The room contained a long table piled with

papers, a pallet bed, and off to the side a small table about a
foot high, the kind usually placed on a kang in North China.
This became my desk. The shifting of prisoners from Yingmen
had brought a flurry of clerical work, and Captain Yang decided
to make use of the newly arrived university student as an assistant. My job was to maintain the prisoners' files, making mul-
tiple lists of their ages, places of origin, and former occupations,
as well as the nature of their crimes. From that moment on, I
became a special prisoner.

Except for sleeping and meals, when I returned to the barracks to join my squad, I spent all my time in Captain Yang's
office. The other prisoners passed much of each day sitting on
the kang, listening as the hours passed to someone reading
aloud from newspaper editorials and Party documents. Sometimes they would go out to labor. About once a week they held
a struggle meeting to criticize a prisoner who had been stubborn
and had failed to admit his guilt or accept responsibility for his
crimes. I felt fortunate to have escaped that routine.

Each day I worked carefully at my small table, not knowing
exactly what was expected of me and trying to avoid mistakes.
I understood the importance of thoroughness and secrecy. On
Captain Yang's desk lay stacks of documents about prison policy
as well as each individual prisoner's personnel file. All of this
was highly classified information. Whenever I approached him
to ask a question, I averted my eyes and looked pointedly at the
walls or windows to make clear my trustworthiness. I often
witnessed Yang's outbursts of anger, and I felt as if I were living
with a tiger.

The others in my squad noted my absence. I said nothing
about my new work, but they knew I had moved close to the
captain, and they began to set me apart. I realized I would pay
a stiff price for my special status. During evening study sessions
in the barracks I felt ostracized. I could see the resentment and
contempt in some people's eyes. During the day I felt like an
obedient dog with an unpredictable master. More and more I
would wag my tail, as if I genuinely liked sitting at Captain
Yang's feet and doing his bidding.

Only a thin wall separated his office from the interrogation
room next door. When Captain Yang questioned prisoners who

had been reported for petty theft or attempted escape, I would sometimes hear screams. During those sessions his voice remained steady and cold. "What's going on? What have you done? Confess your crime! You must examine your actions and criticize yourself completely. I'm warning you this time. . . ." I would hear his chair scrape against the floor and smell his pipe. And I would picture the scene, with the accused prisoner standing opposite the desk and two or three duty prisoners waiting for orders, sometimes delivering blows before bringing in the next victim. I tried to block out the sounds.

Soon I became one of Captain Yang's favorite prisoners, similar to a duty prisoner except that he never asked me to report on the others. Nor did he summon me for work in the interrogation room next door. I was a special running dog, a paperwork running dog. He must have decided that my temperament was not suited to informing on others or beating them. I accepted the bargain. Then one day as I worked, Captain Yang walked into his room carrying a box of cigarettes. "Leave the paperwork for a while," he ordered. "Do you smoke?"

"No, I don't smoke," I answered cautiously.

"Draw up a list of the prisoners in each squad who do smoke and divide the cigarettes among them."

During the famine years the supply of cigarettes throughout China was extremely limited. These were the coarsest kind, made by local factories and costing only eight or nine cents a pack. I had never seen either of the brands before—the Double Fish or the Handshake. They may not even have contained tobacco.

So now, I realized, I was helping the captain to manage the prisoners' lives. I had taken another step closer to the police. I drew up the forms and sent one to each squad with instructions that the completed lists be returned to me. Other prisoners began to wonder who I was and whether I was in fact some kind of assistant officer.

The completed forms listed 375 smokers. After I divided the cigarettes equally, fifty-four remained left over. I asked Captain Yang how to handle the surplus.

"Take them, if you like," he answered.

Cigarettes in the camps could be very useful. They were

just like cash. With them you could buy prisoners' souls. I knew Captain Yang was offering me a privilege, but I had not yet lost all my integrity.

"I don't smoke," I replied. "I don't want them."

"Mmm, maybe you can use them." Captain Yang knew what he was offering.

"No," I insisted quietly. "I don't want them."

"Fine," he said, showing me a little respect by accepting my decision. Then his tone changed. "I've read your file. You're a Catholic?" He would not allow me to refuse his favor without paying a price.

According to Communist Party doctrine, you could become a true Marxist only after renouncing all belief in God. Beginning in 1950 Christians, Buddhists, and Muslims had all been attacked fiercely in a series of national political movements. I had seen some of my middle school teachers criticized and condemned for spreading the poison of a foreign faith. Communists were expected to be materialists and atheists, and I knew Captain Yang was challenging me to repudiate my early faith. "When I was young," I replied carefully, "I was baptized in middle school."

"What is baptism?" he replied sarcastically. "Isn't it just like a bath or a shower?"

Yang was an ignorant man, but now he was playing the cat, and in return I had to play the mouse. Even though he favored me, I had seen his capacity for cruelty. Shrugging, I answered carelessly, "I'm not too sure about it, really. I think it's a serious ceremony."

"Catholics say that a human being is made by God. How did he do it? Did he just take some dirt in his hand and blow on it, like some kind of magic?"

However remote my Catholic beliefs had become, I felt my anger rising, and I knew I had to end this conversation. "You are a Party member," I began respectfully. "You must be a materialist." He nodded. "Would you tell me where humans came from?"

Full of confidence, he seemed to welcome this chance to educate me. "Men evolved," he pronounced, "from apes."

I feigned ignorance. "So that means the monkey was our ancestor?"

"I think so . . ."

"So when I go to the zoo, I can see your forefathers?"

Yang's face clouded. "A monkey is a monkey; my ancestors are my ancestors. There is some connection. I'm not exactly sure . . ."

I put on a confused look as well, but inwardly I felt satisfied at having deflected his attack and defended my own beliefs. The only difference between this man and a monkey is that monkeys don't smoke cigarettes, I thought. For the first time I acknowledged fully my feelings of contempt for my master.

"Anyway," Yang continued, "your God is no help to you here."

"How do you know?" I asked.

"He can't get you out of here, and he can't get you food," Yang continued.

"That's true," I replied cautiously, "but he hasn't really left me alone. And he does offer me another kind of food."

"What use is that?" Yang persisted. "I guess sooner or later you'll give him up."

"Someday I'll give up my body's life, but not my spiritual life," I stated quietly. At that moment of testing, I felt my faith in God strengthened and reaffirmed.

"You are very stubborn! You have a long way to go to reform yourself. The people of this country are working hard to live by Chairman Mao's thoughts. You must also try to reach this goal!"

Suddenly the traditional practice of footbinding came to my mind. We have switched to headbinding, I thought. It's no longer the fashion to bind a woman's feet, but they bind a person's thoughts instead. That way the mind can't move freely. That way ideas all take on the same size and shape, and thinking becomes impossible. That's why they arrested me. That's why they want to change me, that's why they force me to reform.

I returned to my squad for the afternoon meal with a troubled heart. I had applied Xing's teachings, but I had made many compromises during nine months in the camps. I didn't know what I believed, what I could condone. My confusion faded when a prisoner in his late fifties named Qi San approached me outside the barracks with a slight bow and an unusual tone of respect. "Can you possibly find me some extra cigarettes?" he asked politely. He knew I had helped distribute the cigarette rations earlier that day. I was only twenty-three, and his deference startled me. I realized that I had assumed a position of power among my fellow prisoners, and I wanted to maintain that status.

Qi San had been labeled an "historical counterrevolutionary" because of his work as a bookkeeper in a government office before the Communist victory in 1949. Like me, he had committed no crime but had been arrested as a political enemy in 1960 when the Party tried to eliminate any source of unrest. For most of his life, Qi San had smoked two packs of cigarettes a day. His body craved tobacco, and without it his hands trembled, his eyes watered, his throat wheezed. I had watched him gather leaves to wrap into cigarettes, but he was always in need of paper. Sometimes he would tear a small piece from the day's newspaper before it was returned to the security office, always worried that the study leader might notice the ripped page and demand to know who had damaged the people's property.

Qi San listened carefully for any news about a visit to the camp from a family member. Prisoners at the mine were allowed to receive mail, and he always would find out who had gotten a package from home and beg for cigarettes, even butts, anything to feed his craving. I knew the degree of his need for nicotine when I saw him trade one of his two wotou for four cigarettes at breakfast one day. After that I sometimes brought him small scraps of paper from Captain Yang's office.

When Qi San pleaded with me to give him some extra cigarettes, at first I refused out of an ingrained sense of fairness. Then I reconsidered. What use were such values in this setting? When the guards received a second shipment of cigarettes, I added my name to the list of smokers in my squad. I still refused to take extras from the office, but I would accept my share of the tobacco rations.

After the cigarettes were distributed, my squad leader approached me furiously. "What are you doing? You've never smoked! Why do you want to reduce the number of cigarettes the rest of us get? What are you up to?"

"I've started smoking," I replied.

"I've never seen you," he shot back.

Ever since I had begun to work in the captain's office, the squad leader had resented my immunity to his authority. Now he saw an opportunity to challenge me by removing my name from the smoking list. I took a chance. "This form goes only to Captain Yang," I answered boldly. "Go ahead and complain that Wu Hongda never smokes. See if the captain refuses to add my name to the list." The squad leader glared at me and turned away. He knew I was safe, but his resentment of my special privilege grew.

According to one of the twenty-five regulations that governed camp discipline, cigarettes could not be exchanged or given away. The police realized that power relationships formed around the exchange of goods and watched for such transactions. In order to help Qi San without risking serious criticism, I smoked my cigarettes halfway, snuffed them out, slipped them into my pocket, and passed them quietly to my friend.

After that, cigarette rations arrived every month, and I smoked for the rest of my stay at Xihongsan. At the beginning I coughed, but later the smoke in my lungs felt good, and I began to think that I too needed cigarettes. Perhaps at a time of such meager nourishment, my body acquired the habit more readily than if I had been strong and fit. Smoking also provided some psychological comfort, some small respite from the physical deprivation of camp life.

My sudden habit of smoking affected my health, and in the late spring I developed a lung infection, a kind of pleurisy. The camp doctor, a man in his mid-thirties named Ouyang, had been labeled as a counterrevolutionary because during the Anti-Japanese War he served as a medic in the Manchurian puppet army under Japanese command. A native of China's Northeast, Ouyang had studied medicine after the Japanese occupied Manchuria, receiving excellent training. He could tell immediately that my left lung had filled with fluid. Even I could hear the dull, heavy sound when he thumped my chest, so different from the clear, hollow sound of the right lung. Dr. Ouyang gave me some kind of medicine, but my condition did not improve. Then he proposed withdrawing the fluid with a syringe, a procedure that could be performed only at the steel factory clinic an hour and a half drive down the mountain. Four times Dr. Ouyang arranged for me to ride with him to the factory on a supply truck. There he performed this treatment, and several weeks later the infection disappeared.

Idleness and deprivation began to cause restlessness and discipline problems among the prisoners as the famine wore on. Previously everyone had received the same rations. Since no one performed regular labor, no distinctions in food allotments according to work assignments could be made. Then in November Captain Yang decided to institute a variable rationing policy designed to bolster prisoner control and reform. Instead of routinely receiving two wotou at each meal, prisoners had their food rations decided by the police captains. Each squad received a set number of buns to be distributed according to a quota system. Those who cooperated with the guards would be rewarded with extra food deducted from another prisoner's rations.

In my squad of eleven, seven people would receive what were called the standard B-rations of two wotou per meal, while two people would receive A-rations of two and a half wotou, and two would receive C-rations of only one and a half buns. We all knew the importance of these distinctions in a situation of such scarcity. Three criteria determined the allocation of the portions: your political attitude, your adherence to camp regulations, and your age, size, and labor potential. It was understood that political prisoners could never receive A-rations. They were considered harder to control and reform than common criminals because they held their own ideas and had their own moral standards. Also they were generally not experienced at physical labor.

Qi San, as an historical counterrevolutionary, was a political prisoner. He was also over fifty and therefore deemed undeserving of large rations. I was not only a political prisoner but a student wearing glasses, clearly not skilled at physical labor, and thus also a candidate for C-rations. The third prospect in my squad was another older criminal, considered able to survive on smaller portions of food because of his age. Two among the three of us would be allotted reduced rations.

The squad leader hated me because of my special relationship with Captain Yang. "Wu Hongda," he announced to justify my C-rations, "is a serious rightist. He has never done physical labor so he needs less food. The old fellow has had long experience at labor, and because of that he deserves to receive B-rations.''

Listening to the squad leader, I again heard Big Mouth Xing's words. No one would take care of me but myself. I didn't want to grow any weaker, and the squad leader's decision would mean half a bun less per meal, one bun less per day, thirty buns less per month. I couldn't think about the older man. I decided to fight with my life against this decision. "No, this is wrong,'' I declared. "He is fifty years old and I am twenty-four. My body needs more food.''

I stepped down from the kang. "If you don't think I am stronger than he, we can have a fight to decide who is more fit to do labor.''

The squad leader grabbed my arm. "What did you say? You want to fight? Are you opposing camp discipline? You absolutely deserve C-rations!'' He shouted to the study class leader to list me for the smaller food allotment on the form. I couldn't risk opposing his authority any further. My burst of anger left me defeated.

The next day after the squad leaders had returned the ration forms to Captain Yang's desk, he called me over. "What is this? How did you get assigned C-rations?''

"I don't know,'' I replied, looking at the floor. I could think of no convincing way to argue my case. Yang made a note on my squad's ration form.

"Is someone causing trouble for you?'' he asked, dropping the form onto the pile on his desk. Not waiting for a reply, he resumed his paperwork. The following day my A-rations began. No one could object. The master had thrown a bone to the dog. I accepted. Food meant life.

The approach of the Lunar New Year in February 1961 made everyone's thoughts turn to home and family. The three-day Spring Festival, the most important holiday of the year, brought an occasion for reunion and feasting in every family. It was a time to gather with close friends. Prisoners always dreaded the emptiness of this holiday, and their emotions grew more volatile. Some became depressed and withdrawn while others grew hostile and aggressive. I overheard two of the younger ones in my squad talking about escape, even though we sat on a remote mountain slope with steep rock walls rising overhead and a wilderness of barren mountains stretching in all directions. The only exit was the road down to the Yanqing Steel Factory where armed officers with dogs guarded the gates.

One morning the guards discovered that two prisoners from squad ten had escaped. At noon Captain Yang called me, along with three duty prisoners, to his office. He divided us into pairs with orders to search the top of the gorge. He sent two of us up the north hillside, two others to the south, while several armed security officers set out to hunt the escapees with dogs. "If you spot them, one of you keep them in sight, the other return to report," he instructed me. I knew he calculated that the prisoners would not attempt to escape by the road but would hope to find a way out across the top of the gorge.

The wind blew hard on the mountainside. We searched until past dark. By the time we returned, the guards had already found the two prisoners at the railroad station. I had no idea how they had gotten so far. All I knew was that I was cold and hungry. Captain Yang wrote an order to the kitchen to give us extra food.

The cook provided us with steaming bowls of vegetable soup and as many wotou as we could eat. My eyes bulged at the sight of so much food, but I could consume only four buns at one time. The German shepherd that had tracked down the escapees ate wotou beside us in the kitchen, while the two prisoners lay locked in solitary confinement cells. The running dogs and the guard dogs got fed together.

At that moment I thought again about how close I had come to the police. I was a running dog, I was trusted, and I had power. But I had lost my self-respect.

At the evening head count the next day, Captain Yang read aloud a bulletin from Beijing. "The Public Security Bureau will provide one special meal for prisoners over the Spring Festival holiday. Each person will receive four ounces of lamb, two pounds of carrots, one pound of wheat flour, two apples, some hard candy, and a package of cigarettes." The prospect of special food and better quality cigarettes produced great excitement. I understood that such largess was a calculated gesture to raise the prisoners' morale, buy their obedience, and maintain stability in the camp, but I joined in the rejoicing.

"If during the three-day holiday," Captain Yang continued, "anyone makes a mistake, he will go directly to the confinement house. Tomorrow we will assemble in the yard to prepare dumplings. The squad leaders will make sure that everyone participates and no one remains in the barracks."

Captain Yang had been a prison guard for more than ten years. Like most of the Yanqing personnel, he was a demobilized PLA soldier. He understood prisoners and the ways of the camp, and he knew that the introduction of special food would bring trouble. To allow prisoners to join together to roll the dough and mix the meat filling for traditional Spring Festival steamed dumplings was to invite an outburst of fighting and stealing.

Captain Yang organized the proceedings carefully. From the kitchen came wooden plates, newspapers to lay on the ground, and wooden rods to roll out the dumpling skins. When everything was ready, he sat on a chair in the midst of the circles of prisoners, watching everyone. Despite his presence, disruptions began almost immediately. Everyone waited for a chance to grab a raw dumpling and stuff it into his mouth. When that happened, the other squad members, angry that they had lost some of their allotment, would jump up and hit the thief, whom Yang would then order sent off to confinement.

A number of fights broke out that morning. By noon six prisoners out of the five hundred in the yard had been sent to solitary cells. Not only would they miss the dumplings, the cigarettes, and the apples, but they would receive starvation rations. We all knew the penalty, but when faced with a few ounces of real meat, raw or not, some simply could not resist the temptation. The rest of us feasted, grateful for the chance just once to satisfy our hunger.

After the holiday we all grew increasingly fixated on food. In March when the weather grew warmer, Captain Yang announced that he needed a hundred and fifty men to repair the dirt road leading up the gorge from the factory. Ruts had to be filled with sand and gravel, and the rubble from winter rock slides cleared away. Volunteers would receive one extra wotou each day. "Do you want to go?" Captain Yang asked me privately. For an extra wotou, I knew most of the prisoners would volunteer, but not everyone would be selected.

"Okay, I'd like to go," I agreed. Actually I had been wanting to stop working in Captain Yang's office, and this seemed an opportunity to extricate myself without offending my patron. Ever since I had shared the extra food in the kitchen with the German shepherd after the escape attempt, something had changed in me. I didn't like the person I was becoming. Captain Yang approved my name on the list and arranged for me to serve as a squad labor leader responsible for organizing and overseeing one of the work teams.

For four hours a day, I labored alongside the other prisoners, digging sand and gravel from the hillsides, carrying it in large baskets, shoveling it into the holes in the road, and tamping it down. Even more difficult than the physical exertion was the effort to regain my fellow prisoners' respect.

One member of my squad was a young Beijing hoodlum. He was strong and accustomed to physical labor, and he tried to make trouble for me. In our squad only he and I received the A-ration of two and a half buns per meal, in addition to the extra allotment we earned each afternoon for doing roadwork. Soon after we began to labor, he approached me with a sneer. "We get the same rations," he said. "That means we should do the same amount of work."

He knew I had been a student and had never done strenuous physical labor. Like the others, he hated me because I was a running dog, and this was a chance to challenge my authority and make me lose face in front of the other prisoners.

"I am the leader," I answered sharply, taking off my glasses. I knew that I had neither the strength nor the skill to accomplish the same amount of roadwork that he did each day. "You follow me." He swore at me and then let fly a punch. I fell down, and he drew close to kick me, but I grabbed his foot and bit into his ankle as hard as I could. I bit until the blood flowed and still kept biting. I didn't care about anything else, and I didn't let go. He shouted in pain and fell down.

Several prisoners ran to separate us. Hearing the row, Captain Yang appeared. His voice sounded surprised. "You're a student. How can you fight like this?" He seemed impressed. I was tougher than he thought. He told me to wipe the blood from my mouth and without any reprimand turned away.

In this way the hoodlum learned that I was not an easy

target, and he never made trouble for me again. I was determined to put Big Mouth Xing's lessons into practice. If I could not be strong, I could not survive.

As the spring wore on, idle time in the barracks became increasingly devoted to discussions of food. Before going to sleep at night, we would take turns presenting the others with elaborate descriptions of a favorite dish, sometimes a specialty of our native province or a secret recipe from our family. We would explain in detail how to cut the ingredients, how to season them, mix them, and arrange them on the plate. We would describe the smell and then the taste. Everyone would listen in silence.

Evening after evening we held these food-imagining parties. You tell me tonight, I tell you tomorrow, again and again, day after day, trading descriptions of the meals we longed for. In earlier weeks the hoodlums had often talked about sex or about how to fight and steal, relating their exploits on the streets and bragging about how they had beaten up other young toughs who challenged their authority. Gradually their attention shifted, and even their talk turned to food.

At home I had never had practice at cooking, but I tried to imagine how our cook would have prepared my favorite dishes. I told my squad members about the famous pork spareribs made in my family's native city of Wuxi. Even though I had never cooked them, I created delicious stories and later described other meals of fish and chicken. I envisioned every detail of the cutting and seasoning and frying. In telling these stories, we tried to satisfy not only our empty stomachs but our empty hearts as well. Hunger comes not only from the body but also from the spirit.

Day by day, our hunger became more intense. Without food, the body uses calories stored in muscle tissues and even in bones to provide energy and sustain life. I began to understand the process of starvation. When death strikes in the camps, malnutrition is rarely the direct cause. The heart does not stop beating from lack of nourishment. Depending on your overall health, you can survive for a week, even two, with no food or water at all. In such a depleted state, it is other things that kill you.

Sometimes you catch cold, your lungs fill with fluid, and

finally you stop breathing. Sometimes bacteria in the food cause continuous diarrhea that leads to death. Sometimes infection from a wound becomes fatal. The cause of death is always noted in your file as pleurisy or food poisoning or injury, never as starvation.

The food-imagining stories indicated how much closer we had moved toward starvation. People tried every conceivable way to get food. They grabbed, stole, and searched the mountainsides for edible weeds and grasses. They wrote to their relatives asking them to send whatever they could, but food was scarce even outside of the prison camps. Travel was also difficult, and visits from family members were rare.

My own family lived eighteen hundred miles to the south, but even for relatives who lived in Beijing, visiting someone in the camp entailed risk and hardship. First, you had to ask for time off from work. This meant acknowledging to your Party secretary that you had a family member in the camps, which would prompt suspicions about your own loyalty. Second, you had to arrange for transportation and accommodation for a three-day trip. Buying a train ticket required money as well as hours of standing in line. You had to get permission to sleep the first night at the Yanqing Steel Factory in order to travel to the mine for a thirty-minute visit the next day. Then you slept a second night at the factory while waiting for a return train.

Third, everyone in China except the most privileged Party leaders suffered from a drastically reduced food supply in 1961. Even if you had money, there was nothing in the shops to buy. A relative could send you a package of food only by saving a portion of the family's meager rations. That food, we prisoners said, came from the family members' mouths.

By then, unknown to me, my father had also been labeled a rightist. He remained at home, but he could not write to me. Contact between political enemies was strictly forbidden. My sisters had sent me two packages of food since September, carefully wrapped packets containing a towel along with some biscuits, hard candies, and the kind of small soy sauce cubes that could be dissolved to add flavor to the tasteless soup and wotou. I relished these delicacies but worried about the hardship it placed on my family to save flour ration tickets and money to supply me with extra food.

One evening as I lay on the kang, Qi San told me that his

wife had managed to pay him a visit that afternoon. Instead of happiness, his face showed worry and sadness. He wanted to talk.

"Today my old wife came from Beijing," he said despondently. "The trip took her three days. She took a train from Beijing to the small rail station close to the factory and stayed there overnight. The police let her sleep in a small office. In the morning she got up and went out to wash and to ask the police for help getting to the mine. When she returned to the office, someone had stolen the twenty pounds of cooked wheat flour she had brought me, but two pounds of dry biscuits still lay safe under her pillow.

"She had no way to recover the precious flour and started walking along the dirt road to the mine. Finally a truck stopped for her, but it soon broke down, and she walked the rest of the way. It took almost five hours. When she saw me, she tried to cry, but no tears came. I knew how difficult the trip had been. I didn't want her to go to so much trouble.

"She gave me a cotton padded vest she had stitched at night under the single light bulb in our apartment. 'I knew that beyond the Great Wall the wind would be strong,' she said. 'I wanted to do something for you . . .' She looked very sad. 'I saved the wheat flour from my rations. Now someone has stolen it. I'm so sorry to bring you so little.'

"She was so sad about the wheat flour," Qi San continued. "Even when she handed me five packages of cigarettes, she apologized for not having enough money to bring more. She said her sister had helped her buy the train ticket, and that in three months she would try to visit me again." Qi San paused and wiped the tears from his cheeks with the edge of his quilt. He lit one of the cigarettes.

"I told her not to think about me and not to come again. Then I urged her to go to Tianjin and live with our son. I said it would be better if she could accept that in this world she would not have Qi San anymore. She must go on without me and not set aside any more of her food rations. I told her she was growing older, she had lost weight, and she didn't look well. I could see how thin she was, and I could tell she had not been eating enough. I knew she was saving her food rations for me." He turned his head to the wall.

The next day Qi San was missing at evening count. Everyone felt great surprise. No one could imagine he had tried to escape, as he was too old and thin. I knew how distraught he had felt after his wife's visit, and I feared that he might have decided to end both of their suffering.

Two days later Captain Yang told me the duty prisoners had found him. He didn't tell me where or what had happened. He just instructed me to gather Qi San's quilt and belongings and take them to the office. Beneath his pillow I found four unopened packages of cigarettes. Several days later we heard that Qi San had been found at the bottom of a small cliff beyond the mine. Whether he had fallen or jumped, we never learned.

One afternoon early in April, Captain Yang suddenly announced that orders had arrived from Beijing instructing that all prisoners assigned to the Xihongsan mine would be transferred. Our destination had not been specified. We should prepare to move the next morning and wait for further orders. Just after daybreak four trucks appeared in the yard. The duty prisoners issued everyone a full day's food quota of four wotou and one salted turnip. The trucks made several trips, ferrying us to the rail station near the Yanqing factory. I left in the first group. At the station we marched to a cordoned-off area down the tracks from the platform and sat on the ground. The guards stood watch with their rifles, but we hardly thought of escape. Several hours passed before we had all assembled.

Each time before, my transfers had occurred at night. This was the first time in a year that I had seen normal citizens. From behind a rope I watched the local people. Several of them stared at us. They seemed to be whispering, watching us as they would animals at a zoo. Never before had I realized what it meant to be cast out from the society. At first I dropped my head in shame. Then I raised it again, thinking angrily, what do you know about prisoners? Maybe you will be here someday yourselves.

Late in the afternoon we boarded two prison cars that stood on the tracks several hundred feet from the station. No one told us our destination. This time I didn't try to imagine the conditions we would face at our next stop. Would I still be this hungry? I wanted to look out at the countryside from a window, to see again the normal life of a village, but the train sat at the station for a couple of hours, and it was nearly dark by the time we began to move. They don't want us to see or be seen, I thought. Once we enter the camps, they want us to disappear.

9

Xing's Curse

*N*ear midnight, the train pulled into a small railway station. The platform sign read Chadian. In the cars ahead of us, passengers boarded and disembarked, and workers loaded and unloaded freight. We sat captive behind locked doors. Finally a small engine hitched onto the caboose behind us and pulled our two rear prison cars onto a side track. Several hundred yards from the station, we stopped, and the Yanqing guards ordered us out. A line of policemen waited along the tracks. Word spread among us that these were Qinghe Farm police.

Even when I saw that the guards had rifles and two German shepherds, I felt no alarm. What could they do to me? I had no strength to consider escape, not even enough energy to feel apprehension. I wouldn't care if the guards carried machine guns and brought fifty dogs, or if only one policeman stood guard without a rifle. My only thought was that I felt very hungry and very weak.

Loaded again in the back of a truck, I had no idea where I was heading. The landscape looked utterly flat. In the moonlight I could make out irrigation ditches crisscrossing rice fields on both sides of the road, and sometimes I could see the arched silhouette of a bridge over a canal. The smell of the earth in the night air stirred my spirits. On a farm, I thought, I can find food. At least I will be living on soil, not rock. The smell of the earth bred hope.

The trucks slowed as we approached a brick wall, perhaps eighteen feet high. Guard towers rose from the corners of the compound. The night seemed strangely quiet.

"Get down! Come on!" Police shouts broke the silence after the trucks passed through heavy iron gates. "Form a line! Be quick!" The guards wanted to sleep too. The Yanqing police counted us, called the roll, and handed our papers to the Qinghe guards. Five hundred of us had been confined at Xihongsan, but they seemed to call only about one hundred names. I knew that Qi San remained behind, but I had no idea what had happened to the others.

I heard the trucks rumble off, and the Yanqing police disappeared into the night. Captain Yang, I realized gratefully, had left with them.

The Qinghe guards rapidly divided us into squads of ten. "You go to room seven, you to room eight, you to room nine . . ."

Several prisoners pleaded, "Can't we have some food?"

"Tomorrow. It's too late," came the answer.

I followed my new squad leader back to the barracks. "Come on, come on. Pack in together," he shouted to the eight prisoners already sharing the kang. "Hey! Here's newcomers. Let's make room for them!" The occupants rolled over slowly or sat up, grumbling as they moved. "Shut up!" the squad leader shouted, silencing the complaints and pushing some of the slower ones, cursing as he moved them. He was tall and large boned. They obviously feared his strength.

One squad member slept obstinately with his head beneath his pillow. The first time the leader shoved him, he didn't respond. The second time he jumped up and shouted angrily, "Sonuvabitch . . ."

He glared in my direction. Then his face widened in all directions. It was Big Mouth Xing. He looked as dirty as ever.

"Hey, Wu Hongda!" he shouted. "How did you get here? I never thought I'd see you again."

I told him I had just come from Yanqing. "Stream water flows from different mountains, but it reaches the sea in the same river," I said. "Maybe it is the same for prisoners."

Xing moved over to make room for me and announced, "Wu sleeps here, beside me." By the time I had spread out my quilt, Xing had fallen back asleep.

At roll call the next morning, the guards told us we had been assigned to Section 583 of Qinghe Farm. They distributed those of us newly arrived from Yanqing among the eight existing labor teams, each of which numbered about 150 men. Twenty of us joined company three. I never knew what happened to the other eighty from Yanqing. It didn't matter. At Xihongsan I had never even learned most of my fellow prisoners' names.

The prisoner who had slept on my other side introduced himself as Chen Ming and told me he had been arrested as a "thought reactionary." His quiet reserve made me sense immediately that he was the kind of person I would want to know in times of trouble.

"Where did you come from?" Chen asked in a low voice.

"Yanqing," I answered.

"Oh, we've heard it's a good place. The prisoners say you have plenty of food there."

"How much do you get to eat here?" I asked quickly.

"You'll see. What did they give you at Yanqing?"

"Every day two meals, every meal two wotou."

"Wotou? That's fine! What kind of wotou?"

"Half sorghum, half wheat chaff," I answered.

The prisoner on the far side of Chen Ming spoke up. "That's not so bad."

My hopes sank. "What do they give you here?" I repeated.

"Wait, you'll see."

Lined up outside for the morning meal, I watched the duty prisoner using a wooden paddle to scoop out the rations of limp, steamed buns. Instead of the two small, hard wotou I had gotten used to at Yanqing, he handed me one large, soft one. The dough was an ivory color, almost white, and too flaccid to hold its shape in my hand. Next he poured a ladleful of soup into my bowl. A few leaves floated on top, coloring the water a light brown. I tasted the wotou and thought of sawdust.

Chen Ming saw the expression on my face. "This is a new creation," he said, nodding at the wotou.

"What's in it?"

Chen's answer was precise. "Twenty percent corn flour, eighty percent ground, fermented corncob. Steam-baked

twice." At Yanqing I had read an article in *People's Daily* intro-
ducing the method of double-steam baking. Any grain, the newspaper announced, could be double-steam-baked to add more
bulk, help assimilate nutrients, and give the stomach a fuller
feeling.

The next day my bowels moved more freely than they had
in months. My whole body felt relief, but the sensation lasted
for only one day.

"When you go to take a crap," Xing advised me, "you'd
better squeeze tight or your insides will pour out."

That afternoon I looked carefully at the prisoners along the
kang. For the first time I saw a person with one leg swollen and
the other as thin as a stick. I began to recognize the symptoms
of edema. First someone's foot would swell so that he could not
wear his shoe. Slowly the swelling would move up through the
ankle, the calf, the knee, the thigh. When it reached the stomach
and made breathing difficult, a person died quickly.

It was a week or so before I realized that several of the
people around me were dying of starvation. Before this, I had
thought only of how weak I felt, not really grasping the ultimate
consequences of continued hunger. Now I saw what lay ahead.

When I went out with my new company to labor, Xing again
became my teacher. Our task was to clean out one of the irrigation ditches in the rice field. "Maybe we'll find something
exciting, you'll see," Xing said as we walked. This was my first
taste of farm labor, and I was just beginning to get used to the
shovel when I saw Xing digging at top speed.

"What are you doing?" I asked, puzzled by his sudden burst
of energy.

He only dug faster, slicing dirt from along the surface of
the soil and expending great energy despite his weakness.
"Come here," he called. He had spotted a hole and hoped it
would lead to a cache of food stored underground by a mouse
or a rat. After several minutes Xing sat down disgustedly in the
dirt. "Sonuvabitch! Where did it go?" Disappointment and ex-
haustion weighed down his big bones.

"Never pass by a hole," he advised me as we walked back
to the barracks that afternoon. "One day you'll get rich. The
best fortune comes from a rat hole."

From Xing I learned that the weather in late spring was

still too cold for frogs and snakes to emerge from their holes and thus the perfect time to search for underground nests. He also showed me every edible kind of grass and root. The first few times I saw him stuff a handful of weeds in his mouth, I tried to stop him. "No! You have to wash the grasses and cook them. You'll get sick."

Xing smiled at my caution. "Little scholar, there's no need for all that. Nothing will happen."

Two men controlled my squad, the leader, whose name was Lang, and Xing. Because I was Xing's friend, none of the others bothered me or touched my food.

That first day only about seventy out of the hundred and thirty prisoners in my company went out to labor. Some felt too weak, some simply preferred to stay behind. Because of the famine, the workday had been reduced to six hours, and no production quota was required. The prisoners took advantage of this unusual leniency and labored at a leisurely pace.

In the fields we didn't work very hard and sometimes even sat down to chat. The guards never shouted or ordered us back to work. Sometimes they even sat down and talked with us. They understood our condition, and though they were not starving, they too were hungry. They worried about their families, who received only half a pound of meat a month per person, two ounces of oil, often no sugar, and never eggs. The quality of their own wheat flour and corn was bad, though not as stale and moldy as ours, and their stores were empty. They needed to conserve energy themselves.

One day on the way back from labor, I saw a prisoner whose face I knew. It was Ling, the study class leader from the Beiyuan Detention Center. I barely recognized him. His face was so swollen that his eyes were nearly hidden, and he sat propped against the barracks wall to save his strength. He wore a dirty blue cotton cap and had wrapped a grimy white towel around his neck for warmth. I could see that one of his feet was much larger than the other.

Ling must have been around thirty years old, but the person before me looked fifty. The previous fall he had been healthy and a favored prisoner who had gained the trust and confidence of the guards. I couldn't imagine what had happened. How had he come here? Had he made some mistake? I walked closer.

"Hey!" I said. "Do you know me? Can you hear me?" He raised his head slowly, focused his eyes, and nodded. "How did you get here?" I asked. "How long have you been here?" Still no answer. Perhaps these were unpleasant questions, I thought, so I asked, "Where is Xi?" The two study class leaders had often been together at the detention center.

"He left the camps," came Ling's weak reply. "His boss helped him go back to Beijing." I had always assumed that as a Party member Xi would someday return to normal life. No doubt he crawled his way out of the camps, wagging his tail to his master the whole time. Not only was he a lackey, but he scorned all those beneath him. I thought back to my own experience as a running dog. Even though my physical situation at Qinghe was much worse than at the Xihongsan mine, I felt relief not to be assisting Captain Yang any longer. I had lost my privileges, but I had regained my self-respect.

Back on the kang, I told Xing I had seen Ling. "He won't live much longer," said Xing, spitting as he cursed between his teeth. Suddenly his hand swept off his cotton cap, and he parted his hair. "Have you seen this?" he asked, pointing to a two-inch scar on his scalp. "That sonuvabitch kicked me like a dog, so he can die like a dog."

"Just let it go," I replied. "That's in the past. It's over. No need to dwell on it. Do you still have the energy to hate?" I asked. "Why don't you use that energy to help me instead? I still need a lot of help from you."

He looked at me strangely, undecided whether to frown or laugh. "Okay," he said finally, "but everyone from Beiyuan remembers that sonuvabitch Ling. They still hate him. They grab his food and hit him. Not me, but he deserves it."

Xing's disclaimer was false. Several days later his friends in Ling's company grabbed the weakened man's food. Xing had given the order. The police captain "opened one eye and closed the other." A month later, we learned that three prisoners in company eight had died in a single day. One was Ling.

As the weeks passed, I became friends with Lang, my squad leader. He was my age and had been the leader of a small Beijing street gang. I had never known such people at the university, and Lang interested me. He was known not for prowess with women or skill at stealing, but for fighting. His stories taught me a great deal about street life and street language in Beijing, and about how such people think and talk and assert authority. One day Lang showed me a scar on his upper arm. He had tried to stop a fight between two rival gangs, he explained. When neither side would listen, he had pulled out a knife, slashed his own arm, and declared, "If anyone keeps fighting, his blood will flow like this." Afterward, so he said, Lang became the head of both gangs. I didn't know whether to believe his story, but he taught me a lot about how to labor, how to save energy, and how to survive in the camp.

One day I saw Lang beating another prisoner from our team. "Why?" I asked. "With all of us so weak, why beat someone?"

Apparently the prisoner had found a bone somewhere in the fields and split it with his sickle. In the latrine out of the wind, he had boiled it in his basin to soften the marrow. It might have been a pig bone or an ox bone, no one knew. It was bleached white and looked, I was told, at least two years old. Somehow word spread that the prisoner, desperately hungry, was cooking a human bone. Others objected, but he kept right on stirring and boiling his find. He was about to scrape out the marrow and eat it along with the broth when Lang arrived and kicked the whole pot over. "Hey! What do you think you're doing? You can't eat that," Lang had shouted.

"This is mine!" the prisoner had insisted, and they fought. Lang had just knocked him down with a kick when I intervened.

"Did you think that was really a human bone?" I asked Lang a few days later, wanting to understand the reason for the fight. "Maybe it was from a pig or an ox, that's not so bad."

Lang flew into a rage from having his judgment challenged. "It had sat out in the field for two years. It was dry and white without a speck of nourishment, and someone said it was human! That's enough." I stopped asking.

As the weeks passed and our diet remained unchanged, more and more prisoners died. Once seriously weakened by hunger, the body grows increasingly susceptible to disease. The smallest cut brings tetanus. Some prisoners succumbed to fever. But the most common death was from dysentery. People would die in the latrine, having lost control of the sphincter muscle.

One evening Lang told me his bowels had begun to run. I

urged him to use all his strength to constrict his muscles and cut off the flow. If he didn't, he would lose too much energy too fast. He said that nothing helped, his bowels kept running. I told him not to squat down but to stand leaning against a wall, anything that would make it more difficult for the bowels to run. He said he would try.

The next morning I brought back from labor some tree bark and burned it to ash, thinking the ash would leach moisture from his stomach and dry up his digestive tract. I mixed it with boiling water for Lang to drink, but on the third day he fell down dead at the trough in the latrine. His skin was a bluish color. His large bones protruded through his skin, his stomach was distended, his chest caved in. Such a strong young man, gone so suddenly. Perhaps in starvation, I thought, the strongest are the first to die.

Even in death, Lang instructed me. Many prisoners picked grass, brought it back to camp, and boiled it to make it safe. I knew that Lang ate a lot of grass. Because of his height, he seemed to require more food than most of us. Perhaps one day he picked some grass that wasn't clean and didn't let it boil long enough. From Lang's illness I learned to be careful and boil everything I ate. I also recalled how angry Lang had gotten over the bone. Maybe he had wasted too much of his energy in unnecessary emotion, I thought.

Lang was the second in our squad to die. The first was Ma, a peasant with no education who had been arrested for stealing a twenty-pound sack of corn seeds from his production brigade during the famine to feed his starving family. I had watched the swelling travel up Ma's body. His skin stretched so tight it became bright and smooth like glass. During his last days he seemed to experience increased energy and cheerfulness. His thin, pale face regained some rosy color. I later recognized those changes as typical of the last days of edema. "The last redness of the setting sun," we said.

By then I had been at Qinghe's section 583 just over a month. After Lang's death, the security office appointed me squad labor leader. In that situation the title meant very little, and the responsibilities were few. Labor was perfunctory as we were too weak to work effectively. I could hardly take care of myself, let alone oversee the actions of others.

While working in the irrigation ditches one morning, one of my squad members discovered a hole in the canal bank and called for my help. I grew excited, hoping it might lead to a rat's nest full of stored rice and corn and wheat. As Xing had said, that would be a fortune. "Let me try," I said and grabbed his shovel.

I dug and dug, following the tunnel as it meandered up and down the bank for more than twenty feet. Even if the rat had escaped, I knew its home would be stocked with treasure. Suddenly I noticed a few pieces of grain along the passage. That meant the prize was near. I stopped digging, straightened my back, and shouted at my squad member, "Get out of here!"

"Why?" he asked angrily. "I called you for help."

Without hesitating, I drew back my fist and hit him hard in the nose. He fell to the ground, and I called loudly, "Xing, come here, quick!"

"Take him away," I ordered, as Xing ran up.

After a few more swipes, my shovel broke into the rat's nest. The hole contained perhaps two pounds of corn, two pounds of soybeans, and a pound of rice, all hoarded over the winter months by the rat. I wrapped the fortune in my coat. Every day that week I built a fire in the latrine and cooked portions of the food in my basin.

The latrine was a rectangular building with a roof of woven reeds, cement block walls on three sides, open at the front. A cement trough inside sloped toward the back wall of the building, where the excrement would be removed through an opening and distributed later in the fields as fertilizer. The corners of the latrine building, between the trough and the walls, provided enough shelter from the wind to keep a fragile grass fire burning.

Prisoners became very resourceful with the enamel basins issued for washing and carrying water. I learned how to raise my basin on two bricks, gather some dry reeds or cornstalks from the fields, and boil whatever edible grasses or roots I could find. I trusted that the cooking process would kill any harmful bacteria from the fields and also make the weeds digestible. As I cooked, I often squatted beside someone moving his bowels.

I shared my feast of corn and rice with Xing and Chen Ming. No one dared approach us with Xing standing guard, but

I couldn't still my conscience after hitting the squad member who had discovered the hole. The second afternoon I asked Xing to give him a portion of the food in my bowl.

"No way!" Xing declared. "He gets nothing. He makes me sick."

"Why?" I asked. "I don't want to make another enemy. Why not share some with him?"

"We have only one goal, to stay alive. Besides, he's disgusting. He likes men. He loves men. He lived with a man. He sold his ass. Yech!"

"How do you know this?" I asked, unconvinced.

"That's the reason he's here. He confessed at the study class. You don't believe me? You can ask anyone."

Xing seemed to adhere to the opinion, widely accepted in China, that homosexuality is a crime. I dropped the idea of sharing my food. My twinge of compassion disappeared. I acted as if the fittest alone deserved to survive.

In May 1961 the Chinese government issued a new policy about reeducation through labor, imposing a definite sentence on counterrevolutionary rightists. In study sessions we each had to make a confession, think again about our crimes, then state the punishment that we thought we deserved. The most serious counterrevolutionaries certainly deserved the maximum sentence of three years, the captain stated.

I paid little attention to the request and wrote out the list of my crimes routinely, stating that I was a serious counterrevolutionary rightist, that I was an enemy of the people, that I had committed many terrible mistakes, and that I needed three years, the maximum sentence, to reform myself. At the time I could not think seriously three years ahead. I cared only about the next wotou. I wondered whether I could survive for the next month.

As hunger and disease worsened in the camp, more fights broke out at mealtimes. Duty prisoners always transported the food in separate cartloads to each company, but prisoners had started jumping the carts and stealing the food. To solve the problem, the police guards announced that each man would go to the kitchen's serving window to pick up his portion himself. When this system proved too slow, the squad leaders received orders to come to the window and claim their members' allotted food. After that I waited for squad six to be called, then reported to the kitchen where the duty prisoner dished out ten wotou and ten bowls of watery soup. My squad members stood nearby, and we each carried our own food back to the kang so that we could protect our individual rations.

I stayed especially alert that first day on my way back to the kang, but even so, someone ran past me, grabbed my wotou from my hand, and dashed away. I chased him, shouting, trying not to spill my bowl of soup. As he ran, he put my wotou in his mouth, but he stopped as soon as he had finished swallowing. He had gotten an extra meal. He was thin and slight, and I knew that if I wanted to waste my energy, I could beat him. There seemed no point, so I left.

From then on, I told my squad, we would walk back from the kitchen together to protect each other's food. Even then, our rations were at risk. Three men came after one of my squad members the next afternoon, and two of them grabbed him while the other stole his wotou. They had organized themselves to work together. Then other squads, including mine, began organizing against this band of three. I went out with four of my squad members the following day. We found the three and gave them a beating.

By then I had learned how to fight. To avoid wasting energy, your first blow had to knock your opponent down. You would aim for his eyes or his nose. "Close his eye in one shot, never two," Xing had taught me. If you hit him in the chest, he would still try to grab your food. One strike in the right place. You must protect your meal.

All of us were becoming desperate as the spring of 1961 passed into summer. "I must talk to you about something," Xing said one day in early July. "I warn you, we must be completely honest with each other." He paused, then blurted out his question nervously: "Do you want to escape with me?"

I didn't know how to answer. I knew Xing trusted me, and I knew he would never reveal his plan to anyone else, but I also thought we could never succeed.

Xing sensed my hesitation. "At least if we die, we won't die in the camps. We'll die like free men."

"Where would we go?" I asked him. "Where could we get food? We would have to steal to eat. We couldn't stay alive that way for long."

"Maybe so," Xing answered slowly, "but I cannot keep on like this."

"We don't have the strength to get out of 583," I added, "and if we did escape, I'm not sure how far I could walk."

Xing dropped his head in silence. I had never known him to lose his fighting spirit, but that day I saw it begin to die.

Soon after that, Lang's trouble came to Xing. He could not stop his bowels. He would eat a lot, trying to replenish himself, but the more he ate, the more he lost control of his bowels. Grasses and roots were no substitute for real food.

Increasingly Xing began grabbing others' rations. He became more aggressive and daring, not caring what chances he took. Once he learned that a package of food from a prisoner's family had arrived at the security office, and he sneaked in, opened the package, and ate.

Xing's offenses did not pass unnoticed. One morning the police captains assembled our whole company and lectured us about maintaining discipline. Then they announced that Xing would receive a punishment of seven days in solitary confinement.

"No, no!" Xing shouted, asking for forgiveness and promising never again to steal food. "I promise, I promise!" he pleaded. "Please give me another chance to correct myself." Xing knelt down in front of the entire company, but the captain refused to yield. The authorities rarely used confinement as a punishment in 1961, knowing that cutting back the rations of a malnourished prisoner often proved fatal. This time they must have decided to make Xing an example. "You know the rules," the captain barked. "The decision comes from 583 battalion headquarters."

Suddenly Xing jumped up and grabbed a spade from a pile of tools nearby. "I promise, I swear I will never steal. Don't send me to the confinement house!" He brought the spade down, cutting deeply into the little finger of his left hand. "I will use my finger, my own blood, to swear!"

The captain ordered Xing taken to the prison doctor. His rash act brought deliverance from almost certain starvation in the confinement house, but his finger began to redden and swell painfully. Within a few days he lay on the kang with a high fever. Two weeks later Xing died from tetanus. At the edge of death, he kept muttering deliriously. "Sonuvabitch! Sonuvabitch!" Xing's curse rang in my ears. Those were his last words of abuse for an indifferent and hostile world.

10

No Time for Dreams

*I*n early August of 1961, the Beijing Public Security Bureau instituted a new policy to counter a growing demoralization within the labor camps. The rising number of deaths over the summer at the height of the nationwide famine had bred a sense of desperation and panic among labor-reform subjects. Insubordination, fights over food, and escape attempts at Qinghe Farm and at other camps had made prison management difficult. In order to lift morale and maintain stability, the Qinghe headquarters decided that those who had reached an advanced stage of starvation would be sent to a different compound within the sprawling prison complex, out of sight of healthier inmates. What had previously been known as section 585 was renamed the Prison Patient Recovery Center.

I listened carefully when the Qinghe commander explained the new policy. "According to the decision of the Central Committee of the Communist Party," he announced, "and also according to Minister of Public Security Luo Ruiqing, all labor camps will use strong management to prevent vicious and malignant incidents involving prisoner uprisings in the camps. To the best of our ability in this situation, we will try to do the best for you and improve your lives. You must take care of your health and follow good sanitation in order to reduce the risk of disease.

"To this end, the Qinghe Farm headquarters has decided to establish a patient recovery camp for sick prisoners in both the western and eastern sections. At these camps we will offer special treatment in order that prisoners will recover more quickly and return to labor. Only through labor can you reform and become new socialist people. If you cannot labor, you cannot reform yourselves. So we want to give special attention to all sick prisoners. In the western region, section 585 will be the patient recovery camp. We hope that there you will become more comfortable and regain your health, return to labor, and never forget to reform yourselves and become new socialist people."

The first group left for the new recovery center in late August. Over several weeks the clinic doctors examined every prisoner in section 583. They checked our weight, our blood pressure, and our other vital functions, then divided us into three ranks. I never learned the medical criteria for the different categories, but I could see that those assigned to the first rank looked the closest to death. A second group of prisoners left for 585 in mid-September and a third in early October.

"When I call your names," the police captain announced as he notified the third group, "stand by the wall and wait for instructions." I had mixed feelings when I heard my name listed for 585. The decision to set up this separate compound for the seriously ill and malnourished, I reasoned, had come all the way from the Communist Party Central Committee. The goal was to provide a place where prisoners could rest and regain their strength. Maybe in 585 we would receive special treatment, maybe we were fortunate.

I could hear others waiting to be transferred speculating aloud that at the recovery center our rations were sure to be increased. A few ventured that we might receive real food instead of substitutes, maybe some vegetables, maybe two or three ounces of meat every month, maybe even two or three ounces of sugar. The anticipation spread. I could see some of the prisoners left behind watching enviously as we prepared to leave.

But I wondered. Those left behind looked healthier than we, and no one knew what would happen at 585. Perhaps we had been eliminated from the race, while they were still running. I tried to stifle a growing anxiety.

Not more than three miles separated the two compounds, a distance a healthy person could walk in less than an hour. Because we had no strength, four oxcarts arrived to carry the eighty of us to 585 in several trips. Chen Ming and I rode with four others in the lead cart. We rolled along step by step for about two hours. An ox never moves quickly, and these must have been too old to give milk and too bony to slaughter for meat. As we bumped over the rough dirt road, I tried to empty my mind. I could spare no energy for useless apprehension.

Vaguely I wondered where this journey would end. There may have been thirty of us in all loaded onto the four carts in that first trip. I didn't know. I had no interest in counting or keeping track. I didn't notice the color of the sky or the kind of fields we passed along the way.

"Yuiii!" The cart driver, a "resettlement prisoner" who had been released from labor reform but not allowed back into civilian life, shouted to the ox. I heard the reins tighten as the cart stopped, and I raised my head to look over the side. A single guard rode slowly past on a bicycle. For this transfer of prisoners, no rifles or dogs were needed. Above me I saw a high brick wall strung with electrified barbed wire and in front of me two heavy black gates. Section 585 looked identical to 583, I thought, as I lay back down on the cart floor.

The oxcart jerked into motion, and we plodded through the opened gates. I heard the clang of metal behind us and once again raised my head to look around. The gray brick barracks and the mud-packed inner yard appeared indistinguishable from those I had just left. When we stopped, the guards ordered us down from the carts and assigned us to barracks. Chen Ming and I went to company ten, squad six. Without speaking, we both seemed to realize we would be each other's only friend in this new setting. Around us all were strangers.

It was nearly noon, and I saw prisoners scattered around the yard, standing or sitting against the barracks walls, trying to soak up some warmth from the autumn sun. Many looked scarcely human. The brow bones above their eyes protruded under tightly stretched skin. Their mouths hung slightly open below hollowed cheeks. Their gaunt necks seemed unnaturally long. Their blank faces gave no sign that they had noticed our arrival. With a start I wondered whether I looked the same.

In the year and a half since my arrest, I had never seen myself in a mirror. I stared down at my washboard ribcage and realized that I must have look equally wasted and unkempt, with my face unshaved, my hair long and uncombed. Those people must once have been doctors or teachers, factory workers or peasants, I thought, each with his own heaven and hell, his own hopes and problems. Now they are virtually indistinguishable. If Chairman Mao were to spend a year in the camps, he would look no different. My anger flared briefly. Were these the new socialist people that Chairman Mao wanted to create? Was this the glorious result of reforming yourself through labor?

Inside the barracks that first evening I surveyed my fellow prisoners more closely. Several of my new squadmates had begun to swell, some in only one leg, some in both, one already above the waist. I was one of the few not yet affected by edema, but I feared their fate awaited me. Perhaps my own emaciation was more extreme than I knew. I recoiled from the thought that these ravaged people were my mirror.

Why had I been sent to this place where all the prisoners seemed so seriously ill, so close to starvation, I wondered anxiously. I thought back to the prison doctor's examination in August, when my weight had been just over eighty pounds and my blood pressure very low, sixty-five over eighty-five. The fluid in my lung no longer troubled me, but I felt very weak and always cold. Perhaps I had lost my resistance to disease. Perhaps my condition was dangerous. I fell into a troubled sleep.

At ten o'clock on my first morning in 585, a tall, balding cook named Wang, stern and almost toothless, arrived with two buckets of gruel hanging from a shoulder pole. I guessed from the bitter taste that we were eating a mixture of half cornmeal and half food substitute, probably ground corncobs. While it clearly lacked nourishment, the warm liquid felt soothing and filling as I drained my bowl. Then a duty prisoner handed me a small packet made out of folded newspaper that contained two ounces of what he called "health, richness, and relaxation powder." I had never heard of this tonic, but it tasted slightly sweet. Others said that it was mostly ground yellow beans with a bit of sugar. I watched some of the prisoners mix the powder into their gruel, while others ate it right from the envelope. I felt grateful for even this meager source of protein.

At 583 two clinic personnel had been responsible for the entire compound of a thousand prisoners, but at 585 four medical workers from the clinic checked on our progress. Their primary job was not to treat our illness, as they had no medicine to dispense, but to report which prisoners drew close to death and then to record the cause of death in the person's file. One of the clinic workers told me later that he spent each day folding the small envelopes out of newspaper and measuring out the special powder.

On our second day the duty prisoner instructed all newcomers to register for supplies and then to submit the request forms in the afternoon. With the small sums remaining in our prison accounts from 583, we could purchase toothbrushes, toothpaste, envelopes, letter paper, or stamps if we wished. Cigarettes were not available as we were considered too ill to smoke. In my room an older prisoner approached me when the duty prisoner left. "Hey, would you order some toothpaste for me?"

"I don't know," I said, wondering at the request. "Why should I?"

"Just help me."

"Why? For what?"

"I need it."

"Okay." I was not sure why I agreed except that I had given up brushing my teeth and had no interest in toothpaste. Such efforts at hygiene seemed pointless, and I didn't want to use energy for an unnecessary task.

Later in the morning another prisoner came to me, speaking quietly. "Would you order some toothpaste for me?" Obviously there were things about the new compound I did not yet understand.

"Okay," I agreed again. I registered for two tubes of toothpaste and turned in the form.

That evening the duty prisoner stormed into the room. "What are you doing?" he shouted angrily, his finger pointing at me. The sharpness of his anger scared me. "Why are you ordering two tubes of toothpaste? Spread out your things!" I drew my personal belongings down from the shelf opposite the kang. "I knew it," he said. "You still have toothpaste. Why are you ordering more?"

I couldn't understand the problem. I had no idea why the others wanted extra toothpaste, yet I was about to be accused of trying to deceive the prison authorities.

"Never mind about the toothpaste, just forget my order," I replied.

"You're new here," the duty prisoner huffed, confident that he had frightened me into submission, "but don't try this again!" He left the room. I should have guessed that the prisoners used toothpaste as a substitute for food.

Shortly after the next morning's meal, I said to Chen Ming, "How about going outside for a look?"

"Nothing worth looking at," he answered flatly from his spot beside me on the kang.

"Let's just go outside anyway," I persisted.

"Don't waste the energy."

"Come on, come on," I repeated impatiently. I wanted to see my surroundings and also to stir my friend from his lethargy. Chen Ming slowly roused himself, and I supported his weight by draping his arm around my shoulders. The gruel and the bean powder had given me a small spurt of energy. I squinted as I stepped into the sunlight.

Walking slowly, we made our way around the compound yard. At 583 the identical barracks had held two thousand inmates, but these seemed about half occupied. I estimated that about twelve hundred men had been transferred to 585 over the past six weeks. It looked to me as if at least half had already lost the ability to move about.

Inside the latrine I could see two prisoners tending small fires. What could they be cooking, I wondered, when no one is permitted to leave the compound to search for food? We all had matches left from our cigarette rations in 583, and they could have gathered dried leaves and scraps of paper as fuel, but I couldn't guess what they would find to boil. I drew closer, and they watched me carefully, like wolves ready to defend their food. One prisoner said that he was braising his wotou in water to make it expand. "That way you feel fuller," he declared. I thought of our food-imagining evenings. The other more fortunate prisoner was boiling a small handful of wheat flour that he must have received in a package from a family member. He had added just enough flour to his pot of water to make his stomach feel fuller. How many ways we found to satisfy our need for fullness, I thought.

I turned back toward the yard to see three prisoners rush toward a duty prisoner carrying a wooden bucket of food. The three men fell to their knees to lick up some spilled gruel from the hard-packed mud. I remembered vividly the moment nearly a year before when Xing had lapped up the Spring Festival soup, unable to control his urge for food. I also thought of the opening scene of *A Tale of Two Cities*, which I had read in middle school, when starving Parisians lapped up spilled wine from between the cobblestones on the streets.

"Let's go back," muttered Chen Ming, steering me toward the barracks. Strangely his space on the kang had been occupied in our absence. I tried to rouse the prisoner who had taken Chen's spot, but my effort was pointless. The man was dead. Someone had already reported the death to the security office, and two duty prisoners arrived almost immediately to wrap the body in a reed mat and carry it to a small storage shed nearby.

For some reason as I lay on the kang that evening, I thought of Noah's ark. All those animals, driven inside in pairs by the flood, had lived side by side for forty days. They must also have faced a shortage of food, and they didn't know whether the flood would ever end. I wondered how they survived, whether they fought each other, and whether the wolf tried to eat the rabbit. Since they had all managed to reach shore safely, I assumed they must have aided each other during the weeks of flood. Maybe, I thought, humans can also help each other until the waters recede. I remembered for a moment the teachings and the comfort of the Church, and once again I prayed, asking God for help.

In 585 the days passed differently than at any camp I had known before. There was no labor, no political study, and almost no fighting. I saw only one actual fight during those first weeks, like a slow-motion film with the prisoners' fists hardly clenched, falling powerlessly through the air, as if paper men were trying to strike each other when they could have just blown each other down.

Without the energy or the will to move about, we lay hour

after hour with our heads to the wall beneath our quilts and with our chipped enamel bowls on either side of our pillows, one for urine and the other for food. I felt more comfortable without clothes, and most of the other prisoners also lay naked unless they had to get up. Hardly anyone spoke. We rarely even walked the short distance across the yard to the latrine since our bowels moved only every three to five days. Usually we knelt on the kang to urinate and then emptied the bowls outside twice a day. I seemed to grow steadily weaker.

The late October air carried the first cold nip from Siberia. Fewer and fewer in my squad ventured outside. Only at noon would the most robust among us step into the sunshine. More and more we remained on the kang day and night.

Old Wang the cook stopped outside our room twice a day with our gruel. He clanged a big iron ladle against one of his buckets to rouse us for mealtime. "Dong! Dong! Dong!" Around the kang eyes opened and people slowly drew themselves to sitting positions, taking care to keep themselves covered by their quilts. They moved their food bowls to the edge of the kang, watching each ladleful as Wang moved around the room dishing out the watery gruel. He handled his ladle with precision, pausing with it poised above the bucket to drain off the overflow, then with a steady hand pouring the contents into a prisoner's bowl and tapping the ladle against the side to dislodge the last drops. His movements, watched intently, always drew protests.

"Hey! Mine's not full!" a prisoner would shout.

The cook filled the ladle again.

"Hey! The spoon's not level!" He tried again.

"Hey! There's some sticking to the ladle!"

When the food was gone, we licked our bowls slowly and thoroughly, then replaced them beside our heads. They never needed washing. Some men urinated, some walked outside to empty their urine basins. Soon we had all climbed back beneath our quilts to await the next meal.

One prisoner in the room had a spoon, which allowed him an additional eating activity to enhance the pleasure. He could count each spoonful. Even though we were eating a bitter, unpalatable porridge, the prisoner with the spoon ate every mouthful extra slowly, enjoying the process, careful always to hold his spoon exactly level.

"Sonuvabitch! Yesterday I had twenty-five and a half. Today it's only twenty-five. Half a spoon less. Old Wang," he shouted angrily at the cook, "I hope you die soon, I hope your whole family dies!"

After the meal someone would ask, "How did you do to-day?"

"Today, okay. Twenty-seven." Always the words came low and slow.

"Not bad."

"But it seemed thicker yesterday."

Chen Ming grew more dispirited and dejected. At 583 I had known him to be a quiet man, never easily excited or moved to action. He had never been muscular or strong, and he loathed physical conflict, refusing to struggle for food or power. If someone struck him, he turned away. But at 585 he withdrew even more. He seemed to have given up and to be waiting for the end to come. Then early one morning his lethargy seemed to disappear. He turned to me on the kang, unusually animated, with a puzzled look on his face.

"I had a dream," he said.

"Come on," I chided. "Now is not the time for dreams."

"I dreamt that a group of people were using knives to cut me up and then putting my meat in a huge pot. They cooked it and ate it, but I was still alive. I sat there watching them eat like hungry tigers, as if my meat were delicious."

"What was your feeling?" I asked.

"I wanted them to give me a piece and let me taste."

"Come on," I interrupted. "Don't dream about that."

Chen Ming's grim vision made me also think about the end. I reached behind my pillow and handed him a piece of paper I had prepared several days before. "Here is my family's address in Shanghai," I said quietly. "Maybe one day I will go. If you are still alive, please let them know I have gone."

Chen Ming took the paper and handed me his address in exchange. "Yes, it's time. I have only my old mother left. Just tell her I was thinking of her."

For the next few days Chen Ming seemed eager to talk. He wanted to think over his life, to recall the dreams left unfulfilled. "Don't talk," I said to him one morning as he started remembering. "If you don't have money, don't buy. If you don't have food, don't waste energy. Don't even dream or think. Cover your eyes with a towel. Save your strength."

"Save it for what?"

"Don't ask," I answered impatiently. "Why do you even wonder what to save your energy for? That means you are thinking."

"I can't stop my mind. How do I stop thinking?"

"Just forget it. Don't even ask how to save your energy. That is still thinking. Don't think."

I had found refuge in blankness.

11

Death Watch

*I*nside the 585 barracks it became more difficult to distin-
guish the dead from the living. At a glance there seemed
no difference. Much of the day and night we lay in a state of
near stupor. No longer did we pay attention when someone
reached the end and went into last gasps or tremors. Death
arrived almost unnoticed.

The only sign that a prisoner had died was that he failed
to sit up at mealtime. One morning I noticed that the ladle
banging did not rouse the person next to me. When the cook
reached out to fill my bowl, I said only, "Lao Wang, there's
one."

Wang barked gruffly, "Okay," and went on to the next
empty bowl. After the meal two duty prisoners came to remove
the body. They placed a six-foot-square woven reed mat in the
aisle beside the kang, set the body onto it, rolled it up like an
eggroll, and carried it outside to the storage room. I knew that
the next day they would load it with the other eggrolls onto an
oxcart headed for someplace they called 586. This was the final
destination of the dead.

Others told me that bodies had previously been placed in
crude wooden coffins made of boards salvaged from packing

crates, but by October when I reached 585, people were simply rolled up in mats.

I don't know how many sick prisoners died that October. I don't even know how many died in my squad. The number in my room fluctuated too much to keep track. Dead bodies went out and live bodies came in almost daily. I paid no attention. I never even learned their names.

As the days passed, the only prisoner who still bothered with conversation was the one who counted the spoonsful of gruel at every meal. Then one morning when Lao Wang banged on the bucket, the spoonful counter didn't sit up.

"Lao Wang," someone said quietly, "today no one will complain about you after you leave."

"What?" Old Wang, busy ladling, had not noticed that one person had failed to sit up. The speaker sat on his haunches pointing across the aisle to a prostrate figure.

"Why should he complain about me anyway?" Lao Wang grumbled.

"He always said you owed him half a spoonful," I answered.

"You know how careful I am to hold the ladle level," Lao Wang protested. Our cook was a Muslim, older than I, tall and balding, and he had lost many teeth. He spoke in a loud, blunt voice, but I could sense his concern and observe his scrupulous honesty. "I never cheated him," Lao Wang continued. "Anyway, it doesn't matter now." He made a wry face and moved on to dish out gruel for the next prisoner. Lao Wang had become our only link with the world beyond the walls of our room.

In late October the duty prisoners stopped bringing reed mats to carry out the dead. I assumed the storehouse must be running out of supplies with so much demand. They simply rolled the dead prisoners in their quilts, twisted the corners and, each taking an end in one hand, carried them out. The bodies were all very light.

The 585 clinic workers observed us frequently, taking our blood pressure and pulse, checking our eyes and the color of our tongues, then making notes in our files. They didn't bother to bring a scale to measure our weight, since many of us were too weak to stand. I could tell I had shed a few more pounds.

Curiously I felt almost no hunger during those weeks. I swallowed the helpings of gruel and the special tonic powder twice a day, but I had no appetite. I didn't feel as if I were suffering. My thoughts, my feelings, my pain all went away.

In 585 I thought very little. I didn't want to reflect on my surroundings or think about what lay ahead. Even when I tried to dream something or to remember, my mind refused. I didn't want to lose entirely the capacity to think, so sometimes I pushed myself to recall my family, my girlfriend, or some incident from my happy youth. Maybe I didn't have the energy or maybe the lack of nourishment had affected my brain, I don't know. But for two months I was conscious of nothing beyond the small events that happened on the kang.

One day Chen Ming became unusually talkative. He spoke haltingly as if speech were difficult, stopping to rest between each thought, determined to tell me again about his youthful dreams.

"I went to Beijing because I wanted to be a teacher. I was the smartest in my village school. My girlfriend said she would wait for me ... a peasant girl ... very clever. I wanted her to be proud of me. My uncle lived in Beijing. I found a job teaching ... in a primary school ... geography. I showed my students the map. I told them many things. I told them that Taiwan is a beautiful island ... that its people fought off invasions from the Dutch and the Japanese ... that they are brave and proud. I wanted my girlfriend to join me. I thought we would have a new life in Beijing. But it didn't happen.

"She came to Beijing ... but she married someone else. They had a baby. One day my mother came. I took her to Tiananmen Square ... it was very crowded ... we got separated. The police came just then and took me to jail. For what, I don't know."

I had heard Chen Ming's story before, but never at such length. I admired his ambition and his wish to leave his village behind and make a new life as a teacher in the national capital. Like many others, he had not been able to pursue his dream. When the antirightist movement came with its quota of enemies to be filled in every work unit, he was labeled a "thought reactionary" for having spoken favorably about Taiwan and for implying that the Nationalist stronghold could resist an invasion from the mainland.

I listened on and off to Chen Ming's words, a towel covering my eyes, my attention drifting in and out. The next morning he scarcely stirred, and at the four o'clock meal, he didn't sit up. I nudged him, but he didn't move.

"Lao Wang," I said when I had finished eating, "another one."

The duty prisoners arrived for Chen Ming in about an hour. It was almost dark and by mid-November very cold. They twisted the ends of his quilt and carried him away. I found a small envelope and two books under his bedding on the kang. With one motion I swept them under my quilt. That was all I could do to take care of Chen Ming's affairs. I felt nothing. My heart had grown cold, and my tears would not flow.

Long after dark, maybe near midnight, I heard shouting and police voices. Two duty prisoners laid a body down beside me. I saw that it was Chen Ming.

"What's happened?" I asked.

"We heard the duty prisoner in the storage room shouting," one duty prisoner told me excitedly. "He saw a hand reach up and shake the door. There were seven bodies on the kang. In the morning they would be taken out to the ox cart. The duty prisoner thought he saw a ghost and shouted for the security guard. Everyone was scared. It seemed this body had come back to life. Then they realized that one prisoner was not yet dead."

I guessed that Chen Ming had lost consciousness and when he awoke had crawled to the door and rattled it to get someone's attention.

"Oh," I spoke up, "remember that Chen Ming has missed a meal."

"Wait until tomorrow," said the captain. "The meal is over and he's missed it. That's all."

"But he is not an ordinary prisoner," I persisted. "He has come back from hell." This was one favor I could do for my friend.

The captain hesitated, then ordered the duty prisoner, "Get Lao Wang." The cook arrived and verified that Chen Ming had not eaten the last meal.

"I think you should order an extra meal," I persisted.

"Go ahead, you write the request," the captain agreed, handing me a piece of paper.

"Team ten, squadron six, prisoner Chen Ming, missing

afternoon meal. Please supply it," I wrote. It was the first time I had written anything in half a year.

Lao Wang returned with two wotous made of real corn, not food substitutes. I knew the difference immediately by the rich smell. Pulling the towel from my eyes, I sat up. Lao Wang held out a plate to Chen Ming. The two wotou glistened with a golden color even in the dim light. Steam curled from the buns, wafting the fragrance to me. I had never seen anything so delicious in my life. This was food reserved for police captains.

I shook Chen Ming's shoulder. "Get up, get up." I didn't have the energy to lift him. He opened his eyes.

"Here, here. It's for you, eat some," Lao Wang offered.

Suddenly Chen Ming rose to a sitting position. His eyes opened wide and shone more brightly than any eyes I have ever seen. They fixed on the corn wotou.

"For me?"

He grabbed the two buns from the plate and stuffed them both in his mouth at once. Pieces of wotou smeared around his lips. He chewed and swallowed and picked up crumbs from the kang in a frenzy. It took only a few seconds. Then he grabbed his stomach and shouted loudly in pain. His face contorted, and he fell back. He was dead.

"I'm sorry," I whispered, touching his face. His skin felt hot. His weakened stomach could not digest so much rich corn swallowed so quickly.

For a long time I had not seen a face look as red and healthy as Chen Ming's did that night. I watched his look of pain disappear. His body relaxed, and a calmness spread over his face. I closed his eyes. The color drained away.

It was November 1961. For the third time in the labor camps, my thoughts turned to God. I prayed that He would accept Chen Ming. "He is one of your sheep," I prayed, "returned to be with You in the radiance of Your love."

No one in the room showed any interest in Chen's death. I was the only one sitting up. For the first time in weeks, I began to think.

First I thought about Chen Ming. He had told me his dreams, but they were past, his life was over, he was gone. Had he died for anything meaningful? It seemed that a human being could be destroyed so easily, just like a thin sheet of paper, just like a candle blown out.

The authorities could say whatever they liked about Chen Ming, that he was a criminal, a thought reactionary, an undesirable. The whole world could accuse him, but nothing more could happen to my friend. He could suffer no more abuse, no more pain. Nothing could touch him. He was at peace.

I began to think about myself. What was my own life worth? What did it mean? Why did it continue? Why did I even want to live? If tomorrow I followed Chen Ming, what would any of it matter—my girlfriend, my stepmother, my father, my baseball team, my future? It was all nonsense. For Chen Ming, for Xing, for Ling, for Lang, everything had passed, nothing mattered. Everything seemed like nothing.

Why, I thought, did I want to survive? For what did I hold on? Did I continue living for my girlfriend or my family, to become a professor or to play baseball? To do my best, to do my worst, either way meant nothing. By tomorrow it might all be gone.

I lay down again and drew the quilt around me. I had no answer. If I die tomorrow like Chen Ming, I thought, my life will have been worth nothing. But somehow I didn't want to give up, I didn't want to surrender. Something inside me cried out, where is my God, my Father? Help me. Guide me. Bless me. Then my mind emptied. The rest of that night I slept peacefully.

Before the morning meal the duty prisoners came to take Chen Ming's body to the ox cart. They had just begun to wrap him in his quilt when I sat up.

"No, leave it!" I said in a firm voice, stretching myself across his body.

"What are you doing? He's dead," said one of the duty prisoners, astonished at my behavior.

I didn't answer. I just lay with my chest pressed against Chen Ming's cold body.

Unsure what to do about such strange behavior, the duty prisoner reported me to the security office. A young captain newly assigned to 585 named Zheng approached me.

Every security captain begins his encounters with prisoners

by shouting. Captain Zheng was no exception. "What are you doing?" he yelled. I didn't answer, and I didn't move.

"Get away, get away!" he commanded. When I still didn't respond, the captain grew angry. "Move him away," he ordered. The duty prisoner pulled at my arm. I said quietly, "I want to stay with him."

"He's dead. He's going to be buried. You can't stay with him."

"Yes," I said quietly. I didn't know why those words jumped out of my mouth.

Captain Zheng's surprise overwhelmed his anger. In 585 prisoners rarely expressed emotion. No one can respond to so much dying. He paused, then relented, "It's okay, you can go. Go with him."

A duty prisoner pulled me to my feet and told me to put on my clothes. I dressed slowly. He supported me as I walked to the ox cart and helped me climb in at the rear, next to Chen Ming's rolled-up body. Six other corpses lay at the front. The two duty prisoners sat beside me. This was their daily job.

I had no idea what I was doing. I heard the crack of the whip and sat propped against the side of the cart, staring out as we passed through the gates of 585.

We followed a curving path along the base of the camp wall. As we rounded the guard tower, I saw a large open area stretching behind 585. The ox cart left the path and rolled through a bumpy field. I shifted from side to side, then realized I was riding over grave mounds. I had entered a burial ground.

I could see small pieces of wood marking the graves with names written in black ink. Some of the grave sites remained mounded quite high, as if recently dug, while some had flattened as if the earth had settled over time. I could see no end to the mounds. There may have been thousands. This was the area of Qinghe Farm known as section 586.

I could see where some holes had been dug up, and I wondered if wild dogs had eaten the bodies. Even some of the fresher mounds had been half dug away or tunneled into. I saw a few scattered scraps of clothing.

The cart finally stopped when we reached undug ground, and the duty prisoners set to work with their shovels. Soon five of the bodies had been buried. Chen Ming was among them.

"Hey," one of them called. "My hole is big enough for two." They dropped the last two bodies into the single hole, then covered everything hastily with loose dirt. When they had finished, pieces of quilt stuck out from the shallow mounds. They had brought no grave markers. Chen Ming disappeared.

The diggers climbed into the ox cart beside me. No one spoke. Before we rounded the guard tower to pass again through the gates of 585, I looked back. My mind noted with a strangely detached curiosity the different heights of the graves, the crude wooden markers, the occasional shreds of clothing. I had felt nothing when they put Chen Ming in the ground, but that last glance at 586 seared itself into my memory.

Suddenly my mind became animated, and I had what seemed almost a revelation. Human life has no value here, I thought bitterly. It has no more importance than a cigarette ash flicked in the wind. But if a person's life has no value, then the society that shapes that life has no value either. If the people mean no more than dust, then the society is worthless and does not deserve to continue. If the society should not continue, then I should oppose it.

At that moment I knew that I could not die. I could not simply slide into nothingness and join Chen Ming. I had to use my life purposefully and try to change the society. In that way my own existence would not be mere dust but would have some value. My burst of thought came briefly, unexpectedly out of the expanse of human waste that was 586. Then my mind shut down again.

12

The Coldest Winter

*T*he winter of 1961–62 was the coldest I could remember. I passed the weeks of December and January lying on the kang, huddled beneath my quilt, my mind blank. One noontime in January, a new captain named Cao toured the barracks. "Get up! Everyone get up. Outside," he called. No one wanted to move. I pulled on my trousers and overcoat slowly, then wrapped my quilt around my shoulders. I wondered what additional hardship he would inflict.

Outside we sat slumped against the barracks wall, trying to find shelter from the wind. "According to new orders from the Beijing Public Security Bureau," Captain Cao declared, his voice encouraging, "everyone will receive one additional ounce of food daily, starting tomorrow." He waited for some reaction, some excitement, but no one moved. What kind of food, I thought. Would it give real nourishment or just fill our stomachs with more ground bark or corncob powder? Would it ease our hunger? What difference would one ounce make when we were starving?

"Also beginning tomorrow, each squad will muster outside at noontime to take some fresh air. Sunshine will improve your health," Cao continued. "Even a healthy person grows weak if he stays in bed all day. You must move around as much as you

Harry (bottom, third from right) with his two younger sisters, his second youngest brother, three cousins, and (top) his elder brother and elder sister, in Shanghai, 1950.

Harry (second from right) in the only surviving photograph of the whole family, taken before his elder sister left for Hong Kong, in Shanghai, 1950.

Harry's stepmother on the day of her wedding to his father in Shanghai in 1942.

Harry's stepmother outside their home in Shanghai in the winter of 1952.

Harry a few days after he was labeled as a counterrevolutionary rightist, in Beijing, 1957.

Harry (right) with his father and elder brother, in Shanghai, 1953.

Harry (top, second from left) with the all-Beijing baseball team after winning the national intercollegiate championship, summer 1956.

The entrance gate to the section of Qinghe Farm previously known as section 585, called the Beijing Qinghe Shrimp Farm, in June 1991.

The Yinying Coal Mine, also known as Shanxi Province Number 2 Labor Reform Camp, in June 1991.

A view of Qinghe Farm's section 583, in June 1991.

Prisoners digging a ditch at Qinghe Farm, June 1991.

The entrance to the Wangzhuang Coal Mine, also called Shanxi Province Number 4 Labor Reform Camp, in June 1991.

Prisoners marching to labor at the Qinghai Hide and Garment Factory, also known as the Qinghai Number 2 Labor Reform Camp, in August 1991. Harry took the photograph with a concealed camera.

A rear view of Qinghe Farm's section 585, near the site of the 586 graveyard, in June 1991.

Harry testifying before the United States Senate, displaying the shoulder bag that concealed his camera, Washington, D.C., October 1991.

Harry testifying before the United States House of Representatives about his recent visit to China's labor reform camps, Washington, D.C., September 1991.

Harry receiving the Freedom Award from the Hungarian Freedom Fighters'
Federation, Washington, D.C., October 1991.

can. Get exercise, however much you can manage. The people's government and the Communist Party don't want you to die but to be reformed into new socialist people." Those last words I had heard repeated many times before, but the rest of Cao's speech and the mild tone of his voice seemed to convey some genuine personal concern, some human feeling.

The following morning each prisoner received one small extra wotou. We could tell immediately by the taste and texture that it contained more than the usual amount of grain and less food substitute. We didn't ask where the additional corn had come from. Maybe the government wanted to stop the flood of prison deaths. Maybe the famine had abated. We didn't know. All we knew was that for a long time bodies had been carried away every day to 586.

At noon Captain Cao again walked through each room shouting, "Come out! Come out!" He didn't force the prisoners to leave the kang, but he did try to rouse them. Maybe twenty percent of the company ventured into the sunshine. I went with them.

Cao strolled through the yard, chatting in turn with the prisoners clustered along the barracks wall.

"How're you getting along?" he asked me.

"The sun is too strong," I replied, surprised that a police captain would concern himself with my condition.

"Stay outside a little at a time. Try again tomorrow. Gradually you'll get used to it. Don't stay out too long today. Are you able to walk?"

"It's not easy."

"Lean on the wall, lean on the wall," he urged. "Give it a try. If you can go twenty feet today, that's enough. Tomorrow maybe you can go twenty-five feet. Little by little you'll do more and more. Later it will get easier."

The barracks measured about sixty feet. That first day, even supporting myself against the building, I could barely walk its length. I stopped to catch my breath several times. Cao came by often to encourage me. "You're doing very well. You'll be fine. That's enough for today. Go back to rest."

Two weeks later, his face animated, he gathered all the company members in the yard, about one hundred seventy prisoners. This time he urged even the weakest prisoners to come outside. Then he announced, "I've discovered a garden plot that has some carrots still frozen in the ground from last year's planting. It won't be easy, but we'll dig them out. Tomorrow anyone who can walk that far will come with me." Cao was the first police captain I had ever known to take such initiative on behalf of prisoners.

The next morning the duty prisoners made ready some pickaxes and shovels. Only twenty of us felt strong enough to walk the quarter mile to the garden adjoining the police living quarters. The wind blew hard. Even with my quilt draped around my shoulders over my padded overcoat, I still felt numb from the cold. I kept walking only because Captain Cao had promised we could keep for ourselves whatever we dug up.

"These carrots were planted late in the season so they never reached full size," he explained as we arrived at a small square of ground surrounded by a windbreak of reed matting. "No one bothered to harvest them, and they stayed in the ground over the winter." I watched as he scraped away a layer of dried leaves and pointed out several dark nubs just visible above the frozen soil.

Squatting down to clear away more matted leaves, I spotted the tops of several other carrots, blackened from frost. I knew they were mine if I could dig them out, but that morning the temperature was perhaps minus ten degrees centigrade. I knew the earth had frozen to a depth of about eight inches. I raised my pick and let it fall. A white chip of icy dirt glanced off the blade. I lifted the pick again and again, but I managed to chip only a shallow ring around one carrot top. Then I tried using my fingertips, scraping and digging, ignoring the sharp pain from the frozen dirt jammed beneath my fingernails.

"Did you find one?" asked Cao. "I'll help you." He threw off his military overcoat and reached for my pick. Tung! Tung! Tung! The pick bit through the frozen earth. Chips of dirt flew out from the hole. Several minutes later, his face flushed, he handed me the carrot.

I didn't speak. The shriveled carrot sat in my hand, about five inches long and as thick as my thumb. I wiped it clean on my sleeve. My mouth opened, but I forced myself to remember how Xing had died. I dared not eat it raw.

Once Cao had broken through the frozen soil with that first

hole, I could loosen the surrounding ground more easily, and I soon dug out another carrot. In two hours I had managed to scrape out six more. I wondered where my stamina had come from.

Several prisoners could not hold themselves back and immediately consumed whatever they could dig out. I saw one who had chipped out a carrot only halfway lying on the ground to gnaw it off. I wouldn't let myself take the risk. Back in the compound, I filled my washbasin with water and cooked my carrots in the latrine. I ate four and drank the carrot soup, saving the other two for the next day. They would give me the energy to dig more. I knew that if I wanted to survive, I had to calculate every move carefully.

Over the next several days, after hours of digging, I ate many carrots. The additional nourishment gave me more energy and more strength to dig. By the end of a week, I had managed to save twenty carrots. I carried them, wrapped in a towel, everywhere I went. I even slept with the bundle under my pillow.

When I walked to the latrine to boil water each evening, I took along a shovel for protection. I thought of nothing but my stomach, and I warned away anyone who approached too closely. I no longer had any friends among the prisoners, and I helped no one, offering nothing to those too weak to dig. I had no thought of kindness.

With twenty prisoners working the plot, we exhausted the carrots after eight days. "Today is the last chance," Cao announced as the winter darkness fell. In the adjacent field I watched a tractor plowing its final rounds, preparing the still-frozen earth for the early spring planting, and wondered where we could turn next for extra food. The heavy tractor blades cut through the soil, turning over large clods of dark earth. Then I noticed that some of the furrows were dotted with small white lumps.

"What was planted in that field?" I asked Cao, pointing out the flecks in the soil.

"Cabbages," he replied, "but they've all been harvested. There's nothing left. Go check for yourself."

Picking my way across the jagged furrows left by the tractor, I scraped out several of the white chunks. They were pieces of cabbage root. There's more food here, I thought excitedly. I returned with bleeding fingers to show Cao my handful of treasures.

"Okay, okay," he nodded his approval. "You can come back tomorrow."

Inside the compound I washed my small pile of roots, each the size of a small child's fist, split them lengthwise with a sickle, and then plunged them into boiling water. The outer membrane was fibrous and hard as tree bark, but the inside was soft, white, and tasty.

The following day ten of us returned to the field to collect cabbage roots. The furrows left by the plow had frozen harder overnight, making walking even more difficult. I stumbled often, but the thought of the warm vegetables in my stomach pushed me on. With new strength I used my pick to loosen the chunks of cabbage root, then clawed them out with my hands, ignoring the stinging pain under my fingernails.

The smell of boiling vegetables at night in the latrine prompted more prisoners to join our expeditions. Each day the cabbage chunks became harder to find, but I never returned to the barracks empty-handed. I could tell I was growing stronger. Not everyone in my squad was so fortunate. Sometimes I would return and see an empty space on the kang.

On the fifth day, I stood watching a tractor make sweeping circles in the adjacent field, wondering if that section would yield anything edible to scavenge. I jumped back when the driver took too wide a turn just a few feet away from me. His blades swiped into the canal bank that separated the two fields, uncovering a small hole. I leapt forward, plunged my hands into the three-inch-wide opening, and pulled out a tangle of twelve hibernating snakes, still twisted together. Each was more than a foot long and as thick as my thumb, with green backs, white bellies, and dark red spots on their heads.

Like an animal I huddled over my prey. This meat was mine, all mine, I thought. I watched over my shoulder, concerned that someone in the field might notice what I was doing. Working quickly, I grabbed the snakes one by one and counted as I bit off twelve heads. Then I tore off their skins with my teeth and ripped out their insides. In just a few minutes I had stuffed a large handful of raw meat into my knapsack.

That afternoon I headed immediately for the latrine and

boiled the snake meat for an hour in my washbasin. A shovel lay at my feet as a warning that this meal was mine alone. I savored the pungent taste as the steamed meat spread a feeling of warmth throughout my body.

Early in February 1962, the duty prisoner walked through our barracks room by room. "If I call your name, report to the captains' office," he said, reading from a list. Then he called, "Wu Hongda." I was the only one from my squad, and I joined four other prisoners from my company outside. We walked together.

In the office Captain Cao told us, "We're going to transfer you. Don't hurry. Get your things ready by this afternoon. Don't forget anything."

"Where are we moving?" I asked.

"We don't know, but don't worry, you'll be picked up this afternoon." His voice sounded reassuring.

In the early afternoon an ox cart arrived, and we five prisoners climbed in. A police captain rode beside us on a bicycle. From him I learned that our destination was Qinghe's section 584. I felt completely resigned to my fate, totally passive, blank. My brain had turned to wood. I had no fear because I had no hope.

Inside the walls of 584, the midafternoon mood was energetic, almost lighthearted. I saw prisoners greeting each other and carrying their bedding to their assigned barracks. They looked much stronger than the five of us from 585. Then someone told me that these prisoners were all rightists. Underneath their worn, faded clothing, I thought, these were all intellectuals like me. A police captain called to us, "Go to room eleven, squad five." Then he pointed at me. "You're the squad leader," he said and handed me a list of names.

The four long brick buildings in front of me looked identical to the rows of barracks I had left behind in sections 583 and 585. I knew that each would measure roughly one hundred feet by thirty feet, and would contain ten rooms opening off a narrow corridor. What made this arrival different was not the setting but the occasional sound of conversation as prisoners settled in. Many of us had been in contact primarily with penal criminals, hoodlums from the cities or illiterate peasants from the countryside, for as long as four years. To find ourselves

surrounded by political prisoners with backgrounds and educational levels similar to our own brought almost a happy mood
despite our grim setting.

The room assigned to squad five looked the same as the
one I had just left in 585. Against one wall stretched a mud brick
kang, six feet deep and two feet high. Along the other wall,
across a four-foot aisle, ran a rough shelf where squadmates
stored their basins and mugs, toothbrushes and towels, and below it a row of hooks where we hung our overcoats and extra
trousers. The five of us from 585 sat down on the kang exhausted
after carrying our belongings in from the yard.

"What squad is this?" a handsome prisoner of about my
age called to me from the doorway.

"Squad five," I replied, hearing a familiar accent. "Who
are you?"

"I am Lu Haoqin."

"Where are you from?" I asked.

"Jiangsu province."

"What county?" I pursued.

"Wuxi."

"Ah ha!" I exclaimed, excited at this common bond. "We
have the same roots." A traditional saying sprang to my lips:
"When fellow countrymen meet, their eyes brim with tears."

Lu looked somehow different from the rest of us. His
clothes were as old and worn as mine but were much cleaner
and more neatly patched. The brownish tinge to his close-
cropped black hair also set him apart, as did his smooth skin
and delicate cheekbones. I guessed that fieldwork would not
be his strength, but he seemed healthy and agile. He grasped
my hand firmly and volunteered that he had studied motor
vehicle manufacturing at Qinghua University. I knew that in
the mid-1950s only the brightest students were admitted to
this specialized field, considered critical to China's modernization.

One by one the others assigned to squad five arrived, and
the room grew more animated. After an hour nine people had
gathered on the kang and begun exchanging names and backgrounds. I wondered about the person who had not yet appeared, since as squad leader I had to parcel out the kang space.
Using a branch as a measuring stick, I began dividing the length

of the twenty-five-foot kang by ten, marking off each interval with a sharp stone. We all waited for the last prisoner. If he failed to arrive, we could each take three additional inches of sleeping space to add to our two and a half feet, a considerable increment. I stepped outside to speak to Captain Wang.

"Is anyone else coming to squad five?"

He checked his list. "Ao Naisong is coming. He's often late."

"What's happened to him?" I persisted. The captain seemed to know this prisoner, perhaps from another section of Qinghe, and I felt impatient to settle the question of kang space. Then someone appeared at the far end of the corridor, walking very slowly and carrying a small sack tied with a piece of worn rope.

"Is this squad five?" he called.

"Are you Ao Naisong?" We both nodded. I guessed my last squad member was no older than I. Deep lines fanned out from the corners of his large eyes, creasing a face that had darkened from labor in the sun.

"Where's your bedroll?" I asked, looking at his sack.

He gestured toward the outside door. "Hold this for me. It's a lute."

Never had I known a prisoner to own a lute. I wondered why Ao had not brought his bedroll along, why he walked so slowly, and why the captain seemed to humor him.

I turned again to Captain Wang. "What's wrong with him? Is he sick?"

"Don't worry about him," the captain answered dismissingly. "He's always like that."

That afternoon at four o'clock as I stood in a line for food, my stomach again commanded my thoughts. Would our rations increase in 584? Would the wotou contain more grain? At a distance I could see the duty prisoner ladling scoops from a huge wooden bucket into outstretched bowls. As the cart drew nearer, I couldn't believe my eyes. Prisoners were being served rice porridge. I held out my bowl, raised it to my lips, and the warm, soft kernels slid down my throat. The amount was hardly enough to ease my hunger, but for half a year I had not tasted rice. Everyone talked excitedly about this special treatment, optimistic that the special food confirmed rumors of our early release.

"Do you think they'll give us rice every day?" I asked Lu Haoqin beside me. He shrugged. The next morning I waited outside the barracks to ask the duty prisoner about the food as he made his rounds. "You're getting top-quality rice," he replied, "grown right here in the Qinghe fields. Enjoy it while you can, because it's not meant for you. There's been a problem with the transport system, and they've used up all the corn in the 584 storehouse. This rice should be sent to the state market. Soon you'll be eating corn again." Who cared about the months ahead, I thought, as long as we had rice in the present? Maybe by the time the transportation resumed, we would already be released.

At 585 I had been isolated, but that first day I heard talk among the rightists who had come from other sections of Qinghe about the "Three Originals" policy adopted by the Communist Party Central Committee at its Guangzhou Conference in 1962. People said that the new directive provided for rightists to return to their original places of employment, resume their original positions, and receive their original salaries. No one knew when it would be implemented, but it gave us all hope. I realized this must be the document Captain Cao had referred to on the morning we left 585. Perhaps the famine and the economic disasters of the Great Leap Forward had made the Party realize it needed the talents of the teachers, students, scientists, and newspaper editors it had imprisoned with such impunity beginning in 1957.

Captain Wang had heard the excited buzz of conversation among the newly arrived prisoners. At the evening count he tried to put an end to our speculation. "You rightists have all been grouped here from your different compounds," he told us, "and you've all been asking about the Three Originals policy. I'm here to tell you that I've heard nothing about it. According to orders from battalion headquarters, you have come here as labor-reeducation prisoners. You are here to accept your reform, remold your thinking, and transform yourselves through labor. You will act in strict accordance with prison discipline. Tomorrow those of you who are not sick will begin work clearing the reed pond. You will continue to labor and continue working to reform yourselves."

In the morning we counted off, then those of us who were

still too weak to labor stepped back. Captain Wang understood the situation in 585 and did not force us. We five returned to the kang while the others marched in lines of four toward the compound gates. On the third day, excited by the activity of normal camp life and the conversation of the other rightists, I decided to join them. The frozen marshes looked just as I remembered. The reeds growing through the ice stood taller than my head. Everyone carried a sickle and a large sack. In a clearing two duty prisoners set up a simple scale to weigh the bundles that the laborers would carry on their shoulders throughout the day. The duty prisoners prepared to tally each person's labor quota. Nothing had changed.

Once as I paused to rest, I saw Lu Haoqin, my squadmate from Wuxi, kneeling on the ice not far away, arranging a stack of reeds. I smiled to see him nestle a large stone in the pile and conceal it carefully as he tied up the stack. He adjusted the load on his shoulders before heading off toward the scales.

In the fields Captain Wang didn't force me to labor. He knew I could not meet the daily quota and let me sit down often to rest. The temperature hovered below zero, and the wind blew hard across the frozen swamp. With only the morning wotou in our stomachs, we felt the cold sharply. When we reached the compound, the captain ordered the duty prisoners to bring an ox cart full of dry cornstalks as fuel for the kang stove. We ate, then settled down for two hours of political study. At least, I thought, we would be warm that night.

In the labor camps a strict protocol, established by the order of sleeping space on the kang, determines the assignment of prison chores. As squad leader, I slept first in line, closest to the door, and I would usually have been responsible for building the fire under the kang that night, as this was the first chore needing to be completed in my squad. But that evening the captain had asked me to fill out a set of forms listing the prisoners' names, ages, crimes, and family backgrounds, and I felt extremely tired after participating in the day's labor. I didn't want to have to stand outside the door in the cold, feeding cornstalks into the small stove beneath the building, waiting for the heat to pass along the duct beneath the bricks of the kang. I decided to pass that job on to Lu Haoqin, who occupied the space beside me.

"How about filling the stove and lighting the fire tonight?" I asked him.

"No," he answered loudly, "that's your job. I'm the second in line, not the first."

I thought quickly. Everyone had heard this challenge to my new authority, and I couldn't back down. "Even though I'm the first in line, I have other work to do tonight," I explained firmly. "I'm asking you to do this task for everyone's benefit."

"No, this should not be my job," Lu insisted.

I could not let him defy me this way. To pass the job on to another prisoner would confuse the regular order of chores even more, and the next person would likely refuse as well, which would jeopardize my leadership. I could not give up my power so soon.

"Follow my order," I shouted, "or you'll regret it." Lu shook his head.

I stood up and grabbed his foot. "Do it!" I said, and twisted his foot hard.

"Let go of me, I'll go," Lu cried, and the tension passed. He went outside to fetch the cornstalks from the ox cart and load them into the stove.

I had finished filling out the forms, and the other prisoners were chatting among themselves when Lu returned after half an hour, his hands stiff with cold. "Sorry I had to do that," I apologized as he sat down.

"Never mind," he answered, seeming not to bear a grudge after my outburst.

"I have no family here in the North," I continued, wanting to heal the rift and assuming that Lu must share my homesickness for the life south of the Yangtze River that we had both left behind. From Lu's silence I guessed the degree of his loneliness and said no more. I knew that for some prisoners reminders of the past aroused not nostalgia but pain.

"Do you feel warm yet?" Lu asked, letting my comment pass.

"Oh yes, tonight we'll sleep well," I replied, grateful for his companionship.

"When you are full and warm," said Lu, repeating a traditional saying, "you begin thinking about sex. Our stomachs may not be full tonight, but the warmth of the kang will certainly make me think of sex."

"Nothing like that will come to my mind," I replied awkwardly. Then I thought about holding Meihua in my arms. "Anyway, I have no one to desire." I wanted to end the discussion and not remember the pain of her loss.

"How can you stop thinking about sex?" Lu asked. "It's only human." He drew his quilt around his shoulders and turned away to sleep.

13

Kite Dreams

During our first days at Qinghe Farm in February 1962, we clung to the hope that an order for the release of counterrevolutionary rightists might still come. Silence from the authorities brought terrible disappointment to the prisoners. We chatted among ourselves less frequently and avoided mentioning the Three Originals policy. Outwardly I tried to remain optimistic with my squadmates, but inwardly I believed that at best the directive had been postponed. More likely the idea of restoring the freedom of so many intellectuals, and thereby implicitly acknowledging the injustice of their treatment, had faced opposition from those top Party officials, like Deng Xiaoping, responsible for leading the antirightist movement.

After the most severe cold lifted, our work assignment changed from cutting reeds to repairing the irrigation ditches that divided the rice plots. I had recovered some of my strength, and I could begin using the heavy picks and spades to dig out sections of the mud walls that had collapsed over the winter. This work required much greater energy and endurance than cutting reeds from the frozen marshes, so I began slowly at first. Captain Wang did not push us too hard. He knew that many among us still suffered from the effects of the famine. One morning when I arrived at the labor site, I counted only nine men. Ao Naisong had left the compound with the rest of the squad, but he was nowhere to be found. Only after Captain Wang had finished measuring out the length of ditch to be repaired by squad five, did I see Ao still a quarter of a mile away, walking slowly toward us.

By then I knew that Ao suffered from painful hemorrhoids, which made him unable to move quickly. I watched him start to dig, but by the end of the morning, I had cleaned ten feet of ditch, while he had cleaned only two feet. I could see that he was having difficulty. Each shovelful seemed a struggle, and he spent much of his time standing still, as if lost in thought. Dirt streaked his face, and his feet had sunk almost ankle deep in the mud that lay just beneath the thin layer of frozen soil. I knew his shoes would be soaked through, his feet painfully cold. Even back in the compound we had no way to dry our cotton padded shoes. If you let your shoes get wet one day, your feet would be frozen for two.

Toward the end of the afternoon, I heard the captain ask Lu Haoqin, who always completed his work efficiently, to help Ao finish his assignment.

"Sorry," Lu replied quickly, "but we all have the same amount of work to do, we all eat the same food. I won't do someone else's job."

According to 584 regulations, everyone received the same food rations. As a result, those who worked hardest and expended the most energy felt the greatest hunger. Who would volunteer to do extra work when everyone, no matter how much work he had done, received the same amount of food? Lu had learned how to take care of himself in the camps and refused to concern himself with others' needs. The captain could not force him to take on extra labor, but some of the others in the squad seemed to think Ao deserved special consideration because of his physical pain. Two of them joined me, and together we finished Ao's part so that we could complete our squad's labor quota for that day.

The following evening Ao stepped over to my place on the kang before the start of our political study. To my surprise, he began to talk, despite his customary reticence, and even mentioned his father's name. I recognized at once the byline of a famous photographer whose work had often been featured in the monthly news magazine *China Pictorial*.

"What was your own work before you came here?" I asked, hoping to draw him further into conversation.

"I studied in the optical instruments department of the Beijing Industrial College," he answered.

"You must come from a good political background," I replied, aware that Ao's college was administered by the army and that it accepted primarily the children of Party members. Ao again fell silent. I had heard from another squadmate that Ao's father had renounced him, "drawing a line" to separate himself from the political mistakes of his son, and I wondered about Ao's family life.

When Ao turned away, not wanting to speak about his personal problems, I realized that for the first time since my friendships with Big Mouth Xing and Chen Ming, I had begun to care personally about a few of my fellow prisoners. I wanted to know why Lu Haoqin and Ao Naisong had been arrested, what crime had led them to be accused as counterrevolutionary rightists, what lives they had led before being sent to the camps, what suffering they had endured during the most severe months of famine. But prison regulations strictly prohibited any exchange of information about the circumstances of an individual's crimes. The authorities wanted to prevent friendships, alliances, and sympathies from developing among us.

As February passed, we looked forward to the Spring Festival holiday. During those three days we would miss our families more than ever, but we would be able to rest and eat better food. The tradition of making dumplings at Spring Festival remained precious to all of us. We recalled how at home we would always gather around a table at midday with our family members while everyone chatted and looked forward to the feast. The men would sip wine and snack on pickled onions while the women mixed the dough, shaped it into logs, then sliced and rolled it into thin rounds to be stuffed with fragrant pork and cabbage, finally wrapping and folding the crescent-shaped packets. This holiday was a time of great warmth in the Chinese family. Even in the camp we all hoped this would be a time of good feelings, as much like that within a family as we could manage in these surroundings.

On the first morning of the holiday, the duty prisoner handed me a voucher bearing Captain Wang's personal stamp. "Squad five. Ten people. Ten jin of flour and one container of meat mixed with vegetables." The thought of our first tasty meal and our first bite of meat in a whole year spurred our preparations. The captain assigned me to take charge of the arrangements. I asked Lu Haoqin to find and wash the three enamel basins in our squad that had the fewest rust spots. Then I set about sawing off the end of a spade handle to use as a rolling pin and scraped the wood smooth with a piece of broken glass. We spread several sheets of newspaper on the kang space and sat down to wait.

When the duty prisoner shouted, "Team seven, squad five!" we moved quickly. Three men helped me carry the basins and two others accompanied us as guards. We dared not relax the vigilance developed over months of near starvation, even though we were all intellectuals. Someone could easily slip a handful of flour into his pocket, planning to mix it with water the next time he was alone. I had no confidence that any of us retained enough integrity to overwhelm our basic instinct for survival, but in fact, we carried back our allotment of food from the kitchen without incident.

At that point I had to act like a military commander delegating tasks. Don't make any mistakes, I told myself. Keep the group harmonious, keep the mood happy, keep everything working smoothly. I delegated two men to mix the flour and water and decided to roll the dough into logs myself. I asked Lu, the most meticulous worker, to slice the logs evenly and roll out the flat skins. Several men had asked for that job, but I knew that not everyone had the patience or dexterity to make dumplings of exactly equal size. If some pieces ended up larger than others, we would never be able to resolve the arguments about whose dumplings were bigger. Three others placed exactly equal portions of the meat mixture onto the individual wrappers, then folded and sealed the dumplings. One person counted the finished products and stacked them in piles of ten so that none could disappear. Still another watched everyone else. The only one not helping was Ao Naisong.

"Ao, what job can you do?" I called out.

"I can only eat," he replied with a trace of humor.

I didn't want him to be left out. "Why don't you play some music?" I asked. "That can be your job." He seemed pleased.

Ao's spot on the kang was at the far end in the corner, and his lute hung above him on the wall. He pulled it down and began to play while we worked. The mood became warm and convivial, as much like a family celebration as we could manage.

More than a hundred squads would be waiting their turn to use the giants woks that morning, and we were eager to begin. When the dumplings were nearly wrapped, I sent someone to stand in line at the kitchen to reserve our time. Three men helped me carry the basins of raw dumplings and another three accompanied us. The need for protection seemed greatest at this point. A stuffed dumpling could slip easily past someone's teeth.

When at last the basins of steaming dumplings stood at my place on the kang, their aroma filling the room, everyone fell silent. I moved along the row of seated men, counting dumplings into each bowl. Everyone counted with me: "One, one, one . . . two, two, two. . . ." We had wrapped perhaps five hundred dumplings altogether, and I had no idea whether the final number would be divisible by ten. "Forty-five, forty-five, forty-five. . . ."

When I had finished distributing the dumplings, four remained to be divided among ten men. The simplest way would be to cut each leftover dumpling into five pieces, but I had an idea of turning the process into a game.

"Hey, I have a suggestion," I called out. "What if I make ten slips of paper, with four of them marked, and we draw lots for the four dumplings? That way four people will each win an extra whole dumpling. What do you think?"

"No!" Lu Haoqin was quick to object. "Maybe I'll get nothing. I want my two pieces."

"Let's do it," someone countered. "This will make it more fun." No one else complained, so in good Spring Festival spirit we gambled for the dumplings. I didn't get one, but Ao did. He tried to control his delight but laughed in spite of himself. "I got one! I got one!" he shouted.

Lu pulled a blank slip of paper. He crashed his fist to the kang and swore.

"The results are fair!" I shouted. "I didn't win either, so don't get upset." Lu's protests continued. Angry at this sudden disruption of the cheerful mood, I took a dumpling from my own pile of forty-five and thrust it in Lu's basin. He looked away, refusing to eat, very angry. All conversation stopped. Everyone had seen me give him an extra dumpling to soothe his feelings, and the tension rose.

Then Ao stood up from his end of the kang, replaced his lute on the wall, and carried his extra dumpling down the aisle. He threw it on the kang mat beside Lu, looked at me, and said quietly, "Take yours back." Returning to the kang, Ao muttered between his teeth, "Ridiculous!"

I retrieved my dumpling from Lu's bowl, but the incident had disrupted our good cheer. Then Lo, another squad member, broke the stillness with the first line of a familiar Russian folk song called "Siberian Cattle Driver." Its haunting melody described an injured driver's last cattle run across the steppes. Approaching death, the herdsman asked his friend to carry a message back to his village. "Give my black horse to my father. Send my love and respect to my mother. Tell my wife not to be sad and worried. If she can find another, she should forget me." We all sang the words together, our shared melancholy driving away the antagonism.

Knowing that a year would pass before we could enjoy another meal of dumplings, we sprawled on the kang, relaxing with our bellies full. Someone suggested that we talk about the customs of our native provinces, and we started sharing memories of our favorite regional foods. Then Lo suggested another topic.

"Let's have everyone think about something really happy," he urged. "If today you could leave the camp, what is the first thing you would go? Let's imagine something better. Wu Hongda," he said, pointing to me, "you start first."

For me this was not an easy subject. I always felt uncomfortable talking about personal matters. Maybe I wanted to see my father, maybe I wanted to go back to my college, maybe I wanted to find my girlfriend. All these possibilities raced through my mind at once, but I hesitated to speak. Everyone waited. Lo broke the awkward silence.

"If this is too difficult for you, let me go first! What I would do immediately is take all the money I could get my hands on to a restaurant and eat two, maybe three, jin of porkhead meat."

Everyone laughed boisterously. "Great! Great!" shouted Lo, happy to have stirred our enthusiasm.

"No! Two or three is not enough," someone else joined in.

"I'd eat four jin, maybe more than that!"

"Here's both hands in the air to agree with you!"

We all grew excited, as if we could actually savor the meat. When we quieted down, Ao broke his usual silence. "Be careful," he said playfully. "Don't kill yourselves with eating. You'll all bloat to death." Everyone laughed.

The next prisoner began. "First, I would go straight home, see my children, grab my wife, nibble her sweet red lips, then go directly to bed and make love to her."

Lu Haoqin broke in sharply. "Sonuvabitch! Don't talk that way. You may have a wife at home, but some of us can't even imagine what such a moment would be like."

In the camps the topic of physical intimacy was a forbidden area, private and painful to recall, something we never mentioned. Once again the mood on the kang changed, and I called a stop to the conversation, fearing a return of the bitterness we had just escaped. "Say whatever you want, but no more talking about family matters," I insisted. "This is not the time."

The next person to speak lightened the tone. "I'll return to my office and say to the Party secretary who had me arrested, 'Here I am, back again. How are you doing?'"

Another person spoke. "I want to visit the nearest bookstore and see whether they have removed all copies of my books from the shelf."

"When I leave the camp," Lo mused, taking a second turn to speak, "I want to go to a public bath, clean myself completely from head to toe, and wash away every last trace of the camp smell."

"How about you, Ao?" I asked.

He thought for a few moments. "I'll go to the music store and buy two new strings for my lute."

Speaking sarcastically, Lu Haoqin broke in. "Why don't you

go home and see your old father?'' Clearly Lu had not forgotten the insult of the dumpling incident.

Ao's eyes grew rounder. His face flushed, and he tried to speak, but his tongue seemed stuck and no words came out.

"No more talking about family," I announced sharply, conscious of the pain such memories could inflict. "Everyone will leave this topic alone. Now it's my turn." The others had all spoken.

"When I leave the camp, the first thing I'll do is to buy a huge kite. I'll tie on a long streaming tail, let out more and more string, and watch it fly higher and higher. Then I'll cut the string, and watch the kite fly away." I was remembering my boyhood in Shanghai when I never had a chance to fly the kite Father bought me because in our neighborhood there was no open space away from trees and power lines. On that note our fantasies of freedom ended, and we fell asleep.

The next morning, temporarily freed from the routine of daily labor, we again had time to talk. I sat chatting idly with Lu Haoqin behind the barracks, bundled against the steady wind, when suddenly his voice trailed off and his face grew serious. "Hey, do you have a girlfriend?" he asked.

"I had a girlfriend."

"Where is she now?"

"Gone, with everything else."

"What happened? Do you still think about her?"

"Yes, I often think about her," I answered stiffly, "but three years have passed since she wrote to me. Something changed her mind about me, even before I was labeled a rightist. I still love her, but I would only bring her suffering. It's better this way." I stopped, not wanting to remember my love for Meihua. "What about you?"

"Oh, I have a girlfriend," he began, "and I still love her very much." He fell silent, then sniffed and asked quietly, "Did you ever have sex?"

"No," I answered, shocked at the question. In those days premarital sex among college students was almost unheard of, and no one would speak about such private matters.

"I had it once," he rushed on eagerly. "My girlfriend is strong and healthy, and she wanted it, too. The first time was very exciting. Too bad you never had the chance."

"What was it like?" I asked, trying to hide my embarrassment.

"It was on the campus one night," he answered quickly, a light in his eyes, "behind a big tree. It was the first time I touched a girl. I couldn't control myself. I held her, and my hand touched her body. Her skin felt so different. I forgot everything. But something surprised me. I had heard that the first time a girl has sex, she will have some blood. But I didn't find any blood." He paused.

"I'm sorry," I said nervously, "but I don't have any experience with that."

"I keep wondering if maybe my girlfriend was not a virgin," he continued.

"I really don't know anything about it," I repeated.

"Maybe it's because she likes sports, and maybe she lost her virginity running at a track meet."

Uncomfortable with the discussion but curious in spite of myself, I broke into a mild sweat. "I'm sorry, but I really don't know anything about that." I saw that Lu still wanted to talk. "Did you ever have another time like that?"

"No, that was the first and the last."

"Why?"

"We were classmates and for a long time very close. We had been in love for three months. That one night on the campus, we just did it, very quick. Neither of us knew how, and it was awkward. Afterwards I felt as if I had committed a crime. For several days she wouldn't look at me. We both felt ashamed, and we never talked about what had happened. Two months later I became a rightist. That happened five years ago when I was eighteen. It was my only time."

"Do you still think of her?"

"Yes, she's always in my thoughts. I can never forget that night. Sometimes the memory is very clear, sometimes far away. After that I asked some married friends about my experience. They gave me more information about sex. Next time I knew it would be better. If only I could meet her again, I wouldn't hesitate."

As I listened, my thoughts refused to leave Meihua. I wondered where she was and whether she had found someone else.

I also wondered whether I would ever hold someone again, whether I would ever know what Lu had described.

On the third day of the Spring Festival, the wind died down, and we sat in a group behind the barracks in the winter sun after the noon meal. The special meals continued through the holiday, and our stomachs were comfortably full after eating corn flour wotou and a soup made from cabbage, carrots, and small pieces of dried seaweed. As we chatted, Ao began to play his lute. For the first time I had the chance to listen carefully. He played slowly, rhythmically, and I could see how the music stirred his feelings. When he began the haunting strains of "Moonlight Reflecting on Two Springs," I wanted him never to stop. We all joined in singing the familiar words about separation and longing, responding with our own feelings to the story of a man whose betrothed is stolen away by a rich landowner. Everyday he walks through the streets, searching for her, playing his lute. Locked away, she cannot join him and finally ends her own life. We all felt moved by the music, and we hated to have the holiday end. No one knew when such a moment of leisure and reflection would come again.

For the next four months nothing broke the deadening routine of camp life. Every morning at five-thirty a duty prisoner yelled, "Get up! Out of bed!" We dressed and splashed our faces with water, then at six o'clock lined up in our squads to wait for the carts to bring the regular buckets of rice gruel. A ladleful of porridge, a piece of salted turnip, and a single wotou had to sustain us until noon. At six-thirty the police captain shouted, "Off to work," and all the squads lined up four abreast, to count off, listen to the morning's announcements, and learn the day's labor quotas. The entire battalion then moved forward toward the iron gates for a second head count by the armed guards before marching out to the fields.

Captain Wang patrolled our work sites to prevent fights and maintain discipline. We could not talk or rest, and we received water and food only at noontime, when the duty prisoners arrived with the wooden carts. Hungry and tired after four hours of heavy labor, we squatted down to devour two wotou and drink a bowl of thin soup. We had no way to wash our hands before eating. Some would search for sticks to spear their wotou, some would try to clean away the dirt by urinating on their fingers, and some just ignored the mud and wiped their hands on their clothing. We rested for half an hour, then returned to work to complete our quotas. When the sun fell low in the sky, the captain shouted, "Knock off, knock off," and we lined up for another head count before straggling back to the compound. "Dismissed!" he called after we entered our compound.

Those who still had the energy hurried to the water faucet to wash before lining up for the day's two final wotou and the last ladleful of soup. At seven-thirty the captain called, "Study! Study!" and we sat on our quilts to read the newspaper, discuss some new directive, or praise the Communist Party's latest achievements. After a day of exhausting labor, those two hours of political study passed slowly. Finally at nine-thirty we filed outside for the evening head count and Captain Wang's comments about our work efficiency or about how to improve our thought reform. At ten he called, "Dismissed. Go to bed," and we headed for the latrine, then returned to the barracks to fall asleep instantly. Day by day, month by month, this was the life of the labor camp.

After Spring Festival, I realized the effect of adding protein to my diet, and I decided to write to my family to ask if they could send me some special food. Several times that year since my transfer to Qinghe, my sister had sent small packages containing soap, biscuits, and candies. I hoped she could provide something even more nourishing, so I wrote to ask her to send some dried scallops and pressed yellow beans. I knew these foods would cost money, but at least they wouldn't require my family to sacrifice grain coupons to buy biscuits. Several weeks later I received a note saying she would do her best and send what she could.

With my new energy, every day in April and May I went out to labor. In the spring the captains assigned the 584 inmates to the rice fields, sometimes to clean the irrigation ditches, sometimes to reinforce the mud walls that separated the paddies. Always we searched for extra food. During those weeks I perfected the technique Big Mouth Xing had taught me for catching frogs. First you pulled a thread from your padded jacket and tied a small piece of cotton batting from the lining to the end of the string. Next you dangled the bait at the edge of the ditch where frogs hid in the grass and reeds. With luck, a frog would mistake the cotton for an insect and jump at the bait, which stuck briefly to its tongue. Then you grabbed its feet, killed it with your teeth, tore off the skin from the head to the legs, and stuffed the raw meat into your knapsack. If you stayed out of the captain's sight in the evening, you could boil the frog in the latrine.

In April 1962, two months after the first rumors of the Three Originals policy had spurred our hopes, a few rightists at 584 received notice of their release to the status of "resettlement prisoners." The rest of us waited without any word. Then one morning in June, Captain Wang suddenly announced new orders that all rightists remaining at Qinghe Farm would be returned to Beijing. We had no idea what the latest directive would mean. We asked where we would go and whether we would end up in another camp, but Captain Wang insisted he had no further information. We wanted to believe that this move back to the capital at last assured our release.

The four prison trucks took several hours the next day to ferry more than four hundred of us rightists to Chadian station where once again we assembled on the special branch track used only for the occupants of Qinghe Farm. We gazed out of the train windows at the passing fields, believing we might soon be free. Our excitement mounted after the one-hour ride when we left the special holding area for prisoners at the Yundingmen station in the southern part of Beijing and rode for half an hour by truck along the familiar poplar-lined streets on the outskirts of the capital to reach Tuanhe Farm, a sprawling prison facility on the southern edge of the city.

14

Biting Dogs

No brick walls or iron gates separated Tuanhe Farm from the fields of suburban Beijing. No guard towers marked the compound's corners, and no armed sentries stood watch. Only the thin strands of a six-foot-high barbed-wire fence defined the prison's perimeter. Assembled in the yard on that first evening as dusk fell, we stared across stretches of fields, amazed after so many years behind walls to watch city buses pass along the poplar-lined roads outside the farm complex.

The guards from Qinghe counted us one final time before climbing aboard the empty trucks. Their shabby uniforms looked out of place beside the neatly pressed civilian clothes of the Tuanhe captains. For two years I had not seen anyone dressed in the casual grey trousers and white short-sleeved shirts typically worn by government cadres. The difference in clothing seemed to signal a turning point in our prison lives and mark an end to the dehumanizing conditions of our years of internal exile. When captains Gao and Wu announced with unusual courtesy that food would be provided as soon as they had assigned us to barracks, I felt I had returned to civilization.

The Tuanhe rooms were large enough to accommodate twenty men, or two squads. A kang lined each opposite wall, separated by a four-foot middle aisle. Appointed to be my squad's labor leader, I set about measuring the kang space for squad eight that evening, grateful that here we would have three feet of sleeping space apiece, half a foot more than under the best conditions I had known at Qinghe. Next I read out the name list to assign the order on the kang for my ten men. Lu Haoqin and Lo were also assigned to squad eight, Ao Naisong to squad nine, which shared our large room. We arranged our chipped enamel basins and our badly frayed towels on the shelf, then spread out our worn quilts. Here in the more civilized surroundings of the city, I noticed with new eyes the shabbiness of our possessions.

At about eleven o'clock the duty prisoner called us to the kitchen. On earlier transfers, we had missed at least one meal and suffered hunger pangs until morning, but here the cooks served an extra dinner, dishing out a large corn wotou and a bowl of cabbage soup to each of us. These encouraging signs of more lenient treatment made me impatient for the morning's announcements, and I slept very lightly that night.

We mustered quickly in the early summer sunshine that next morning, confident that we would hear some instructions about our release. Captain Gao's trim appearance and respectful greeting reinforced our hopes, but then his voice grew shrill. "I know you have heard a lot of rumors," he barked, "but I have received no information about your release. What happens tomorrow I cannot predict, but today you are prisoners subject to discipline. You will go out to labor and strictly follow prison orders." With those few words our anticipation of freedom once again disappeared. The faces of my squadmates showed disbelief, anger, and dejection.

Numbly I listened to Captain Wu announce we would spend that day laboring in the vegetable fields. I tried to shake off my disappointment. Orders for our release might still arrive in the next few days, I told myself, and at least I might be able to scavenge extra food. Summoning the inertia so familiar from the past, I warned myself not to think ahead, not to consider anything but the needs of the moment. As we marched out to labor, I concentrated on the prospect of tasting fresh vegetables.

At Qinghe my most strenuous efforts at foraging in the marshes, the irrigation ditches, and the cabbage fields had produced no edible plants other than roots and leaves. The first sight that morning of vines laden with tomatoes and beans, eggplants and cucumbers grown for the markets of the capital city distracted my thoughts and stirred my deepest hunger. I didn't care that I had just finished breakfast or that I would have to eat the vegetables raw. My squad members seemed equally ravenous. As we spread out in lines to hoe weeds, all of us bent low between the rows of vegetables, out of sight of the guards, and filled our mouths. Clearly we were trying to satisfy some deeper hunger. I don't know how much I ate on that first day.

After head count in the evening, Captain Gao criticized us in a contemptuous tone. "You act like animals," he shouted. "You just steal everything!" After he dismissed us, I stayed behind to defend one of my squad members, a well-known playwright, who had been caught eating an eggplant.

"Captain Gao," I explained, "you don't know what it's like, but we have spent months being hungry." He just stared back at me, letting my comment pass without response.

After several weeks at Tuanhe, we no longer felt desperate for food. Improved harvests had brought an end to the three bitter years of nationwide famine, and we received more substantial portions of wotou, still made with bitter corn flour but using no more food substitutes. Everyone who fulfilled the daily labor quota was allocated 45 jin of grain per month, enough for one wotou at breakfast and two and a half wotou at lunch and again at dinner. In addition, the kitchen served us cabbage soup, which was strangely dark in color but to us tasted delicious with its thick vegetables and the flavoring of soy sauce and a few flecks of oil.

Nevertheless we continued to forage in the fields at Tuanhe, not so much to ease our hunger but to vary our diet with better-tasting grains and vegetables. I learned how to rub away the husks from the wheat kernels with rapid strokes of my shoe soles, for example, and then to eat the grain raw, and I often hid between the rows of cornstalks, pulled off an ear or two, sucked the juicy kernels, then buried the cobs to conceal my theft.

The monthly allowance of five yuan deposited in our individual prison accounts gave us enough money to buy toothpaste, towels, pens, writing paper, soap, and even thermos bottles in the Tuanhe store. We used the thermoses not just to carry hot water from the boiler room for drinking and washing, but also to cook frogs and snakes whenever we could find them in the fields. The latrines in our compound offered no secluded space where we could build a fire without detection, so instead we plunged the skinned frogs directly into our thermos bottles of boiling water and let them steep for an hour until they were done. Also at Tuanhe Farm more prisoners had relatives nearby, and those families had more food to spare.

In some ways our improved conditions only increased the feelings of isolation and desperation. Freedom seemed close but still unattainable. Because of the minimal security at Tuanhe, I felt certain everyone had at least considered the possibility of escape. I often imagined myself climbing through the barbed-wire fence, running across the fields, and catching a bus to disappear into the city, but each time I decided not to risk re-capture. I didn't want to jeopardize my chance for official re-lease. The other prisoners seemed to reach the same conclusion, and all of us waited, expecting that any day might bring a shift in policy toward the tens of thousands of counterrevolutionary rightists imprisoned nationwide since 1957.

Meanwhile we had 500 mou of land to plant with corn, cotton, and wheat, and another 20 mou of vegetables to tend. The summer wheat had to be harvested in June and July, at the same time that the autumn corn needed planting. As labor leader, I kept very busy. By then I was twenty-five and one of the youngest among the rightist prisoners. Fully recovered from the famine, I could not only carry 170 pounds of wheat on my back, but I could hoist the loads onto a tractor. I knew the captains favored me because of my strength and my enthusiasm for labor.

I also knew that some in my squad, especially three of the older prisoners, didn't like me. They viewed the labor leader who assigned them daily quotas and urged them to complete their work as helping the police. Especially on days when we had to meet a quota designated by squad rather than by person, they complained about the heavy work. Fulfilling the collective quota was my responsibility, and I always insisted that everyone finish, even those who felt hungry or didn't want to work.

Some would openly accuse me, saying, "Hey, you are just like a running dog. Why do you work for them, why do you force me to labor?"

Others understood my position. "He has to do this," my friends would respond. "If Wu Hongda were not squad leader, someone else would do the job."

My friends and enemies alike knew that the position of labor leader carried considerable power, as I could exercise discretion in assigning jobs by favoring certain people and giving them the lightest work. At Tuanhe we sometimes made bricks, and I could give a friend the easier task of carrying the sand rather than the heavier work of carrying the finished bricks. When we planted rice, I could delegate those sections of flooded field where the mud was soft and the seedlings could be pushed in easily to someone I wished to help, making others work in the areas where the mud was harder to penetrate. At harvest time I could choose who would transport the grain, a relatively light job, and who would do the backbreaking work of bending down in the fields wielding a sickle to cut the stalks.

If a squad member opposed my orders, I could call the captain, and he would support me. I could also report at the end of the day that a prisoner had not obeyed me. The police had to rely on me to get the job completed. Our personal quarrels they viewed as merely an instance of dogs biting dogs, and when fights occurred, they imposed punishments only if someone got seriously hurt. More likely the captain would issue a reprimand or ignore a dispute altogether.

For the first several weeks at Tuanhe, the atmosphere remained harmonious. Still hoping that we would return to our former positions and our families, we generally helped and encouraged each other. But this goodwill faded as the weeks of summer passed and we received no word about release. The personal tensions, the continuing fights over food, and the disputes over labor assignments reflected our mounting frustrations and our dwindling hopes. I began to realize that living among intellectuals was not necessarily an improvement, and I thought back almost fondly to my friendship with Big Mouth Xing.

That summer I often got into fights. One day in the fields when I was carrying the rear end of a shoulder pole, transporting a heavy bucket of soil, I saw my work partner kick a dried-up turnip out of the path and into the tall grass beside the ditch. I assumed he would come back to retrieve the turnip, since at that moment a guard stood nearby, preventing any interruption in our labor. I noted the spot and, as if still responding to some basic instinct for survival, returned first, found the turnip, and hurried away to squat out of sight and eat. Anytime I had a chance to supplement the daily rations I seized it. My partner saw me and rushed over, furious at my theft.

"Give it back," he shouted.

"Who says this is yours?" I shouted back. "Get out of here, you sonuvabitch."

"I found that turnip!" he declared, trying to grab it away.

"Get away!" I repeated and punched him hard. His nose began to bleed, and his thick glasses fell to the ground. He scrambled frantically to find them. Suddenly I felt guilty, not about the blood, but because I too wore glasses, and I knew that without his, he was nearly blind. I found them unbroken in the thick grass, handed them to him, and he left. He was weaker than I and had no way to punish me physically, but back in the barracks, he told everyone that I had stolen his turnip. I defended myself, lying and claiming that I had no idea the turnip was his, that I had found it by myself. Several people asked me why I had hit him. I argued defiantly that he had tried to take my food. So great was the frustration resulting from continued imprisonment and so ingrained the habit of self-preservation that I felt no guilt about taking whatever I could get for my own. I never stopped to question the dog-bite-dog mentality that I had acquired during two years in the camps.

Others defined differently the boundaries of acceptable conduct. For me being tough and aggressive in the fields seemed justified, based on my long-reinforced conviction that in the camps only the fittest would survive. But I hated violent, aggressive, or underhanded behavior during study meetings. I felt only contempt for those too weak and cowardly to engage in fights who acted out their rivalries and resentments in a political setting. Maneuvering for favor and power, they would secretly report on others to the guards. They would also offer false accusations in group struggle sessions and join in the prearranged beating of a prisoner being "taught a lesson" for bad political attitudes. I despised this behavior. Sometimes at a struggle meeting I could not escape the pressure to shout accusations, but I never struck anyone, nor did I ever report on another person's words or actions. My scruples were well known, and the majority of my squadmates trusted and respected me.

Those who reported to the police in exchange for special benefits hoped that by demonstrating the progress of their reform, they could secure an early release. Dong Li, the major "reform activist" in squad eight, followed this path. I never understood how he could have received the label of rightist, as he seemed to hold no political viewpoints and never to think deeply enough to disagree with the policies of the Party. Raised in the countryside north of Beijing, he spoke with a slow, country accent, and those of us from the cities looked down on him as a hick, showing the condescension typical of China's educated elite. But more importantly, we believed that he had no basic moral principles.

Not only would Dong Li seek special favors, but he would flaunt them. Prison regulations allowed visiting rights only to immediate family members, but the police permitted Dong's uncle to visit him after he claimed his mother was too old to make the trip. Visitors could officially carry only two pounds of food to a prisoner, but Dong Li's uncle received clearance to bring in a ten-pound package of special precooked flour, called *caomei*. The cache remained in a package under his pillow, and every night before sleeping, as all of us watched, he ate a handful mixed with water in his basin.

Dong Li compounded our resentment by ignoring the unspoken etiquette that governed the enjoyment of special gifts. You were not expected to share personal food with your squad members, but you also were not expected to eat it in front of others. Everyone hated Dong Li for proudly displaying his treasure and smacking his lips with satisfaction when he ate. No one else in squad nine had Beijing relatives who could bring extra food, and our anger grew. "You report us to the police, they let you have your reward, and then you eat it in front of us with great relish," I thought.

One night when Dong Li had left the room, four of us grabbed his package from behind his pillow, divided his flour into quarters, mixed the portions with water, and swallowed the caomei immediately. When Dong returned, he shouted like a mad dog to find his cache gone, but he could do nothing. The next morning he reported the incident to the captain, but he had no evidence to single out any individual squad members as the culprits. The captain had no interest in such petty larceny and saw this as just another case of dogs biting dogs.

A few days later Dong Li took his revenge. He reported to the captain that Lo, the gentle, principled man, who had sung so movingly at our Spring Festival celebration and whom all of the squad members respected, had shouted out reactionary thoughts. Regarding matters of this nature, the captain responded vigorously. Lo denied the charge to no avail. Perhaps Captain Gao wanted to placate Dong Li, or perhaps he decided arbitrarily to use this incident to warn the rest of us about the consequences of resisting reform. Whatever the motive, he ordered Lo placed in solitary confinement for seven days. We all knew this punishment inflicted great suffering. Locked in a tiny confinement cell, a prisoner received starvation rations and lay trapped in his own excrement, unable to sit or stand. Outraged at Dong Li's betrayal, we decided to hold a *mengdao*, or cover-the-head meeting, to give him some education. I made the arrangements.

After that evening's count, we hurried back to the barracks. When Dong Li entered the room, a thick padded quilt dropped silently over his head. The door closed. I stood outside to watch for duty prisoners or security captains. I could hear no voices inside, only the muffled sounds of feet and fists. The beating lasted a little more than a minute, leaving Dong Li slumped on the floor. Only Ao refused to take part.

When Dong Li shook off the quilt and stood up, I could see that one eye was blackened and his nose bled. I knew that his arms and legs must also be bruised. He could easily guess which of us had attacked him and the next day reported the incident to the police, but again he had no evidence. The quilt that had covered his head was his own.

"Tell me who beat you, and I will punish them," said Captain Gao. Dong Li could only answer with silence. Another dog-bite-dog struggle.

After that he stopped reporting on us for a time, but the lesson proved short-lived. We knew he continued to monitor

us, waiting for someone to speak inadvertently, and we tried to
be vigilant, cautioning each other in moments of indiscretion
and taking special care whenever we discussed political events,
which was against regulations and very dangerous. If the wrong
ears heard, you could be reported for spreading "reactionary
thoughts." The crime would be noted in your file and could
even compound the original charges against you. Worse yet was
to be overheard speaking to more than one person at a time,
which put you at risk of being charged with membership in a
"reactionary clique," an even more serious accusation. Knowing the consequences of such conversations, we dared mention
political matters only guardedly and among trusted friends.

In the spring of 1962, we read a number of articles in *People's Daily* asserting that the American imperialists intended to
support the Guomindang government in Taiwan and invade the
Chinese mainland. The conflict seemed too far away to matter
to most of us, but one of my friends in the camp named Zhao
Wei, a former editor for *Beijing Daily*, wanted to discuss the
looming international crisis. As we sat behind a building, relaxing on one of our fortnightly rest days, he whispered, "If the
United States decides to support the Guomindang, this will provoke the Chinese government. For rightists, the influence will
be very bad. Already the Three Originals policy has been ignored, but worse things could happen to us. If there should be
a major crisis, political prisoners will be considered a security
risk within the capital, and we could be moved to some remote
area far from Beijing."

I disagreed. "I don't think the United States will do that.
They've learned a lesson from the Korean War. Why would they
want to make a bad chess move twice?"

The discussion continued as Ao rounded the corner, carrying his basin and chopsticks. He sat down quietly, listened to
the editor's answer, and then suddenly jumped up. Tang! Tang!
Tang! Ao slapped his chopsticks sharply against the edge of his
bowl. "Two wotou and a bowl of soup!" he shouted, continuing
to rap his chopsticks against the rim. "Two wotou and a bowl
of soup!" I thought he was commenting sardonically that the
Taiwan threat was remote, while our immediate problem was
the prison diet. I laughed and turned to leave. Then I saw the
reason for Ao's outburst.

Dong Li leaned against the wall just around the corner, close enough to have heard. Ao had seen him and guessed that Dong would report us to the captain for holding a counterrevolutionary meeting. This would be a perfect opportunity for revenge. The incident passed, but we watched Dong Li carefully, knowing that he could decide to report on us at any opportunity.

Throughout that summer and autumn of 1962, we went out to labor every morning and sat on the kang reading newspapers every evening. We learned from *People's Daily* that the annual meeting for the highest Party leaders at the seaside resort of Beidaihe had resulted in a new political line. Chairman Mao, apparently attempting to reassert his authority after the debacle of the Great Leap Forward, had declared a new, and to us ominous, emphasis on ideology. "Class struggle" was to provide the "key link" for every endeavor, Mao proclaimed. The new emphasis seemed not to affect us until one night in October when the four men responsible for the political reform of rightists at Tuanhe Farm strode through the door. We put down our newspapers, and the room immediately grew tense. We knew either luck or disaster would follow, but we didn't know which.

Comrade Song, our company's political instructor, began to speak, reiterating the most recent high instruction from Chairman Mao. "We must never forget class struggle!" he shouted. "We in the labor camp are not immune from this problem. Right here in this team there is class struggle! You must recognize this evil. We will hold a class struggle education session tonight!"

Then the battalion political instructor, named Zhang, stepped forward. "Following the new high instruction from Chairman Mao, we must carefully consider Comrade Song's words." Zhang declared that one member of our team had recently displayed counterrevolutionary and reactionary behavior. With clenched jaw, he demanded, "Who is Xu Yunqin?"

Immediately the study leader of squad nine, which shared our room, called out, "Xu Yunqin! Stand up!"

Xu looked bewildered and stood beside the kang with his head bowed. Instructor Zhang continued, "We have reviewed Xu Yunqin's file and find that he is a counterrevolutionary rightist and a most savage element opposed to the Communist Party! His attitude is very bad. He tries to reverse previous verdicts.

He makes reactionary statements. Recently he even declared the reactionary words, 'History will pronounce me not guilty.' We have decided to punish this die-hard element, this counter-revolutionary renegade, by ordering him to solitary confinement. But first these two squads will hold a joint struggle meeting!"

The political instructors left to carry Chairman Mao's new high instructions to other squads, but Captain Gao remained to assume command of the proceedings. Wang, the study leader of squad nine, and Mao, our study leader in squad eight, conferred for a few moments with Captain Gao.

I wished Xu no harm, but I recognized the seriousness of these accusations and knew I would have to participate. I also knew that the agenda for this session was being hastily arranged by the leaders. I guessed that Wang and Mao, who worked closely with the captains, were receiving instructions and that somehow Dong Li would play an important part.

When Captain Gao finished briefing the study leaders, he convened the meeting. The first step was for Xu to confess his crime and then to criticize his own attitudes and thoughts. Still seeming confused about what was happening, Xu paused often, groping for words. "I truly am an evil rightist," he began, "and I have committed many counterrevolutionary crimes. The Communist Party has helped me to reform myself, but . . . but . . . I have always recognized my crimes . . . I always try to reform myself . . ."

Mao, the study leader from my squad, grabbed the back of Xu's neck and forced him to his knees, shouting, "First of all we need to help you correct your attitude! Bow your head and admit your error. Ask for punishment from our Great Leader Chairman Mao!"

At this point, a reform activist from Xu's own squad who reported often to the police in exchange for favors, jumped up and began to slap and kick the victim. This harsh treatment was suppose to help a miscreant understand his crime. I noted with surprise that Dong Li remained seated.

Two others wishing to impress Captain Gao joined the attack, shouting loudly, "Down with the counterreform element Xu Yunqin! He refuses to accept reform! He chooses to cut himself off from the revolutionary masses! Long live our Great Leader Chairman Mao!"

Then the rest of us had to join the chorus to show our enthusiasm for the struggle meeting and our agreement that Xu really was an evil counterreform element. We had to demonstrate that we stood with the Party or we would ourselves be criticized. Captain Gao stood impassively on the side watching. He seemed to decide the beating had sufficiently taught Xu a lesson. "Let him stand up!" he instructed, and the study leaders and other activists returned to their places on the kang.

Captain Gao walked to the center of the floor and addressed Xu in a low voice. "Xu Yunqin, people have heard you say that you are innocent and that one day history will judge you not guilty. If your opinion were true, that could only mean that the Party had made mistakes while you were correct. Now tell us what you did in your middle school in 1957. Let everyone hear what you said and did. Let everyone decide for themselves whether you deserve the label of counterrevolutionary rightist!" By then Gao's voice had become a fierce shout. The play was not yet over.

Xu still seemed unsure of what to say, and the shouts resumed, "Speak out! Speak out! Confess! Confess!"

As prisoners we had all learned to keep the list of our crimes clearly in mind, ready for recitation at any moment along with the routine facts of our birthplace, our parents' names, and our class background. A tall, thin, intelligent man from a peasant family, Xu told how he had been a middle school teacher in a small village far to the south of Beijing and how during the Hundred Flowers campaign in the spring of 1957 he had spoken poisonous words criticizing the Communist Party. As far as I had been able to tell, having heard Xu recount his crimes in previous squad meetings when we all took turns criticizing our past errors, Xu had never deserved the rightist label. He had apparently antagonized his school's Party secretary by expressing some sense of superiority toward the less-educated villagers after he became a teacher, but nothing more. At that time personal grudges and petty resentments often became the motive for political condemnation, and Xu had been capped as a rightist to fill the middle school's quota of counterrevolutionary enemies.

Before Xu could finish, Wang, his study leader, interrupted angrily, "The iron facts prove that you are a counterrevolutionary rightist, yet you claim that history will prove you innocent.

Everyone can see you are resisting reform. You are trying to reverse the Party's verdict!"

All of us had grown accustomed to this improbable logic. The Communist Party was always "great, good, glorious, and correct." Therefore, Comrade Song, as the Party's representative, could not be wrong in his accusation, and therefore Xu was by necessity lying.

But at this last accusation Xu's voice suddenly grew firm. "I have always recognized my crime," he insisted. "I have always accepted reform."

"No! You lie! You quibble! You deny!" The shouts began again with renewed vigor. Then the several activist prisoners jumped up, ready to punish such stubbornness and benefit themselves by enthusiastically carrying out Captain Gao's suggestions.

Then Captain Gao intervened. "It would be better for you to confess," he urged Xu, his voice cajoling. "The issue is clear. Unless you confess now, you will lose the chance. You will be accused again, and the results will be more severe!"

Xu remained silent, and confusion again covered his face. Captain Gao sat down. Slowly and self-importantly, Dong Li stood up from the kang. I felt certain his intervention had been orchestrated beforehand. Dong cleared his throat and began his accusation.

"For a long time Xu has refused reform and refused to recognize his counterrevolutionary crimes. He has always hated the Communist Party. Three days ago in this very room, I heard Xu shout, 'History will pronounce me not guilty.' Isn't this a fact, Xu?" Dong Li trembled with self-righteous anger.

Xu's bowed head turned slightly. He stared hard at Dong Li and spit out his response through clenched teeth. "I never said that!"

Immediately Wang and Mao, the two study leaders, grabbed Xu's arms. This time Dong Li participated in the beating, furious that Xu had dared deny his accusation. Perhaps he felt outrage at having his credibility challenged, perhaps he saw this as a chance to move closer to the police, I could not tell, but Xu fell beneath the blows. His head struck the edge of the kang, and blood flowed from a cut somewhere above his ear.

Captain Gao signaled to a duty prisoner waiting by the door

to remove Xu to the confinement cell. Just then Ao interrupted the process by stepping down from the kang and walking slowly toward the shelf where we kept our personal items. The struggle meeting had not yet been dismissed, and we were not free to move around the room. Everyone stared at Ao's breach of discipline. Holding out a pamphlet to Captain Gao, he said quietly, "On that day Xu Yunqin sat on the kang reading this pamphlet aloud. I was the only other person in the room. I heard him read the title: 'History Will Pronounce Me Not Guilty.' Maybe Dong Li heard Xu's voice from the hallway and did not realize that he was only reading."

"How can he dare stand up to the captain?" I wondered, but Ao had more to say. "This pamphlet was issued by the Party. Its title was drawn from a speech by Fidel Castro, Cuba's revolutionary leader." Ao turned and walked back to his place. Had he tried earlier to swim against the tide of the struggle meeting by making his statement sooner, he would certainly have become a target of the Party's attack. He had no way to save Xu from the initial blows, but he could try to influence the subsequent punishment.

I had also read the pamphlet, which was published by the Chinese Communist Party in 1962, shortly after the Cuban missile crisis, to instruct people about the international situation. Captain Gao turned the pages slowly, apparently trying to make up his mind what to do next. Then Dong Li spoke again. "It's true that the title of this pamphlet comes from Castro's speech, but it's also true that the counterreform element Xu rebelled against the peasant class. He read the title of that pamphlet out loud on purpose. He meant to declare his innocence. He meant to accuse the Party of making a mistake. He is an enemy of the Party!"

Captain Gao seemed to lose interest at this point. He must have decided the problem was not so serious after all, that it was merely another instance of dogs biting dogs. Without another word, he walked out the door. When Dong Li continued to attack Xu, insisting that he must criticize himself, Ao stepped down from the kang once again.

"History will judge everyone," he said slowly, "so why do we hurry to pass judgment now? Maybe history will decide that Xu has committed a crime and maybe not. Let history decide."

Those were definitely "black words," the most dangerous of all utterances, in that they denied the ultimate authority and unassailable correctness of the Communist Party. No one spoke. I decided to use this moment to try to end the meeting before any more accusations could erupt. "Dong Li," I called, "how about going to Captain Gao to ask for instructions about tomorrow's work assignments?"

"No! The struggle meeting must continue!" shouted Dong Li. "We are all here to reform our thoughts. Class struggle is the most important thing. You must not use production as an excuse to weaken our political task."

"Then I will go report to Captain Gao that I cannot be responsible for tomorrow's labor," I replied firmly, and I moved toward the door.

Ao stood up and said, "I'm going to the toilet." Several others followed his lead, and I left to speak to Captain Gao. When I returned, Dong Li remained seated on the kang, staring at Xu, his face rigid with anger. Ao lay lost in thought. Two of the squadmates had washed Xu's wound, and we waited for further punishment, but the duty prisoner never reappeared to take Xu to confinement. I fell asleep thinking about Ao's courage and wondering how he could maintain such a deep sense of justice.

15

Confinement

During 1963 almost half of the five hundred rightists transferred to Tuanhe Farm with me in June 1962 were "released" from labor reform. Transferred to another section of the Tuanhe facility, they continued to work under supervision as resettlement prisoners, or "forced job placement personnel." Their new status did not bring freedom, but it brought a number of benefits.

They received monthly salaries and the opportunity on fortnightly rest days to leave the farm and visit a restaurant, buy extra food, or see a movie. They purchased their daily meals from a cafeteria like ordinary workers, so they could order meat and vegetable dishes whenever they liked. And perhaps most important in making them feel no longer like prisoners, they did not report for evening head count. Restless and impatient, the 261 of us who remained in the Number Two barracks counted the days until May 24, 1964, the date when the maximum three-year sentences for rightists would end, so that we too could terminate our status as labor-reform prisoners.

The sense of some objective ahead bred a new spirit of cooperation. As the date of release approached, we became more polite to one another, arguing and fighting less frequently. Lu Haoqin, for example, became less self-absorbed and sometimes helped others complete their labor quotas, and even Dong Li changed, no longer seeking reasons to report his squadmates to the prison authorities. In our moments of free time, we began to prepare for our transfer, anticipating the opportunity to visit friends and restaurants in the city twice a month. Lo washed and mended his shirt, his clumsy hands wrestling with the tiny needle. Another squadmate wrote a letter that he planned to post to his wife the moment he received word of his change in status.

We told ourselves not to worry that the government had never announced an official policy about the discharge of rightists because the date had been firmly set in 1961. A few prisoners even revived the hope that the end of this three-year sentence would bring complete freedom from confinement, but most of us expected to remain at Tuanhe Farm under the supervision of the Public Security Bureau. Even so, we could look ahead to being treated more like workers than prisoners. We would at least have taken a step forward.

On the evening of May 23, we waited to see whether the captain would summon the labor leaders with orders for the next day's work. Instead, an excited duty prisoner arrived with a notice from the camp commander's office. "Labor for tomorrow is canceled," he read. "An announcement will be made in the morning." Even though he served the police, he too had been sentenced as a rightist, and he was as eager as the rest of us for news.

After the final head count that night, I lay sleepless on the kang. Beside me Lu Haoqin tossed back and forth. Several times I got up and walked into the warm night air. "Stay inside!" the duty prisoner yelled each time one of us appeared in the doorway. "Stay on the kang, don't come outside!"

Wide awake at the first light, we swallowed our morning wotou and returned to the kang to await word of our fate. Finally at ten o'clock the duty prisoner's voice echoed down the hall, "All squads to the yard! Form lines!"

We rushed out the door and again waited expectantly until Captain Gao stood before us. "Comrade Ning has come from battalion headquarters to speak to you," he announced. I felt encouraged at these words. A company captain like Gao, I thought, was not important enough to deliver the order for the final release of rightists. A higher official had been delegated to make the announcement.

"Today is May 24," Administrator Ning began, shuffling a sheaf of papers. "For every prisoner with a three-year term, today should be the last day of labor reform. You have all been waiting for this moment, but as yet no order has arrived from the Beijing Public Security Bureau. Everyone must be patient and continue to wait. Until we receive official word of your release, you will proceed as usual. I urge you to remember," he added, "that thought reform is a lifetime effort. I hope all of you will continue to work hard to reeducate yourselves and become new socialist people through labor. Dismissed!"

No one moved. Ao stood next to me. After several minutes I broke the silence. "What does this mean?" I asked him. "Has the sentence been extended with no release date?"

Ao's face betrayed no emotion. "Of course," he said at last, "this is hardly a surprise. What else would you expect?" On his lips I saw the faint trace of a sardonic smile.

"They have to announce our release today," shouted Lu Haoqin angrily after we had returned to the barracks. He sat rigidly beside me on the kang, his face twisted with emotion. "How can they ignore our sentence? Where is the law?"

"Don't yell," I answered, frightened at the extremity of his distress. "Maybe . . . I don't know what will happen . . . we have to wait . . ." I thought fast, wanting to calm him. "Tell me what you would have done if you had been released today."

"I would have gone immediately back to Beijing to find my girlfriend," Lu raged. "I can't stop thinking about her. I can't sleep at night. I think she is there, lying with me. Now what will I do?" His voice sounded desperate.

"Yes," I said, "I know you think of her. And every night you do something in your quilt."

He looked at me. "How do you know that?"

"Every night I feel you shaking beside me, and you make a lot of wet maps on your quilt."

Lu dropped his head slightly. "Is that right? I wake you? I didn't know. I keep thinking about her. I can't stop."

Lu's emotions had always been volatile. I turned to face him, wondering how to help him accept this latest disappointment. "If you really love her," I said firmly, "let her live in your heart. Don't waste your energy. If you do too much of this activity, you will damage yourself. Then when your girlfriend really comes back, you will feel great regret."

"But I can't control myself," Lu replied.

Ao overheard our conversation. "Think carefully about this," he urged. "You don't need to stroke your pipe so much."

"Besides, this kind of handicraft industry is illegal," I interrupted, joking awkwardly to ease the tension.

Ao looked directly into my eyes. "To stroke a pipe isn't against the law," he said.

I had only wanted to help Lu, not to discuss law or moral truth. Slightly angry, I said, "What are you talking about? If he continues like this, it will damage his health."

"Personal business," said Ao simply.

"Do you also engage in this?" I shot back, annoyed at his rebuke.

"I have never developed this kind of handicraft interest," he answered calmly, "but I do think it is Lu Haoqin's private business. You need to understand that this is only human nature."

Chinese commonly believe that masturbation drains energy from the body. I assumed this to be true and felt that especially now, after such a serious disappointment, it would weaken Lu to masturbate so often. I thought he looked paler than usual, and I worried that his health had already suffered.

Lu had always been one of the most skilled workers in the fields. He could labor all day bent forward, cutting wheat or plunging seedlings into the mud. He never needed to stop and rest his elbows on his knees the way the less resilient squad members did. But one day during the previous week I had heard him grunt sharply and grimace with pain.

"What's wrong?" I had called out.

"I fell . . . yesterday," Lu had answered hesitantly. I feared then that he was stroking his pipe too much.

Concern about Lu kept in check my own outrage at the authorities' flagrant disregard for our release date. For the rest of that day, no one bothered to speak. We sat alone with our distress, wondering what would happen next.

After a few days had passed, Ao approached me after dinner.

"What do you think now about our prospects for the future?" he asked.

"I don't know. I don't think about it anymore," I replied.

"If you don't think about a future, why do you bother to go on living?" Ao asked flatly, his face expressionless. "What is life for, anyway?"

"I really don't know," I repeated. "I just live on, perhaps to learn the end of the story."

Later that week during study session, I went to the toilet and noticed Ao squatting over the trough in the opposite corner of the latrine. He didn't see me come in. I glanced over my shoulder and noticed that he was having the longest bowel movement I had ever seen. It was perhaps six inches long, and it never dropped down. I turned away, then looked back to see the dark red shape still dangling. It took me a moment to realize that this was not a bowel movement but a hemorrhoid.

I waited for Ao to finish. Using his fingers, he painstakingly pushed the hemorrhoid back inside his rectum. Then he stood for a long time with his hands pressed against his back.

"Hey," he said as he turned to leave. He didn't even seem surprised to see me.

"Now I know how you suffer," I said, my voice low with sympathy. I had developed a deep respect for this courageous but inaccessible man.

"Yes," he said with his sardonic smile. "Maybe too much suffering. Maybe someday it will all come to an end."

By June our hope of release at the end of the three-year sentence had largely passed, but not our disappointment. Weeks merged into months as we planted corn and wheat, cotton and rice. We fed pigs and chickens, and we built pig sties and chicken coops. We tended fruit trees and harvested grapes. With no reason to think our sentences would ever end, we struggled against dejection. I wrote to my family explaining that no release had come on May 24. Sometime later that summer I received a harsh note from my older brother. Perhaps he had returned to Shanghai for vacation and read the letters I had written over the years to my family. "What are you thinking?" his note began. "The family is suffering, they have no extra money, and you ask them to buy that kind of bourgeois food?" He was referring to my request two years earlier for my sister to send me some scallops and yellow beans. "It is very difficult for us to maintain our own lives. Our stepmother is dead. Our father is a counterrevolutionary rightist. How can you reform yourself when you still want to lead a bourgeois life? We have all drawn a clear line to separate ourselves from you. You must follow Chairman Mao's teachings and work hard to reform yourself through labor."

The coldness of my brother's rebuke stung me, but the news of my stepmother's death struck my heart. I had wondered why she never wrote to me, but my sister always responded to my queries about her health by saying she was fine. A few weeks after my brother's letter, my sister also wrote, "I'm very sad to tell you what has happened in our family. Our stepmother is gone and our father is a counterrevolutionary rightist. Continue to study Chairman Mao's thought, and work hard at your reform." I had no idea what had prompted the letters from my family. Perhaps they had been waiting for my release to tell me the truth, and after hearing that my sentence would not be dismissed, they had decided to inform me about the family's situation. My brother may have thought I had continued to be obstinate and deserved to remain in labor reform. I had no way to guess what my father thought or whether he shared my brother's condemnation.

Concern about my family distracted my thoughts during study sessions that summer when we often read articles in *People's Daily* about the Socialist Education campaign that had brought administrative practices in the countryside and educational policies in the cities under intense scrutiny. Party work teams were reported to be waging class struggle in an effort to root out "revisionism." They were investigating charges of corruption and misuse of authority in the villages, as well as the return of "superstition" and "capitalist tendencies" in the countryside. Work teams had been dispatched as well to middle schools and universities to review textbooks and lesson plans and to inspect students' class notes for evidence of reactionary ideas.

Inside Tuanhe Farm the ideological debates, power struggles, and shifts of political line within the Communist Party seemed remote and irrelevant. The latest campaign had no bearing on my life. Counterrevolutionaries arrested in the past continued to be forgotten. Another year passed.

During the summer of 1965, one of the younger prisoners in my company named Guo Jie began to ask my opinion about contacting people in the outside world. He wanted to make known the fact that rightists still languished in the labor-reform camps even when their terms were over. Guo felt frustrated that he could not even send a letter to his mother explaining that he was not being released and that his term had expired. She was a Party member and also the head of her residents' committee in Jiangxi province, and the captain had let him know that such a letter from a labor-reform prisoner might be damaging for her. But Guo insisted that he could not continue just to endure passively the injustice of our confinement. He wanted an explanation for why we remained prisoners without a reason, and he wanted to call attention to our fate.

He urged me to help him write a letter directly to Chairman Mao to inquire when we rightists could expect our labor-reform sentences to end. Guo grew more determined about this idea and soon proposed writing letters as well to the Communist Party Central Committee and to the Beijing Municipal Party Committee. Surely someone, he reasoned, would see the injustice of our punishment and initiate a change. I thought the idea might bring results, but I urged Guo to take care so that his statements could not be labeled reactionary. Almost certainly the letters would be traced back to the camp, and anyone involved would then have to defend his actions to the prison authorities.

Another friend, Chen Quan, had confided to me his outrage at our continued imprisonment, and I asked him and another long-term squadmate named Li to join Guo in planning the letter-writing effort. I also privately consulted Zhao Wei, the former newspaper editor whose opinion I valued. Zhao was six years older than I and an astute observer of political affairs. Over the course of several weeks, whenever we were sure we were not overheard, Guo and I discussed how to word the appeals. Most important was not giving the impression that we formed a "reactionary group." This was the most serious crime inside the camps. One prisoner making remarks judged to be counterrevolutionary would be punished, but two or three together voicing such ideas would be treated with much greater severity.

Guo took responsibility for actually writing the three letters. "We know that the Party's policy is intended to help everyone reform," he began. "We know that the policy regarding the reform of rightists has been very successful. With the Party's guidance we have managed to reform ourselves during our years of reeducation through labor. Even if we ourselves have not yet been thoroughly reformed, some of those reeducated alongside us must by now have achieved this goal. Why is it that no rightists have been released since May 24, 1964?" At the bottom of each sheet of paper, he signed, "A Counterrevolutionary Rightist." Then we waited for an opportunity to send the letters undetected through the mail.

Nearly a month later, on a sunny Sunday in September that was one of our fortnightly rest days, Captain Gao called me to his office. "Take three people with you to the canal to pick peaches," he ordered. Usually I would have resented such an unofficial work assignment, knowing that the fruit would end up on the captains' tables, but this time I jumped at the chance for a few hours without surveillance. I knew Gao trusted me, even though he added quickly, "Take along the study leader."

I had often hoed weeds from the roots of the peach trees that lined one section of the irrigation canal on the southern boundary of the prison farm, and I knew that no fences marked that stretch of the border. I had watched ordinary peasants working in the fields across the canal and trucks driving along the narrow country roads. I had also noticed a postbox about two hundred yards away.

That Sunday, returning to the barracks, I asked Guo and Chen to collect four large wicker baskets and join me. They understood this was the chance we had waited for. I also informed Fan Guang, then our squad's study leader, about Captain Gao's instruction. Li stayed behind. Dressed in shorts, undershirts, and wide-brimmed straw hats, the four of us walked half a mile to the canal in the bright autumn sunshine.

I volunteered to take the hardest job, picking peaches from the top branches of the tallest tree, to show my earnestness about fulfilling the captain's orders. Then I assigned Fan Guang to work on the smaller trees closest to me, sending Guo and

Chen to pick at the far end of the row where they would be out of Fan's sight. I whispered that they should work for one hour, then wade across the chest-deep water to the far bank, holding their shirts and shoes stuffed in their straw hats above their heads. I calculated that it would take them only ten minutes to reach the postbox and drop in the letters. The plan worked perfectly. Their shorts had dried almost completely by the time they reported to me at noon with their baskets of peaches.

After dinner the next evening, we lined up as usual in the yard for the head count and the daily admonishments to work harder and reform ourselves through labor, but ten minutes passed with no sign of Captain Gao. When he appeared from the security office, Administrator Ning stood at his side. Everyone waited, knowing that some disciplinary problem must have arisen. Then Ning stepped forward. From behind his back, he pulled three envelopes. "The person who wrote these letters knows clearly what he did. After the count, he is to report to the office and explain his actions. The Communist Party's policy is 'leniency to those who confess their crimes and severity to those who refuse.' I don't need to say more. Dismissed!"

Guo Jie whispered as he fell into step beside me, "So fast! Now what should we do?"

I felt amazed at the Beijing Public Security Bureau's efficiency. The letters would have been collected only that morning, yet by evening they had already been returned to the camp. Back on the kang, I waited nervously for a summons to report to the office, but nothing happened. Fan Guang had disappeared during study class, presumably because the authorities knew only the four of us could have had access to the postbox across the canal. They would order the study leader to make a full report, then simply wait for the rest of us to confess.

Always the primary measurement of a prisoner's success at reform in the camps is his willingness to "draw close to the government, actively inform against evils, and report them to the authorities." Any person who meets this standard receives praise and personal advantages, perhaps even a reduction of his sentence. Such inducements are compelling. Fan Guang was in his mid-forties and physically weak. He was outspoken in his belief that "drawing close to the government" was the way for him to assure his own benefit and survival.

The five of us involved in writing the letters had discussed at the outset what to do if the envelopes were returned to the camp authorities, and we had decided we could gain nothing by admitting our act. Crossing outside the prison boundary and mailing petitions to China's highest leaders would be considered serious crimes. Once the letters had been returned, we were already like meat on a cutting board.

At around ten o'clock on Monday night, the duty prisoner appeared and ordered Chen to report to the team office. He had become one of my closest friends over the past year, teaching me to play elephant chess in my head whenever we had leisure time. The game served as a pleasant diversion and also a means of strengthening our memories. I hated to think of what Chen faced. He looked away as he passed my space on the kang.

On Tuesday morning I learned that Guo Jie had also been called out from his squad during the night. I went off to work in the fields, distracted by thoughts of my friends' interrogation. At midday Zhao Wei squatted down hurriedly to talk. "The incident has to be covered up," he said. "We cannot let them link us together as a group. Guo Jie will never confess, but Chen Quan is less sturdy. If he reveals that other people knew in advance about the plan, the captain will assume we have formed a counterrevolutionary clique. Then the consequences will be very serious."

"What should we do?" I asked.

"You must go to them yourself and confess," Zhao stated firmly. He had obviously thought hard about the problem before deciding to speak to me. "One person placed in confinement is better than two. That will reduce the danger of exposure."

I did not answer. I knew Zhao was right to assume Guo and Chen would be released if I accepted full responsibility and insisted the others had known nothing about my plans. But during more than five years in prison, I had never been tortured or placed in the confinement cell, known to us all as "the small one." I couldn't summon the selflessness to take on voluntarily that extreme suffering.

Back from the fields that afternoon, everyone jostled in line outside the boiler room, eager for a drink of hot water and a wash after the day's labor. Zhao stopped beside me long enough to whisper, "Have you made up your mind?" Before I could

reply, he continued, "It's the only way. We will think of a plan."
I knew he would do his best to help me survive.

During the study session that evening, the duty prisoner
shouted from the doorway, "Wu Hongda, report to the security
office!" My squad members seemed to assume I was being called
to discuss the following day's labor assignment, but I knew I
might never come back.

Sitting around the table, their cigarette smoke filling the
air, Captain Gao, Captain Wu, and Administrator Ning looked
up as I stood in the doorway. The tiny office was already too
crowded for me to enter. "Report what happened last week on
your day off when you went to pick peaches," Gao commanded.

"I want to confess right away," I began immediately, not
permitting myself time for second thoughts. "I was the one who
mailed the three letters. It had nothing to do with Guo Jie and
Chen Quan."

They exchanged glances. Captain Gao looked at me intently. "We have already investigated the incident. We believe
it unlikely that you did this, so we have placed Chen and Guo
in confinement to force them to tell the truth. What more do
you want to tell us?"

I knew that Fan Guang would already have reported working alongside me for the entire morning while Guo and Chen
had picked in trees farther away. Thinking rapidly, I explained
that Fan Guang had picked peaches from the trees adjacent to
mine part of the time but that he had not been able to keep me
in sight continuously. "While Fan Guang was busy, I swam over
to the other side of the canal," I reported. "It took me only
fifteen minutes to mail the letters."

Administrator Ning yelled to the duty prisoner, "Call Fan
Guang!" A moment later Fan appeared and confirmed that during some periods of time, he had not actually been able to observe me working.

"Release Guo Jie and Chen Quan!" shouted Gao. "Return
them to their squads, and have the kitchen provide them with
food. Tomorrow they return to labor. Place Wu Hongda in confinement."

Many times I had seen from a distance the row of ten confinement cells along the southern edge of the prison compound.
As the duty prisoner marched me closer, I could see that a brick

wall screened the barred cell openings from outside view. A rough path led alongside the doorways, where the duty prisoner who supervised this section grabbed my arm, opened one of the barred gates, forced my shoulders down, and pushed me inside. Expecting to be able to stand up after I stooped through the entrance, I nearly fainted when my head banged hard against the cement ceiling in the darkness. The iron bars grated against the floor as the guard shoved my feet inside. Then the key turned noisily in the lock.

Feeling the shape of the cell with my hands, I tried to move my head toward the entrance. The structure was about six feet long, three feet wide, and three feet high, slightly larger than a coffin. It smelled dank and moldy. The night was silent, and I didn't know if prisoners occupied any of the other cells. I wondered if anyone could hear me if I shouted. Squatting on my haunches, I tried to minimize contact with the cold cement floor. Without even straw beneath me, I quickly grew chilled, but I concentrated on planning my confession, determined to leave this concrete cage at the captain's first visit. The fact that I had not been handcuffed gave me hope that my treatment would not be too harsh. I fell asleep curled up with my back against the wall.

At daybreak I crawled over to sit beside the iron gate. I could see nothing but the loose stones and weeds that covered the pathway between the line of cells and the brick wall. I wished I could see the sky. Then I thought about the animals I had visited as a child at the Shanghai zoo.

Outside the gate beyond my reach stood a metal bucket. I shouted for someone to come so that I could relieve myself. I shouted louder, then raised myself up on all fours, but it was hard to urinate with my back pushed against the ceiling. Finally I slid off my pants and sat on the ground. The urine spurted against the iron bars. That was my most important activity during the first day of captivity.

On the second day I waited, but again no one came to bring food or water. A sharp pain grew in my stomach, and my throat felt sticky and bitter. When night fell, I moved toward the inside corner of the cell, trying to escape the mosquitoes that swarmed near the gate. Confused images flashed across my mind mixed with fragments of memories from my childhood as I tried to sleep.

On the third day, the special duty prisoner arrived sometime around noon. He looked about fifty years old, with a strong body and an expressionless peasant's face. "Wu Hongda!" he called.

"Yes," I answered, my voice already sounding weak.

He squatted and moved close to the gate to look inside. "Are you okay?"

I crawled to the bars like a dog. "When will they give me food?"

"Usually after the third day. That's the rule." His voice conveyed no feeling, and I wondered vaguely how many suffering prisoners he had attended.

"Can I have water?" He didn't answer, just stood up and walked away.

Early on the morning of the fourth day, he returned. Without speaking, he opened the gate to let me out, and I crawled to his feet to accept a bowl of water. I gulped two mouthfuls, then sipped the rest. He asked if I wanted to use the metal toilet bucket. Strangely I felt the urge to have a bowel movement and I struggled to stand up, but I could squeeze out only a few drops of urine. "I want to confess to the captain," I pleaded.

"I'll report to the authorities," he answered and locked me inside.

He returned in half an hour carrying a bowl of corn gruel and a piece of pickled turnip the size of my thumb. With trembling hands, I drank the thin porridge, then scraped the sides of the bowl with the turnip. Before long Captain Gao appeared.

"What did you want to say to me?" he asked, his voice almost casual. I tried to remember my prepared speech and explained in a humble voice that I had only wanted to inform Chairman Mao of our situation and to ask him to end my years of labor reform so that I could return to work and help with the goal of building socialism.

"You call that a confession?" Captain Gao yelled. "You believe that you have not committed a crime? You believe that you can decide the Party's policy and choose where you want to be sent?" He strode away. That evening a second bowl of gruel appeared.

On the fifth day my body began to tremble. I feared that I could not survive the continued contact with the cold concrete floor. Until then I had tried to stay curled in a corner, touching the ground as little as possible, but I no longer had the strength to maintain that posture. I could only sprawl on the ground, allowing the cement to absorb my body heat. In the morning when the duty prisoner brought another bowl of gruel and un-locked the door, I had to drag myself to the opening to drink the soup. I had no strength to move outside, nor did I have the urge to use the toilet bucket. Urine would occasionally trickle down my leg, but I no longer noticed the wetness or even the smell.

On the sixth day when the bowl of morning gruel appeared, I called out weakly, "I want to confess to the captain." I knew that confinement terms usually lasted seven days, and I intended to apologize to the Party and express my repentance to secure my release. But Captain Gao never came. I began to hallucinate. Childhood memories mixed with illusions. I got into a fight with the neighborhood children. I sneaked into the Summer Palace in Beijing to catch carp in the lake. I kissed Meihua during summer vacation. I saw my stepmother's long, white hands.

On the morning of the seventh day, Captain Gao appeared. The duty prisoner carried along a low stool so that Gao could sit beside my gate. I managed to drag half of my head and shoulders out of the cell.

"Are you making progress with your self-criticism?"

"I am guilty," I cried. "I committed a crime against the Party, a crime against the people. I failed to follow the government's instructions to reform myself, and so I committed a new crime. I beg the government's forgiveness, I beg for a second chance . . ."

"Describe from the beginning how you wrote those letters," Captain Gao shouted.

I explained how I had taken the letters with me when I went to pick peaches, how I had sent Fan Guang away, how I had sneaked across the prison boundary to reach the postbox across the canal. I struggled to make my thoughts coherent and my voice strong.

"If you want to leave this confinement cell today," Captain Gao threatened, "you will confess not only that you resisted reform but also that you conspired with a counterrevolutionary clique. You will confess the plot hatched by your enemy group. Otherwise you will not leave here!"

He told the duty prisoner to place a second bowl of corn gruel beside my head. "Drink the soup and then confess. I warn you that the government's patience is not limitless!"

Prostrate at Captain Gao's feet, I swallowed the soup. A surge of strength returned. "I know I have not lived up to the Party's trust," I confessed. "I promise I will never do it again. I understand the wisdom of Chairman Mao's teachings. I am a 'die-hard element,' and I must undergo reform for a long time to become a new socialist person. I beg the Party for a second chance . . ."

A kick from Captain Gao interrupted me. "Stop talking nonsense! I already know about your counterrevolutionary clique. I warn you to report what you have done with your die-hard group. Otherwise you will stay in confinement." He left immediately. The duty prisoner pushed my shoulders inside, locked the gate, and carried away the stool.

Clutching the bars, I called out, "Help me! Tell Captain Gao I want to confess further. Tell him I beg the Party for another chance . . ."

"It's against the rules. You missed your chance. I can only report emergencies." I heard him walk away.

Darkness enveloped me, and for the first time I knew despair. I had endured the hunger, the thirst, the cold, trying to hold on until the seventh day. Now I felt utterly abandoned, as insignificant as an ant on the pavement. No one would care if I were crushed beneath a shoe.

My thoughts rambled back over my attempt at confession. I had admitted my crime, I had offered no resistance, I had begged for forgiveness, but I could not incriminate my friends. If that was the price of release, I would die in confinement. I decided not to struggle any longer. Life itself had become a torment.

On the eighth morning the duty prisoner found me collapsed at the back of the cell. When he shouted, I didn't respond. After a few minutes he crawled inside to drag me to the gate. "Drink your soup!" he ordered, but I kept my eyes shut. I would no longer accept their food. I pushed the bowl away, and the gruel spilled onto the cement.

"Oh," exclaimed the duty prisoner, "now he wants to die!" He left to report, then some hours later brought a second bowl, but I didn't move. That afternoon Captain Gao returned. "It's up to you whether you eat or starve," he declared. "The Party and the government do not fear your threat of suicide." I heard him leave, but I didn't open my eyes.

On the ninth morning I heard Captain Gao's voice outside my gate. Through squinted eyes I could see that he had brought along four prisoners and a clinic worker. "Wu Hongda!" he shouted. "I see that you want to resist the Party and the government to the end. I see that you want to cut yourself off forever from the people. Drag him out!" The duty prisoner reached in and pulled me through the gate.

"The Party's policy is to transform you into a new socialist person. The government holds itself responsible for you. We will use revolutionary humanitarianism to save you from the path of death and to keep you from cutting yourself off from the people!"

Then the four prisoners pinned me to the ground, and the duty prisoner, with his strong peasant hands, held my head. The clinic worker fed a rubber tube into my nostril, forcing it in inch by inch. I felt a stabbing, burning pain, and my throat tasted salty. "Far enough," he muttered as he began to pour a thin gruel through a funnel into the tube.

That afternoon I lay on the concrete floor and swallowed the blood that dripped from my nasal cavity down my throat. The Communist Party's revolutionary humanitarianism had kept me from death.

On the tenth morning Captain Gao appeared again. I never opened my eyes, but I could tell from the voices that he had brought along a different group of prisoners. Maybe he wanted others to benefit from this lesson in reeducation, I thought vaguely.

"Wu Hongda!" he called. "Have you straightened out your thinking? Do you want to continue to alienate yourself from the people or are you ready to walk on the bright path of confessing and receiving leniency?"

I did not respond. Again the duty prisoner held my head. "Today change to the right nostril," he said as he fed in the tube. I seemed to feel less pain the second time.

When the prisoners released their grip on my arms and legs, I felt a slight pressure in my right hand. I realized dimly that someone had passed me a small wad of paper. I didn't move. I heard the team leave, and the duty prisoner pushed me inside.

Smoothing the paper, I narrowed my eyes and recognized Zhao's cramped handwriting. "Go ahead and confess. Only Guo and Chen. No need for sacrifice." I rolled up the note and swallowed it immediately. True to his word, Zhao had made a plan to help me.

On the eleventh morning I heard again the approach of footsteps and recognized Captain Gao's voice. "I'm ready to confess," I called out weakly. "I'm ready to eat."

"What is it you want to confess?"

I tried to speak, but the pain in my nose and throat turned my words to a low grunt. Captain Gao told the duty prisoner to support my head so I could speak. The shift in position brought a gush of blood from my nose and mouth.

"Remove him!" ordered Gao. "Send him back to his company and give him three days to write a full confession. Tell the kitchen to prepare sick-list rations. If he doesn't confess completely, he will return."

The ordeal had ended. For two days I could not move from the kang. No one could express sympathy to me, but I could see concern in my squadmates' eyes. They would offer me a drink of hot water or a small piece of wotou. Guo caught a frog in the fields and the second night managed to hand me a bowl of tender, steamed meat. Gradually my strength returned, and I felt amazed at my body's resilience. I felt no hatred for my captors, no desire for revenge. I was alive. Nothing else mattered.

Before my release Guo and Chen had already undergone separate struggle meetings and criticized themselves before their squad members. The police believed the case had been handled successfully and treated my written confession as a formality. They had intercepted the letters quickly, discovered and severely punished the ringleader, prevented a suicide, and extracted a full confession. They considered the matter closed. On my sixth day out of confinement, still weak but largely recovered, I returned to labor. It was September 17, 1965.

16

The Little Woman

On October 7, 1965, Chen Yi, the Minister of Foreign Affairs, met in Beijing with foreign and domestic journalists to announce China's absolute determination to defeat American imperialism. The story covered the front page of *People's Daily*. "We will make any sacrifice necessary to reach this goal. After we defeat the United States, colonialism and imperialism will disappear from the face of the earth. Communism will be victorious!"

Inside the camp, with access to no information other than newspapers and pamphlets published by the Communist Party, we expected that history might well unfold in just that way. Perhaps Communism would triumph in the rest of the world as it had in China. Zhao and I discussed our concern that the initiative to defeat the country's external enemies might have consequences for us, its internal foes.

That same evening an official notice from Tuanhe Farm battalion headquarters announced the transfer of twenty-four rightists from our labor reform team. We knew nothing about their fate except that they would be assigned resettlement status as forced job placement personnel. Li, Lo, Dong, and Ao were among them. Lu Haoqin, Chen, and I remained behind in squad eight. Listening to the names of those being reclassified, I noticed that Zhao and Guo also were not called, nor was Fan Guang. All his efforts to win favor from the police had not succeeded. The announcement of my friends' "release" stirred mixed emotions. I envied their chance for greater freedom, but I also knew their future prospects darkened with this transfer.

Labor-reform prisoners like me, at least in theory, served a fixed sentence. We could maintain some vague hope that Party leaders would someday reevaluate the policy toward rightists and announce a termination date for our prison terms. Even ten years away, we hoped that we might leave the prison system and resume our interrupted lives. The transfer to forced job placement status removed that possibility. Once resettled, the ex-prisoners would receive permanent assignment to a work unit, probably in some remote area, and would live out their lives in a netherworld of internal exile.

After the announcement I thought about how Ao and the others would receive a regular monthly salary, buy their daily meals in a cafeteria, and spend their days off getting their shoes repaired or eating noodles in a small restaurant. But I also knew they could never hope to return to a regular life in society. They would have no working papers, no grain coupons, no housing, no way to exist apart from the network of farms and enterprises run by the Public Security Bureau. Their forced job placement label was a life sentence.

In the labor camps, despite our disappointments, each of us secretly cherished wishes. Even a small wish could pull you along and give you the will to live. If a twenty-year sentence stretched before you, it still offered hope. Someday it would end, and you could look forward to a lavish Peking duck dinner, a comfortably furnished apartment, maybe a happy marriage. The resettlement transfer deprived you of that chance to wish.

Ao knew that after his shift from labor-reform status, very little would actually change. His salary would be half that of an ordinary worker, too small for expensive restaurant meals. He would continue living in a barracks rather than an apartment, and his labor would still be dictated and supervised by the police. He could leave the farm only on his days off and then only with a travel permit. And even if he could find a peasant woman willing to settle down with him in the dormitory, he could not hope to be happy in marriage or to raise children without passing on to them the stigma of his ex-prisoner status. He would gain a measure of freedom, but at the same time he would relinquish his hopes.

More than most of us, Ao had managed to retain his ideals. His lute, his habit of reflection, his refusal to engage in fights, and his belief in justice and fair treatment had always set him apart. I worried about how he would respond to the prospect of his entire life being spent at manual labor, punctuated only by eating, sleeping, and perhaps occasional, perfunctory sex.

Before he left the next morning, Ao drew me aside. He had only a few minutes to talk while the duty prisoners made final arrangements for the transfer. I had never seen his face so downcast.

"When only disappointment awaits you in your life, why continue to exist?" he asked. "For what reason?"

"Don't ask that kind of question." I stared at the ground, not wanting to meet his eyes. "You'll be farther along than I. You'll have more freedom."

"How much farther?" he persisted. "How far ahead? Once there was a wish ahead of me, a wish for release. When only resettlement is granted, I have reached the end. What more can I hope for?"

"Ao Naisong," I began seriously, pulling him around behind the dormitory where we had discussed the Taiwan threat and so many other forbidden subjects during more than three years of friendship at Tuanhe Farm. "Let me tell you a story from my own life."

In fact, I didn't know why I continued to live either. I had no real future in front of me, no reason to believe I faced anything but continued fighting, misery, and pain. What did I hope for? I didn't know, but I wanted to buttress Ao's spirits.

"When I was a boy, I got into a fight with a classmate older and stronger than I," I began. "He punched me hard, but I held back my tears. I ran home, and my stepmother patted my head and washed my bloody nose. Only then did I let myself cry. I remember my stepmother asking, 'Was he bigger and stronger than you?' She felt sorry for me.

" 'Yes,' I told her, sniffing back my tears. 'It wasn't fair. His brother helped him, it was two against one.' My father sat nearby, saying nothing. Then he called to me. I expected he would also offer sympathy.

" 'I don't care who fought against you or how many boys, he said firmly, 'but I want to know one thing. Did you give in to them?'

" 'No,' I said.

"That's right,' he answered proudly. 'Never give in. No matter what, you must never give in!' All my life my father taught me not to show weakness, not to be intimidated, and not to back down.

"I can't answer your question," I told Ao. "I really don't know why I live either. Maybe it's because I still listen to my father."

"Take care," Ao said, smiling bitterly.

"We won't be far apart," I replied. "Maybe we can see each other." My words deceived neither of us, but I wanted to ease the sadness of parting. Trying to sound optimistic, I quoted a traditional proverb. "Two fish trapped in a tidal pool will splash each other to keep alive. When one day they return to the ocean, they cannot forget each other."

Ao turned toward the waiting truck. I tried to find consolation in the thought that perhaps someday those of us rightists who remained confined to the labor-reform camps would be pardoned or "rehabilitated." Perhaps someday, somehow, I would be allowed to resume my former life.

The strain of continued imprisonment without a specified term affected everyone in squads eight and nine after Ao and the others left, but the most disturbed among us during that autumn of 1965 was Lu Haoqin. We who lived closely with him recognized that his earlier problems had grown serious. He became withdrawn in the dormitory and listless at labor. His behavior became more erratic, interrupted by outbursts of anger and distress and by moments of delusion.

Since spring I had worried about how the indefinite imprisonment weighed on his mind and twisted his feelings. One night in April he had turned toward me on the kang and whispered, "Do you know what it means to 'fuck the bottom'?" I had told him that was a dirty thought and not to talk about such things. Then the next morning I had awakened before the duty prisoner's shout to find Lu's hand under my quilt. I pushed it back and told him to stop or I would report him to the police.

For awhile during the summer Lu had seemed to accept his situation, but suddenly in August he had asked the prison barber to shave his head. Someone said derisively, "What a pretty little nun!" I looked at him and thought that Lu really did have a beautiful woman's face. After that, "Little Nun" became his nickname. He didn't seem to mind.

By late summer Lu's behavior had become offensive to several of our squadmates. I tried to ignore his outbursts and understand his needs. He had been in prison for seven years, and he missed sex acutely. Once the date of our expected release had passed in 1964, he lost hope of ever reuniting with his girlfriend, and he truly could no longer control himself. I felt sympathy for him.

Then one noon as I squatted with him to sneak a rest in some shade beside a clump of weeds along the canal, out of sight of the police captain, his expression abruptly changed. We had spent the morning planting rice seedlings. He looked up, tilted his face, and asked, "Hey, aren't I beautiful? Don't you want to love me?"

"What are you saying?" I answered, stepping away. He tried to embrace me.

"I don't like this. We have to get back to work," I said and hurried back to the field. I didn't want anything to do with Lu's affection. A man should act like a man, I thought, and a woman like a woman.

The incident passed, and Lu seemed to control his emotions for several weeks. After squad eight was assigned to construction projects, Lu worked with greater energy and enthusiasm. Like me, he found building pigsties less monotonous than hoeing weeds in the fields or harvesting wheat. Sometimes we carried bricks and wood, sometimes we transported sand and water to mix into cement. Not only was our labor more varied, but we could also move around the camp in pairs with our shoulder poles to collect construction materials. This mobility gave us an unusual sense of freedom.

In November we received orders to construct a high, free-standing brick wall parallel to the road, just inside one of the farm entrances. The structure would serve to screen the prisoners from outside view and would also provide a prominent surface for the revolutionary slogans being painted with increasing fervor in late 1965 on walls and buildings throughout the city. At the start of this project, I took Lu with me to collect some old bricks in a deserted corner of the farm. Suddenly he embraced me and tried to kiss my face.

"Okay . . ." he said, his voice excited and frightened, his breath hot against my neck. "I love you. Now make love to me."

"What are you trying to do?" I asked, pushing him away. Sweating from the labor despite the November chill, he had stripped off his padded jacket and trousers and wore only shorts and a sleeveless undershirt while carrying the heavy loads of bricks. The skin of his shoulder felt as smooth as a woman's against my arm. In spite of myself, I had a quick flash of sexual excitement.

He stepped away and stripped off his shorts. "Let me show you," he said, grabbing and stroking his penis. My feeling changed to anger, but when I looked at Lu's face and saw the degree of his suffering, I wasn't sure what to do. I just stared, confused by my own emotions.

"Come on, come on," Lu said. "I'll play with you. You are my man! You are strong. I love you!"

"What do you mean?" I asked, amazed even to hear myself hesitate and ask the question. Across my mind flashed the face of a student in my middle school. Once I had been shocked to notice the dark seams of a pair of women's nylon stockings showing beneath his trousers. Especially after the Communist victory, homosexuality was regarded not only as a perversion in China, but as a sufficient cause for arrest and imprisonment, and I had always felt disgusted by the idea of sexual contact between men.

Lu tucked his penis between his legs and squeezed them together so it didn't show. He began to turn his body round and round. "See! I don't have one. I'm just like a woman. Am I pretty? Do you like me? Come on, make love to me!" He moved close, pulling at my shorts and trying to touch between my legs.

"Put on your shorts and stop this," I answered. "You are a man. Stand up like a man."

"Why should I?" He made his voice sound higher and more feminine. "I'm a woman now, a pretty woman. You see? Here!" He took off his shirt and shoes. "Wouldn't you like me?"

"No!" The shout rose from my throat, loud and hoarse. "Stop that!"

He tried to embrace me again. Finally, yelling at him to stop, I slapped him. He awoke. Saying nothing, he put on his clothes. We picked up the shoulder pole and carried the bricks back to the work site in silence.

That evening Lu whispered, "Please, don't talk to anyone about this."

"Of course," I promised, still hoping he would somehow control his terrible longing. "Be strong," I urged him. "Press ahead."

But Lu's behavior grew more erratic. He began smoking cigarettes continuously, whenever he could find them. He asked others to sleep with him, or sneaked up behind someone and pulled down his pants. At times he seemed calm and clear-headed and he could work efficiently, but then suddenly he would lapse into what seemed almost a fit of madness. During one of his stable periods, I asked him what he was thinking about when he asked other men for sex.

"That is what I want," he answered. "It's what I need. I've been waiting such a long time. I don't see any chance ever to have contact with a woman again. To stroke a pipe makes me feel comfortable and happy. It's like what I had that one time with my girlfriend. Every time I stroke my pipe, I think I am making love to her again. I feel her body instead of my own. I forget everything. Why not? Some people tell me this is shameful, but I don't agree. It doesn't hurt anyone. It's my own business, and I like it."

"Lu," I pleaded, frightened for the welfare of this man who had become one of my closest friends. "I know it's your business, but it has damaged your health. You've grown weak. You're no longer a strong worker. I'm worried about that. Our situation is still very difficult. You need to have a strong body. Besides, it's dangerous for you. They'll punish you if you don't stop."

"I know." He sounded tired. "I know."

Perhaps two months later Lu waited for me on the kang

after breakfast. On his face I saw a look of despair. "I'm sick. I can't go to the fields this morning. I don't want to labor anymore."

"If you're sick, you need permission from the captain to stay in the camp. That's the only way to be excused from labor. I can't release you."

"Please," he said. "Talk to him for me. I don't want to labor anymore."

I didn't want to labor anymore either. No one wanted to, but we had no choice. Often I had to stifle my own rebelliousness, discipline my resentment, and remind myself to be patient, to wait, to obey, until some change came. Lu's patience was gone.

I forwarded Lu's request to Captain Gao. "No!" he shouted. "Everyone goes to labor as usual. There's nothing wrong with Lu. He's not sick, he's acting. I've heard about him. He's got a nerve trying to peddle his dirty ass here. And you're trying to help him?"

The memory of Lu's haunted face made me persevere. "No, he's really sick."

"Call him out!" screamed the captain. "Call him!"

I didn't know why Lu wanted to stay away from work that day, but I did know that during the night there had been a lot of motion beside me on the kang. I followed the duty prisoner back to the room.

"Ooooooh," squealed Lu, squirming as the duty prisoner tried to pull him to his feet. "Are you trying to rape me?" He was a woman again. "Come on, let's have sex!" He began to strip off his clothes.

The duty prisoner grumbled, "What are you up to? Acting stupid, eh?"

Captain Gao appeared in the doorway. "He's acting again, teach him a lesson!" The duty prisoner struck Lu across the face, then kicked him. I held the man's arm, and Lu ran off. Gao stood silently looking on.

"Don't do that," I warned the duty prisoner quietly, but then Lu returned to the kang, laughing and yelling loudly, his hand on his penis. "I'm pretty, I'm young. I want to have sex with everyone. Come on!"

Two duty prisoners grabbed him. They were about to hit him again when I intervened with the captain. "You can see that he's really sick."

"What do you know about it?" Gao demanded.

"Once he wanted to have sex with me," I said. "So I know. This person is not normal."

The captain looked at his watch. "Leave him here for today," he directed. A hundred prisoners waited in the yard for orders to proceed to the field, but before joining them, I warned the duty prisoner again, "If I come back and find you've beaten him, you'll be the one to get taught a lesson."

That evening as we marched four abreast back into the compound, I saw with alarm that several of the windowpanes in our barracks had been broken. The duty prisoner assigned to watch Lu Haoqin heard us returning and came to meet me.

"I couldn't control him," he said. "Lu took his clothes off again, then he started smashing windows and screaming in a woman's voice."

I rushed to our room. Quilts, pillows, and clothing lay strewn across the floor. The other returning squad members began to shout at Lu, who pranced around naked with his legs squeezed together, asking whoever came near to have sex with him. I ordered the others to leave him alone and take care of cleaning up the mess. Two captains stood in the corridor observing the commotion. I overheard one say, "They'll be here soon."

Half an hour later a jeep squealed to a stop outside our building. Two men in police uniforms appeared in the doorway and ordered the waiting duty prisoners to hold Lu down. Then they checked his pupils, took his pulse, and looked him over. He remained calm, but the moment they released him, he began again to dance around, shouting and laughing to himself. Lu seemed to have utterly lost his grip on reality.

The noise brought two other men from the jeep carrying what they called "peace clothing," a one-piece suit made of thick canvas. It had a full-length zipper, short ties leading from the arms to the torso, and another tie between the feet. They forced Lu into the suit, tying his arms and feet together so that he couldn't move and then pressing some kind of medicine into his mouth. The shouting stopped. They picked him up and carried him off to the duty prisoners' room.

The next day when we returned from the fields, Lu was gone. The duty prisoner told me they had taken him to another camp. I asked where.

"Maybe the Yanqing Brick Factory, how would I know?" came the reply.

I had left the Yanqing Steel Factory in 1961 four years earlier, when it closed down after the Great Leap Forward. Both it and the two iron mines had remained closed. I had heard via the prison grapevine that the Beijing Public Security Bureau continued to use the brick factory as a special facility for prisoners not capable of doing labor. According to my information, that remote, mountainous site confined those whose physical or psychological disabilities prevented them from doing work. I knew it must be a terrible place, and I wondered how Lu would survive.

I thought of Lu often as the winter of 1965 passed. Every day at Tuanhe we labored, and every evening we sat through a session of political study. The newspapers reported the events of the Four Cleanups campaign in the countryside, where allegedly corrupt village cadres were being "unmasked" and "struggled against" by the masses. I had little interest in what happened outside. Nothing mattered to me except the situation inside the labor camps.

I began more and more to envy those prisoners around me who had relatives in Beijing to bring them extra food on visiting days. I longed for other kinds of food to supplement the diet of corn gruel, steamed buns, and vegetable soup. Even though I still managed to steal vegetables from the fields and sometimes to catch a frog or snake, I began to crave the cookies, wheat flour, and meat that I saw other prisoners receive from outside.

Pulling weeds in the rice fields one morning, I found a chance to chat unobserved with a former squadmate named Wang who had been transferred to forced job placement status early in 1964. Always quiet and efficient, Wang had earned the authorities' trust and been assigned to work as a controller for the water supply to the fields. This was a special job, requiring that Wang walk about the camp unaccompanied to check the network of small canals and irrigation ditches that fed the rice paddies. Regulations prohibited a forced job placement worker from speaking to a labor-reform prisoner, but Wang would occasionally find a chance to stop beside me to exchange some information or even to pass me a small packet of biscuits or candies. He wanted to help in some small way by sharing his privileges, and I felt grateful for his generosity.

After his release, Wang had married a simple peasant woman who lived in her own village, passing freely in and out of Tuanhe Farm. One day I asked Wang for help. I desperately wanted some meat from the outside, and I thought he might find a way to get me some.

The next time he stopped in the fields to chat, he told me his plan. His wife had agreed to pose as one of my sisters enroute to the Northeast on a quality-control investigation for her radio speaker factory in Shanghai. She would pretend to be stopping at Tuanhe for a family visit, carrying a package of meat as a gift from my father. Wang had seen earlier the family photographs that I kept in my suitcases inside our company's storage room with the rest of my belongings, and he knew something of my family background. He thought the resemblance between his wife and my second younger sister was close enough not to be questioned, and he checked with me for details about my sister's age and work.

A few weeks later, in January of 1966, the captain called me away from the fields one afternoon. "How are you doing with your thought reform?" he asked.

"Fine," I answered with caution.

"How is your family? Do you have a sister?"

"I have three sisters," I answered, telling him their names. I guessed that Wang's wife must have requested a family visit.

The captain led me to a small office in the company headquarters. Because my "sister" had explained that she could only briefly interrupt her inspection trip from Shanghai, they had given her a special pass that could be used outside of the regular visiting hours. A young woman sat beside the desk, her face covered against the cold by a gauze mask, her head concealed by a wool scarf. I looked closely at her eyes, saw a small scar above one eyelid, and for some reason, having seen two photographs of Wang's wife, felt certain that the woman before me was someone else. Wondering who could have come in her place, I called my sister's name. She nodded her head. A security guard stood close by.

To ease the woman's nervousness, I asked about her trip, then offered a few conventional remarks about myself. "I work very hard and do my best to reform myself through labor," I told her.

"Our family has only one hope for you," she replied, as if on cue. "You must work hard, obey the captain's instructions, and follow Chairman Mao's direction to make yourself into a new socialist person. I really cannot stay longer, but I have brought you some salted meat."

"No," I pretended to object. "I don't want it. My living conditions are fine. I don't need anything more to eat." We could all recite such lines automatically, mindful of our listeners.

The guard also responded predictably. "What? You've brought ten jin of meat? Certainly that is not necessary. Your family must remember that your brother has to labor hard to reform himself. He became a criminal because his life was too easy, and I cannot permit you to give him so much meat."

"Of course, I don't need this food," I answered, continuing the charade. "The food here is adequate, and I must continue to labor to reform my thought. Please take back the meat."

"I cannot make such a decision," protested my sister. "I brought the package at the request of our father."

"You will have to take it back," the guard repeated.

"But I'm not returning to Shanghai," she persevered. "I'm on an inspection trip for my factory." Finally, the guard offered the expected solution. He agreed that I could keep five jin of the meat for my own use, and he would take five jin for the police captains' kitchen. The visit ended, and I walked the woman to the compound gate.

"Who are you?" I asked when the guard stepped briefly out of earshot. She pulled down her face mask for a moment and said, "Look at me, and remember." Then she was gone. I waited for Wang to find me in the fields so that I could thank him for his generosity and ask who had visited me in place of his wife. Some weeks later I learned that he had been transferred to another camp. I didn't know why or where. The woman's gentle face and her extraordinary act of kindness continued to haunt me. I wanted to thank her, but I had no way to discover her name.

17

Revolution on the Farm

$\mathcal{T}$ he violent outbreak of the Cultural Revolution in the early summer of 1966 had no effect on the routine life of the labor camps. Throughout Beijing gangs of politically fervent youths, called Red Guards, rampaged through the streets and terrorized campuses, government ministries, newspaper and radio offices, and apartment complexes. Inside Tuanhe Farm we spent our days as before, planting the rice fields and the autumn wheat. For three months imprisonment afforded a strange sanctuary from the madness and cruelty that swept the city.

Prisoners who received letters and visits from Beijing relatives during those weeks passed whispered comments about young people directing their revolutionary wrath toward their teachers and parents. They told of people in the streets who were accused as "diehard reactionaries," then being humiliated and struck or sometimes beaten with heavy belts. Some had their heads shaved or their clothing ripped off.

I tried to assess the extent of the brutality in June and July of 1966 from *People's Daily*, but I learned only that a serious "two-line struggle" had begun, that Chairman Mao supported the revolutionary masses, and that he had issued instructions to eliminate the "four olds": old thoughts, old habits, old customs, and old culture. In August I read that Chairman Mao himself was addressing tens of thousands of Red Guards from atop the reviewing stand in Tiananmen Square, encouraging them to spread out across the nation, fan the flames of revolution, and sweep away the vestiges of privilege, corruption, and revisionism. Meanwhile visitors to the prison carried reports of Buddhist temples, Confucian monuments, museums, and graveyards defaced, of homes ransacked and personal property seized, all part of the life-and-death struggle to rid the nation of the contaminating influence of its bourgeois past.

In fact, I worried more about China's expanding conflict with Vietnam and its aggravated tensions with the Soviet Union than about the political furor at home. Always I feared that the outbreak of an international crisis would worsen the situation of China's political prisoners. Should the nation's security become threatened, I feared that control would be tightened within the camps, or even that the authorities could decide to execute counterrevolutionaries to rid the country of its domestic enemies.

The grapevine reports of terror outside the camps left me largely indifferent. So accustomed had I become to violence and cruelty that even the most shocking stories made me feel as if I were viewing a fire from the other side of a river. The suffering of others no longer concerned me. I cared little about the two-line struggle or the punishment of reactionary elements until September 17. That night after dinner, a team of twenty Red Guards stormed through the gates into our compound shouting slogans.

"It is right to rebel!"

"Revolution is not a dinner party!"

"We must follow the teachings of our Great Leader Chairman Mao!"

"We must wipe out revisionism!"

The rebels gathered outside the police captains' office, their fists raised, their faces angry. Their leader shouted hoarsely at Captain Gao, "Who is your most stubborn prisoner?" I stood at attention with the others from my squad as the militant youths, dressed in green army jackets and red armbands, glared at the group assembled in the floodlit compound yard.

Even if he had wanted to protect us, Captain Gao could not at that moment disobey the instructions of Chairman Mao's revolutionary vanguard. He had to produce a victim. Pausing for a moment, he pointed at a prisoner with glasses and a square face who stood a few feet from me. "That one continues to resist reform."

"Pull him out!" the Red Guard leader commanded.

I had known Xiu, the designated target, for more than three years. He had previously worked as a civil engineer at the Beijing Construction Design Company. His impassiveness in the face of criticism and his refusal over the years to implicate other prisoners had earned him the reputation of being stubborn. Older than I and unskilled at physical labor, Xiu had done little at Tuanhe Farm to prove himself useful to the authorities.

Two Red Guards led Xiu roughly to the front of the yard and pinned his arms behind his back. Three others began striking him with their fists and lashing him with their thick leather belts. For some moments he cried out in pain, then he collapsed on the ground unconscious.

"This is revolutionary action!" one shouted.

"We will return!"

"If you refuse reform, the punishment will be death!"

"Long live Chairman Mao's Great Proletarian Cultural Revolution! Long live our great leader Chairman Mao!" they chorused. We repeated the slogans mechanically until they left, apparently to carry their revolutionary struggle to other parts of the camp.

I could see Xiu move slightly on the ground. Blood streamed down his forehead. Several of his squad members picked him up and carried him to their barracks to tend his wounds.

Until then I had not felt frightened by the Cultural Revolution. I had believed that my situation as a prisoner with an indefinite sentence could hardly grow worse. Seeing Xiu beaten so savagely shattered even that grim illusion.

Later my squadmates expressed different opinions about what action we should take, given the Red Guards' threat of further revolutionary action. Some thought we should try to escape, since the Beijing Public Security Bureau, disrupted by militants within its own ranks, was apparently in disarray and no longer effectively patrolled the city streets. Some resolved to fight back if the Red Guards returned, believing that after years of physical labor we could defend ourselves easily against these inexperienced kids. Others decided to draw closer to the police, hoping that a display of greater cooperation would prevent their being turned over if the Red Guards came again.

Perhaps a week later, the police captains announced an effort to rid the camp of any possessions that were "old" or reactionary. I was told to turn over my books.

Soon after my arrest in 1960, the Geology Institute had forwarded to me all of my books and course notebooks. From camp to camp, those texts had followed me, along with some unused clothing, stuffed inside the large leather suitcase, the duffel bag, and the small wooden trunk that I had taken with me from home when I left Shanghai in 1955. In each location they remained in the locked storage room assigned to my company. The police held the key to the door, but I kept the keys to my individual trunks. Usually once a month on our rest days, the captain would unlock the room to give us access to our suitcases and boxes so that we could pull out extra clothing or just look through our belongings.

I feared that anything I handed in would be burned in a huge "reactionary" bonfire, so I turned over my Chinese-English dictionary reluctantly, as well as my geology texts. But I didn't want to see my favorite works of literature destroyed. In that summer of 1966, I gambled on being able to save a small packet of books. To execute my plan, I borrowed a spade and a square of plastic sheeting from the prisoner responsible for our labor tools, who was my friend. Then I wrapped tightly my Chinese translations of Shakespeare and Tolstoy, Victor Hugo and Mark Twain, and buried the package near the company's toolshed on the night before the search. The police assumed we would give up any incriminating materials voluntarily, for our own protection, and they looked no further. My few works of Western literature lay safely hidden for more than a year.

The spread of Cultural Revolution violence inside the farm made everyone edgy. Those prisoners trying hardest to demonstrate their successful reform asked for permission to buy the revolutionary buttons worn as badges of political loyalty to Chairman Mao. Their request was denied. Rightists were enemies of the people, our political instructor decreed, not members of the revolutionary masses. We were not entitled to claim

Mao Zedong as our leader or to display buttons with his likeness on our hats or lapels. As enemies of the revolution, we had to study Chairman Mao's works with even greater diligence than ordinary citizens, he asserted. Some prisoners were quick to memorize the Chairman's words, but I often stumbled in the recitation of the longer passages, and the study leader criticized me repeatedly for not being serious about my thought reform. It seemed that I could recall the words easily only when they were set to music.

After Xiu's beating the police also grew wary, fearful that the Red Guards would return and that they would be held responsible for any breach of prison security, even during instances of revolutionary action. No one wanted to commit a political mistake. Like us, the authorities watched and waited. As the weeks passed, I also began to pick up clues that the Tuanhe police had themselves become embroiled in factional struggle. When they supervised us in the fields, they carried red armbands in their pockets, ready to slip on should they need to display their own revolutionary commitment. I approached one of the political cadres one day with a question about the labor assignment, and he warned me against following the instructions of one particular police captain.

The cadre's voice expressed his hostility, and after that I assumed the individual captains faced their own pressure and their own criticism meetings. I became more cautious, wanting not to become caught in the middle of the guards' factional disputes.

A few weeks later the Cultural Revolution's savagery broke out inside the camp a second time, this time within our own ranks. One evening in October a police captain interrupted our study session to summon us to a struggle meeting. We could tell from his face that something serious had happened. There had been an "active counterrevolutionary incident," he shouted, after four squads with some forty-five prisoners had crowded into a large dormitory room. The police captain left. Two rightists whom I knew only slightly stood at the front of the room, their arms pinned behind them, their heads jerked forward by four fellow prisoners. This was the painful "jet plane" position used to torture alleged enemies during the Cultural Revolution. To my horror, the four activists, themselves fellow rightists, began viciously to strike and kick their captives, shouting for them to confess. "Are you too hot?" one of them taunted, seeing the sweat on his victims' faces. Then before our eyes two activists stripped off the helpless men's clothing. One of the men being struggled against slumped to the floor.

"He's pretending to be dead," an activist shouted, "I'll help him stand up." He ran outside to the tool room and returned with a rope. Soon the two victims were strung by their wrists from the crossbeam in the roof. I saw someone come in with a belt dipped in water and begin beating one of the men, against whom I knew he held a grudge. Then the activists, their excitement mounting, claimed these two formed part of a revolutionary clique. Dong Li shouted a third name, then a fourth, and several men ran out to drag in the alleged accomplices. Dong Li, as usual, served as a barking dog but not a biting dog, I noticed.

At that moment I slipped out of the rear door and headed for the security office in the next building. I knew that in fact the men being accused did have some connections with each other, and I wanted to disrupt the struggle meeting. Two men tried to stop me, shouting that I could not leave the room, but I was a squad labor leader and I declared that I was reporting to the police office. They had no authority to stop me. I hesitated outside the captains' door, having no idea what I would say, then ducked into the police latrine, which was off-limits to prisoners, to think. I wanted to find some way to stop the violence from spreading. Inside I saw the fourth man whose name had been called as an accomplice to the two being struggled against. A former professor of Russian history at Beijing University, he looked deathly frightened and motioned for me to keep silent.

I walked to the security office door and knocked. "Report!" I called.

"What is it?" one of the captains answered. Seeing me, he called, "We'll talk about the labor assignment later."

"I have something to report," I insisted.

"What is it?"

"Someone has escaped," I stated in an urgent voice.

"Who is it?" Three captains jumped up. This was serious.

"Fan Ming," I answered, giving the name of the Russian professor.

The captains ran to the dormitory room, shouting for everyone at the struggle meeting to form lines outside for a count. Just as I had reported, they found Fan Ming missing.

"Who's seen him?" a captain yelled as Fan Ming appeared around the corner of the dormitory. He had left the meeting only to go to the latrine, he explained in a low voice. He apologized for using the police toilet but said it was closer to the struggle meeting. The captain shouted a reprimand, then dismissed us. The frenzy of violence was over. I had seen inhuman treatment many times during my six and a half years in the camps, but I had never seen such viciousness.

Not until the next day did I learn about the alleged crimes of the two originally accused. One, named Guo, was said to have written counterrevolutionary slogans on a cigarette package during study class that evening. Dong Li had been sitting beside him on the kang and claimed he observed Guo writing in tiny characters "Down with Chairman Mao." Immediately he grabbed the cigarette pack and ran to the police captain to report. The second to be accused and beaten, named Wang, was a fellow squad member who ran after Dong Li to stop him. Wang was a very trustworthy person, always trying to help others, and he warned Dong Li to be careful or he would get beaten. Dong Li had then accused Wang of sympathizing with a counterrevolutionary act. In fact, another squad member explained, Guo had only written the slogans "Long live Chairman Mao" and "Down with Liu Shaoqi" as a way to pass the time, but on the cigarette package the tiny characters had appeared jumbled together. I knew the police must not have found the evidence very compelling, as they had left the prisoners alone to carry out a struggle meeting rather than handling the investigation and punishment themselves.

I found this instance of cruelty inflicted by self-promoting prisoners even more shocking and horrible than that unleashed by youthful zealots caught up in the thrill of waging revolution. After that episode I tried harder not to think and not to feel. Tragedy had come to seem commonplace, survival itself unexpected. I labored, ate, and slept, that was all.

One crisp fall day in late October, a visit from another of the resettlement prisoners working as a water controller roused me from this lethargy. I looked up from repairing a canal to notice my friend Wang inspecting the irrigation ditches nearby. Catching my eye, he fanned himself with his straw hat, a signal that he wanted to talk. The captain supervising our labor stood near enough to overhear.

"Hey!" I shouted to Wang. "Water controller! There's a leak over here. Can you fix it?"

Wang came over and set to work with his spade. "Next movie," he whispered. "Thirty minutes after it begins. Behind the screen." Then he raised his voice. "Okay, this should hold. If it leaks again, call me." I watched him stride away across the flat expanse of fields.

Two weeks later the duty prisoner announced an evening showing of *Tunnel Battle*, a heroic depiction of the Communist Eighth Route Army leading the Chinese people to rise up against the Japanese invaders during the Sino-Japanese War. At Tuanhe we watched films outside in the threshing yard sometimes once a month, and I had seen this one several times before. As darkness fell, I chose a spot on the ground in the midst of my squad members, not far from the white cloth that stretched between two bamboo poles to serve as a screen. The thin sheet rippled in the chill November wind. I had no idea whether Wang would come or why he had taken such care to set this appointment.

Exactly twenty-five minutes after the movie started, I asked Captain Gao for permission to use the latrine. He nodded, and I disappeared into the darkness under the stream of light from the projector. As I headed for the area behind the screen, the tinny sound of gunfire from the movie followed me. I knew that the Eighth Route Army was defending a strategic valley occupied by the enemy forces. Soon the Japanese would try to flood the guerrillas out from their underground tunnel, then to smoke them out with burning straw. Finally a straggling band of Communist soldiers, having conquered great odds, would destroy the enemy and survive. As I crept into the darkness, I hoped I would be as fortunate.

I took care to stoop as I walked, not wanting my head to appear silhouetted against the screen. Around me I could hear prisoners whispering to their friends, conveying messages, or passing food and cigarettes. I lay down behind the makeshift screen and waited. About a hundred feet beyond me a face bobbed up into the light, once, then twice. I jumped up twice in response, then crawled toward my friend. The instant I reached him, Wang passed me a small package wrapped in newspaper. "That's all," he whispered, and he crept away into the darkness.

I slipped the parcel inside my shirt and made my way back, choosing a spot somewhat apart from my squad. With the darkness concealing my movements, I unwrapped half a pound of precious porkhead meat and a pound of biscuits. Then I felt a small square of folded paper. Stuffing the note into my pocket, I began to eat. I swallowed all the meat and biscuits, savoring the taste, wishing I could save some to enjoy later in the barracks. Even then I feared someone would observe me and report my food package to the police. That would have meant confessing the source of my gift and facing criticism for not obeying the regulation forbidding contact between labor-reform prisoners and resettlement workers.

I knew I could not hope to read the note until study class the following evening, as that was the only time any kind of reading was permitted. To try and unfold the note on the kang after the movie, or even in the fields the next day, would be to invite detection. Back in the barracks, I slipped the note under my sleeping mat, hoping that it would not be discovered.

The next evening I made sure to be the first to return to the kang after supper, and I casually picked up a back issue of *People's Daily* from the materials designated for study. Slouched against my rolled-up quilt, I slid my hand under the mat, relieved to find the note undisturbed. I concealed the small square of paper inside my newspaper and finally managed to unfold it and read the cramped characters. At the bottom I read the signature of Li, one of my former squadmates who had been transferred to resettlement status the previous October. The message said that Ao Naisong had disappeared. They were searching for him. They didn't know if he would come back. The date at the top, October 18, 1966, told me the information was already two weeks old.

Upset at the news, I replaced the note and pretended to study the newspaper, thinking hard. I had heard that Ao and Li had been transferred together from Tuanhe to Qinghe Farm several months earlier. I could imagine only the worst. Ao was not the type to attempt escape, and I guessed that my friend had decided to take his final leave.

I thought back to my arrival at Tuanhe from Qinghe Farm four years earlier in 1962. I remembered my first glimpse of Ao as he walked slowly down the hallway holding the sack containing his lute. The memory filled my heart with sadness as I thought that Ao alone among us had retained, despite his own suffering, his fundamental humanity. I retrieved the note from under my bedding and at the bottom of the scrap of paper wrote a short poem.

> Lofty, undisturbed,
> Like a deity in nature,
> A straight pine,
> Forever green,
> Forever true,
> Forever lodged in the hearts of those who knew him.

I hoped that at last Ao had found rest. Then I destroyed the note.

18

Another Day

*I*n January 1967, with no prior warning, the police instructed us one morning to pack our possessions. Orders had arrived that all rightists remaining in Tuanhe's second battalion barracks would move to the more secure compound occupied by the farm's penal prisoners in Battalion One. We guessed that the prison leaders had decided to take extra precautions to prevent escape attempts and also to protect the political criminals in their charge from unauthorized violence at the hands of the Red Guards. By noon more than two hundred of us had moved in to much less hospitable surroundings.

I looked with little concern at the electrified wire that topped the high brick wall surrounding my new barracks and at the armed guards standing at each corner to monitor the movements of prisoners in the yard below. Even though I hated to think of facing tighter discipline and more surveillance, I knew that in these surroundings I would be less vulnerable to revolutionary action from the outside.

Two months later, in March 1967, orders came for us rightists to move yet again. This time trucks waited at the compound gate, and we piled in, our destination unknown. We rode in silence for twenty minutes to reach the railroad station at Yundingmen. Just as before, the police captains herded us onto the side of the special spur line reserved for prisoners. I looked around, curious to glimpse some sign of the chaos that I knew had gripped the country for months, but I saw nothing amiss.

On board the train, the guards told us our destination was Qinghe Farm. I listened to this announcement with indifference. Perhaps we would be safer in a camp farther away from Beijing, I thought. Perhaps I would see my old friends again and learn more news about Ao Naisong. After seven years as a prisoner, I cared little about where I labored. My only thought was that I would miss the vegetables and fruits in the fields at Tuanhe Farm.

At Qinghe it seemed that nothing had changed, except that the food supply had improved. The barracks, the marshes, the electric wire along the wall looked all too familiar. The guards from Tuanhe dispersed us throughout the east and west sections, with twenty or thirty assigned to my team and only one other rightist in my squad. The only other change from 1962 was that now we had to sing Chairman Mao's words as we marched to the fields and back.

As labor reform prisoners, we were expected to show enthusiasm for the opportunity to remold ourselves through work. "Sing a song!" a guard would yell each morning as we lined up, and one of the squad leaders would start off, usually with a passage from Chairman Mao's *Quotations* set to music:

> All those mistaken thoughts,
> All those poisonous weeds,
> All those ghosts
> Must be criticized.
> Never let them run rampant!

In the afternoon, tired themselves after a day in the fields, the guards never bothered to make us sing or march in rows until we approached the gates. Then they shouted, "March in line! Sing a song!"

> Sailing on the sea needs a helmsman,
> The growth of a plant needs the sunshine,
> The rain and dew moisten the seedling crops—
> The revolution is guarded by Mao Zedong Thought!

Shortly after I had settled back into the Qinghe routine, a police captain called to me as I returned one day from labor in the mud of the irrigation ditches. "Hey, Wu Hongda! Come here," he shouted. "Lu Haoqin has come back. He's waiting in your barracks. Take care of him." I guessed that my former association with Lu had been entered into my file.

"How is he?" I asked.

"Go see for yourself."

From the doorway I stood for a moment, watching Lu seated cross-legged on the kang, his back to the wall, an ashtray overflowing with cigarette butts at his knee. He smoked nervously in short, quick puffs. I could not imagine how he had survived for a year and a half in the desolate mountains of the Yanqing camp.

"Hey, Lu!" I called out, excited to see my friend again. "Are you okay?"

"Look for yourself," he answered in a flat voice, never looking up from his cigarette. He didn't want to talk, so I went out to wash up and eat.

"Can I borrow some money to buy cigarettes?" Lu called to me when I returned for study class.

"How can you ask that?" I replied. "How would I have money?"

Seeing Lu's expression, I regretted my remark. He must have assumed that during his absence we had all been released to resettlement status and were drawing a monthly salary. I had not meant to dash his hopes so abruptly.

"I'll try to get you some cigarettes," I offered quickly. "It's just that I spent the last of my money this month," I lied. "I'll see if I can borrow some." I walked from room to room asking for donations and came back with a full pack of cigarettes. Lu thanked me coldly. During the two hours of study, he never spoke, and when the call came for evening count, he refused to move. As labor leader, I was responsible for making my squad members report, but I didn't want to force him. Lu remained in the room.

"Where's Lu?" called Captain Yu, the most rigid of the police captains I had encountered since returning to Qinghe.

"Back in the room," I answered.

"Why didn't he report?"

"He can't come!" I answered.

Evening count was mandatory. Each squad stood in its line,

and the duty prisoner called every name. Only if a prisoner was so seriously sick that he couldn't leave the kang could a squad leader answer for him. This was considered the most important part of the day for the maintenance of camp security.

"Get him!" Captain Yu ordered. When I didn't move, he turned his head angrily toward the duty prisoners, amazed that they had not jumped instantly at his instruction. "Are you going to obey my order?"

Just then Captain Wang, who knew Lu's history, intervened, and the count continued. I wondered what would happen if Lu refused to report the next day.

Back in the room we prepared for sleep. Lu still sat cross-legged, smoking. "Hey, Wu Hongda," he called to me as I crawled under my quilt. "What's been happening here?"

"What do you mean?" I answered. Lu had not made eye contact with anyone since his return. Now he looked straight at me. I wondered whether the Yanqing police had lied about our status, perhaps to give him some hope or to make him cooperative and obedient. Now he wanted to know the truth.

"No change?" Lu continued.

"What kind of change?" I answered evasively.

"How come you still have evening count?"

I didn't answer. Believing that he had returned as a resettlement worker, entitled to meager wages and occasional time off, Lu must have expected that he could search for his girlfriend in Beijing. I didn't want to destroy this hope.

"Tomorrow will I still have to line up for labor?"

"Probably," I said hesitantly. I couldn't lie to him, and he knew the distinction, that reeducation prisoners always lined up each morning in the yard, while resettlement workers did not. "If you feel okay, you'll have to go." I told him the wake-up call came at five-thirty. Then I fell asleep. How long he sat up that night, I never knew, but I found him slumped against the wall asleep in the morning. When the time came to line up alongside the other squads in our company, Lu refused to leave the kang.

I slipped away quickly to borrow more cigarettes. "Just stay here," I told him, knowing he must have slept badly. "When I come back, I want to talk to you." Lu said nothing.

As squad leader I had to call out the number of men present

to the captain. I reported nine members of my squad present. Captain Yu demanded, "Where's your tenth?"

"Lu Haoqin has just returned from Yanqing. He needs a rest," I replied.

"No rest. He must labor! This is the Great Proletarian Cultural Revolution. We must strengthen the dictatorship of the proletariat! We must show no sympathy for the class enemies! Call him out!"

Lu had not spoken a word since the previous evening. I sensed trouble ahead and stood still.

"Get him!" Yu shouted, growing red in the face.

"Would you check with Captain Wang?" I said, hoping that Wang would intervene as he had the previous night to spare Lu Haoqin from reporting for the count.

Captain Yu shouted, "What? You don't respect my orders? You want to ask Captain Wang? Are you trying to change my decision? I told you to get him out here!"

I had no choice. I could not directly challenge the captain's authority, so I went back to the room and found Lu leaning against the wall asleep. An overflowing ashtray lay on the floor beside him. I knew he needed more rest, so I returned to the yard.

"Captain Yu," I reported. "Lu cannot come."

He turned to the duty prisoners in a fury. "Get him out!"

"Maybe you should go see for yourself," I suggested in a low voice.

"What's wrong?"

"I don't know. Maybe he has some problem."

Captain Yu turned toward our barracks, and I followed a few steps behind. He shouted Lu's name as he neared the door, but Lu never stirred. Yu relented. "It's already late!" he growled. "When we get back, I'll talk with him. Let's go!" And we went out to labor.

That afternoon when I returned, Lu had taken off all his clothes and lay on the kang, his eyes closed, his quilt wet, a sign that he had recently masturbated. I covered him and said, "Hey!"

He shook himself groggily, then muttered, "So everything is just like before." His eyes seemed to glaze again.

"Hey," I repeated. "Do you need some cigarettes? Come

on, put your clothes on, okay?" I wanted him to walk outside and talk with the others. Maybe that contact would help him accept the fact that he was still a prisoner. Silently he began to dress. While I waited for him, I scavenged a few cigarette butts.

"Now I understand," Lu repeated when he joined me in the doorway. "Nothing will ever change."

"How about coming out to labor tomorrow?" I urged. "Now's a good time. It's harvest. We can steal some corn or some turnips, maybe find some frogs or snakes."

"Okay," he said quietly. "Tomorrow."

"How was Yanqing?"

He rolled up his sleeves. On his forearms I saw small black and brown scars. He spoke slowly. "The police used electric instruments to shock me. The other prisoners stole my food, beat me, and fucked my bottom. At the end the guards told me I had been released to resettlement. I thought I could go to see my girlfriend. Maybe she is still at Qinghua University. That made me feel better, but they lied."

The next morning Lu came out to the fields. All day he sat on an irrigation bank staring at his feet. Several times a captain came over and told him to get to work, but finally the guard left him alone.

"Today I won't go to labor," he told me the following morning. "I'm tired. I'm sick." When I reported Lu's illness to the police, they let him stay behind. I planned to talk to him as soon as I returned to the compound that afternoon, but several members of our squad reached the barracks ahead of me. From my place in line at the faucet, I heard shouting. I ran toward the room and saw the back of a man's head pressed against the glass of the high barred window above the door handle. The weight of the body kept us from pushing the door open.

"Quick!" I yelled, and we ran to the barred window on the opposite side of the room. I could see Lu's feet hanging about four inches from the floor. Only the window onto the hallway, one of its panes long broken and covered with newspaper, had no bars. I shouted for someone to grab a sickle, then climbed up to the sill, pulled away the paper, and reached my arm inside to cut the rope from around Lu's neck. The body dropped to the floor. I jumped into the room and pulled Lu away from the door. His body still felt warm. "Call the doctor! Call the captain!" someone shouted.

"Go ahead. Call the sonuvabitch," I muttered. Bending Lu's knees, I folded his legs to his chest and pushed hard, hoping to send blood to his lungs.

"What's going on?" Captain Yu demanded from the doorway.

I looked away. We lifted Lu to the kang. "Is he okay?" shouted the captain. I had nothing to say to him.

The doctor arrived, a rightist like us, and set to work rubbing Lu's chest and arms. When his eyes fluttered open, I pressed a cup of water to his lips. Then I stared at the nail Lu had driven into the door jamb and the rope he had fashioned out of the laces from our extra shoes. Lu seemed to be out of danger, so the doctor left him on the kang to sleep.

Behind the barracks that night, my friends and I discussed Lu's desperation. I wanted to stop him from attempting suicide again. I wanted to ask him to be patient, to give him some hope, but I had nothing to offer. I couldn't tell him that our confinement would end and everything would be fine. I couldn't say that someday he could visit his girlfriend or that his aged mother would come to visit or that he could soon eat a fine meal of porkhead meat. I couldn't even promise to keep supplying him with cigarettes. My friends said there was no way to give Lu an incentive to continue living.

One friend named Tang advised, "Let him go. He's suffering too much. Don't save him again. There's only one way to liberate him."

I knew Tang was right, but I couldn't let Lu die. "Tomorrow," I said to Yin, another squadmate, "would you stay in the barracks?" I knew Yin had problems with his feet, which gave him a legitimate reason to request a release from labor. "Stay here and watch Lu, okay? I'll get permission from Captain Wang. Take care of Lu Haoqin until I get back."

That evening Yin reported how Lu had spent the day pacing back and forth in the narrow alley behind the barracks, refusing to talk. Yin watched Lu closely for three days, and nothing happened. On the fourth day he had to return to labor, so I went to the other nine teams in our company to ask if any sick pris-

oners would be staying behind from labor that morning. Most
of those men were penal criminals, but they were my only hope.
One prisoner with a large, ugly head agreed to watch Lu. "Sure,
we'll take care of your friend, no problem. Go ahead, leave him
to us!"

After the day's work, I rushed back through the gate, not
even stopping at the faucet. Inside the barracks, Lu Haoqin lay
motionless on the kang, his eyes open but glazed. Ugly Head
explained that Lu had tried again, this time driving a nail above
the window. The duty prisoner had pulled him down, and again
the doctor had revived him. Lu apparently had planned this
attempt carefully, waiting until the two prisoners on sick list
reported for lunch and stopped watching the door. Ugly Head
shrugged and turned away.

After this, Lu stopped speaking at all. At supper time he ate
only half his portion of wotou and soup. I asked for a talk with
Captain Wang. "If Lu kills himself, it will not be good for the
morale of the other prisoners," I told the captain. "I suggest
we assign someone to stay behind to watch him."

"If he wants to separate himself from the Party and the
people," Wang answered, "he is better dead. We have given him
the chance to reform himself, but he refuses. He is stubborn.
We cannot do anything more. He will make his own choice."
But then the captain paused, no doubt considering the risk to
his own record of reporting a suicide from his company to the
battalion commander's office. "Okay. I will give you one day.
Tomorrow you stay home from labor. Talk to Lu and make him
understand the consequences of his foolishness. If he continues
to resist, we will hold a struggle meeting for him."

For much of that night, I lay awake thinking. I could stay
behind only once. This would be my last day with Lu. I could
think of nothing to say, nothing that would give him a reason
to live.

"How come you didn't go out to labor?" Lu asked me sus-
piciously the next morning.

"I'm sick," I answered quickly.

Sitting on the kang, I began to reminisce aloud about our
native province. I talked about its natural beauty and about
someday looking out again at the dawn mist over Lake Tai, one
of the most scenic spots in China. Lu didn't respond.

I tried asking him about his mother. "I don't know anything about her," he snapped. "Anyway, she's not my real mother. I'm alone."

I tried talking about the food in Wuxi. "Hey," I said, "do you remember the spareribs braised in soy sauce? I'm going to find someone to bring us a box of spareribs, okay?"

"I don't like them," Lu replied coolly, and we sat for the rest of the morning in silence. By afternoon I could think of only one way to save him.

"Hey," I called, my voice soft. "Would you make love to me? Come on. Would you like to?" There seemed to be no other way to call him back, but Lu looked away.

"Do you remember the time you asked me and I refused?" I persisted. "Today we have another chance. For you and for me."

"No," he said, his voice so low that I could barely hear him. "I'm not interested."

I still couldn't give up. "Hey, come on. Try! I'm strong, I'm healthy. Maybe you'll like me."

"No." Lu spoke without interest or emotion.

"But you're so pretty," I insisted, trying to revive his will to live. "You're the pretty woman I saw before. Come on, put your arms around me." I pulled off my shirt.

"Nonsense," Lu answered. He had given up his only passion. We sat together silently until late afternoon when the prisoners returned from labor and filled the compound with their talking and arguing, shattering the stillness.

The next morning I awoke to a piercing shout sometime before the five-thirty call. "Come quick! Someone save him!" I ran outside. Already a small crowd had gathered.

Behind the barracks stood a row of cement posts with strands of wire stretched between them for drying grapes. Except during harvest season, we threw our straw hats on these posts and our dirty work clothes on the wires every night, hoping they would dry by morning. Lu had fastened a belt to the top of one of the posts. I saw that his feet dangled only one inch above the ground. This time Lu Haoqin had succeeded.

"Didn't you see him come outside? Didn't you watch him?" I shouted angrily at the duty prisoner as we stood in the eerie glow of floodlamps behind the barracks.

"Sure, I saw him come out, and I kept my eye on him while I made my rounds. He just paced back and forth, and I thought he couldn't sleep. Finally he leaned against that post. He seemed to be resting. The hats and clothes shaded him from the lights, and I forgot he was there."

More prisoners gathered, silent and expressionless. We heard the wake-up shout at five-thirty. Then the crowd dispersed, heading for the faucet and the latrine. It was time to eat and to labor. Another day had begun.

19

A Larger Bird Cage

*L*ocked away inside Qinghe Farm, I had little contact with the still-escalating political struggles of the Cultural Revolution. Sometimes from the guards, or from prisoners who had received visitors, I heard rumors about schools and universities closed down, factories ceasing production, and "educated youths" being "sent down" to the countryside in growing numbers, presumably to stem the violence in the cities. I knew vaguely that self-styled "rebel fighting groups" within many work units were trying to settle old scores and at the same time prove themselves the true exemplars of Chairman Mao's revolutionary line. But only much later would I learn about the most serious outbreaks of fighting, like the deadly power struggle between military units in the Southwest that battled each other with tanks and automatic weapons diverted from the Vietnam front. In 1967 and 1968 I had no idea that the violence in some parts of the country had moved beyond the level of social turmoil to a kind of civil war.

Isolated and self-absorbed, I worked in the fields each day and repeated slogans about combatting "revisionism" and promoting Mao Zedong thought each evening. As days merged into weeks and months into years, I grew more withdrawn. My family stopped sending letters and food packages to me after the sum-

mer of 1966, fearful of having any contact with a counterrevolutionary relative undergoing labor reform. I no longer cared
about changes in my surroundings or even about the hardships
and injustices of prison life. Having survived the most extreme
scarcity, I adapted indifferently to changes in camp routine,
labor assignment, and living conditions.

My outlook had begun to alter after the ordeal of solitary
confinement in 1965. Having come so close to death, I had
thereafter grown strangely at ease with my daily existence. I no
longer worried about my family or my future. My youth in
Shanghai and my student years in Beijing faded more and more
from memory. Prison became the only reality I knew. Life itself
was all I could ask for.

In the early years after my arrest, I had felt outraged at the
insults of the guards and the petty betrayals of my fellow prisoners. I had chafed under the police captains' arbitrary, sometimes sadistic, authority and later had felt troubled by my own
diminished humanity. All that had gone. Less and less often did
I think about Lu and Ao, who had left all this behind, or wonder
why I didn't join them in their retreat to a final oblivion. Like
an ox in the field, I ate, worked, and slept. One day became
indistinguishable from the next.

My two years at Qinghe Farm during the famine had taught
me how to labor in the mud, the reeds, and the rice paddies.
Back within the same walls in 1967, I began again to search for
frogs in the spring, to gather the leaves of new grasses in the
summer, and to steal the ripened grain from the fields in the
autumn. Inside my jacket I stuffed edible weeds and fistfuls of
dried straw to use as cooking fuel whenever I thought my pil-
fering would go undetected. I knew that the police preferred
to keep "one eye open and one eye shut" and ignore minor
infractions of discipline. Only during the harvest months did
they take seriously their mission to safeguard the state's grain
supply. For most of the year, they hardly bothered to search us
when we returned to the compound.

We all became expert at concealing our paltry gleanings,
dropping handfuls of rice kernels inside our jacket linings and
then emptying out the grain once we had reached the relative
safety of the narrow corridor behind the barracks where the
police rarely bothered to patrol. There we would build small

fires beneath our basins to boil anything edible we had foraged during the day. The guards knew we had no means of escape beyond the compound wall. Preoccupied by their own internal struggles and uncertain whether they would later be held responsible for the breakdown of China's public security system, they cared little about our clandestine cooking ventures. But despite our attentiveness to the patterns of surveillance, we could never eliminate the risk of random inspections.

One evening in August of 1967 when I squatted as usual in the shadow of the shoulder-high inner wall behind the barracks, trying to boil a few handfuls of wheat in my basin over a small fire, I suddenly noticed the prisoners tending pots on either side of me grab their basins, kick out their fires, and slink away. I looked quickly over both shoulders but saw nothing amiss, no reason for their caution, and I wanted to finish bringing the water in my pot to a boil. I got up just to check what had alarmed my squadmates, and met the stare of a police captain who stood just on the other side of the ten-inch-thick wall.

Instinctively I reached down to protect my porridge as he thrust a spade over the wall, trying to knock over my cooking pan. The rusty shovel blade struck my hand, leaving a deep gash above my left thumb. At such a moment my first thought, ingrained from years of hunger, would normally have been to salvage my food from the ground, but the blood flowing from my hand made me angry. I glared into the captain's eyes and ever so briefly sensed his discomfort. He was a human being, too, challenged in his act of petty cruelty and stripped for that moment of any moral authority. Without speaking, he turned away, ignoring my wound. I scooped up as much of the spilled wheat as I could, then reported to the clinic where the medical worker stitched up my wound.

That whole year passed unremarkably inside the farm. The political events ravaging the nation did not impinge on my life again until early in February 1968, shortly before the Spring Festival holiday, when one of our company captains read an urgent statement from the Beijing city government. A directive had arrived from Kang Shen, the Minister of Public Security and one of the leaders of the powerful "Small Group" charged with directing the Cultural Revolution. We would take another step to sweep away the "four olds." The Qinghe authorities, he continued, would resolutely pursue the goals of the Cultural Revolution by eliminating revisionism within the camp. On the following day the captains would conduct an inspection of all our personal belongings to make certain no one had concealed any reactionary materials. Before we reported for labor, we were to leave behind the keys to our suitcases and trunks. I wondered why suddenly one of the Cultural Revolution's top leaders was again attacking the "four olds," but I could not at that time guess that he was carrying out the orders of Jiang Qing, Chairman Mao's wife, to destroy any materials anywhere in the society that might reveal her own "reactionary" past as a movie actress in Shanghai in the 1940s.

I thought immediately about my hidden books. In 1967 before leaving Tuanhe Farm, I had managed to dig up the package containing my foreign novels and hide them beneath some old shoes inside my locked wooden trunk. The books had already sat undisturbed in the Qinghe storage room for a year. Whatever had prompted Kang Sheng's sudden directive, I still didn't want to give my last possessions up, so I said nothing about the contents of my trunk.

Captain Wang released us early from labor on the afternoon of the search so we could help the duty prisoners examine our suitcases. The disarray in the barracks shocked me. Never before had I seen such a thorough inspection. Clothing lay scattered on the floor, our sleeping mats had been overturned, even our quilts had been ripped apart to expose the cotton batting. Before I could straighten up my belongings, a duty prisoner named Zhu shouted my name, ordering me outside. In the yard lay a small mountain of boxes and suitcases. I saw the trunk containing my books in the pile.

"Anything that remains locked will be smashed open," the police captain declared. I could have opened my box right then in front of him and confessed that I had been wrong to conceal reactionary materials, but instead I made up my mind to resist. For some reason I felt determined to protect my books, even though I knew *Les Miserables* had no use inside the camps. I had neither the time nor the inclination to read literature, and if I were ever to return to a normal life, I could easily have replaced them. Yet some inner resolve made me refuse to give up the one thing of value I still possessed. Defiance, or perhaps stubbornness, overwhelmed both my caution and indifference.

I decided to gamble again, as I had in September 1966 when I buried the books at Tuanhe. This time I counted on my usefulness to the police as a labor leader, always reliable and ready to fulfill the daily production quota, to earn me some leniency. "One of those cases is mine," I said casually. "It's still locked because I've lost the key. There's nothing inside but some old shoes. Trust me, I've never lied to you."

"All boxes must be opened," insisted the captain. "No exceptions."

I returned to the barracks as if to search for the key, and told my decision to two squadmates, Wu and Li, both arrested not for political crimes but for petty theft. They urged me not to be foolish, but then they sensed my determination. "Okay, then steal the box back, exchange the contents, and return it to the pile," Li suggested. "It's the only way to save your books."

I asked my two friends to create a minor disturbance on the far side of the yard to divert Zhu's attention. A few minutes later they began to argue loudly. When he left to intervene, I grabbed my box from the pile and walked quickly inside the room. I noticed that my squad's study leader, named Zheng, a long-term Qinghe inmate and an activist who regularly reported to the police, was sitting at his space on the kang. Several other prisoners were also in the room trying to put their things back in order, so I hoped Zheng would not pay attention to me.

Working fast, I pulled a pair of worn shoes from the hole beneath my spot on the kang and thrust my books down inside. With a sweep of my arm, I tore down the length of mosquito netting that hung unused in winter along the wall behind my rolled-up quilt and shoved it on top of the old shoes in the trunk. By the time Zhu, the duty prisoner, had settled the dispute between my two friends outside, my box with its harmless contents sat inconspicuously among the others.

I returned to the kang to see Zheng walk purposefully outside toward the security office. A few minutes later the police captain shouted for my wooden case to be carried over for inspection. Only at that point did I begin to consider the possible consequences of my stubbornness.

After evening count Captain Wang called me in. "Where are your hidden books?" he shouted. "Are you still trying to oppose the government? Do you still want to obstruct Chairman Mao's Cultural Revolution?"

Hoping to counteract my earlier disobedience and my direct lie to my captain, I tried to seem cooperative. "In my room," I replied. Just then Zhu and Zheng arrived to deposit my books in the police office. I considered how pleased the captains would be to report to their superiors such a victorious result of their search.

For two days I waited. Each morning I went out to labor, but I noticed that each evening Liu and Zheng, the two activist members of my squad, would write busily in their notebooks during the study session. From their averted faces I guessed they were preparing reports to use against me in a struggle meeting. Neither of them liked me. This was a chance for them to get revenge and prove their loyalty to the police. Most likely they would accuse me of the triple crimes of lying to the police, cheating the Communist Party, and obstructing the Great Proletarian Cultural Revolution.

On the second night Captain Wang announced that a battalionwide struggle meeting would take place the following morning. I knew I would be the target, but I felt strangely calm. Those days in solitary confinement had relieved me of the fear of suffering. In that cement cell I had reached the limit of my endurance. I had known the black chasm of despair. Afterward nothing could frighten me. Whatever they wanted, I thought as I tried to fall asleep that night, my books, my labor, my youth, my life, they could just take it. I would not interfere. My resignation brought a freedom beyond police control. Waiting for the struggle session, I knew I could not prevent whatever would happen. Just let it come, I thought. Then I slept.

The next morning I heard the duty prisoners shouting for the other companies to come outside and report. When my company filed out, Captain Wang pulled me aside and ordered me to the police office. Standing inside that cluttered room, I imagined the twelve hundred prisoners seating themselves on the ground outside to witness my ordeal. Perhaps ten minutes passed before a duty prisoner led me to the front of the platform on which the company captains and the battalion commander had all taken their seats. Before me on the ground lay my novels, neatly arrayed in a line.

The battalion-level political instructor had arrived to preside over the meeting. He raised high his copy of Chairman Mao's quotations, and twelve hundred little red books waved in response. I waited, knowing that the opening quotation would establish the tone of the proceedings. "Our Great Leader Chairman Mao teaches us that revolution is not a dinner party!" he intoned shrilly. This was the harshest of Mao's teachings, the statement that could be used to justify any cruelty. We all knew the code. I understood that what followed would be terrible for me.

Like every struggle meeting, this one followed a predictable script. First the activist prisoners from several squads positioned in the audience began shouting accusations and slogans to arouse the onlookers and intimidate the victim. After the third chorus the political instructor interrupted: "So what is your judgment of Wu Hongda's crime? Should he be shot? Revolution can never be a dinner party!"

As the shouting resumed, four activists came forward, screaming at me to bend my head in submission. Two grabbed my shoulders, trying to push me to my knees as a further gesture of concession, insisting that I beg the Party for mercy. The other two jerked my arms high behind my back in the excruciatingly painful jet plane position.

When I struggled to remain standing, Captain Wang shouted, "Look at his counterrevolutionary attitude! Look how he opposes our Party, opposes our Great Leader, opposes our Great Proletarian Cultural Revolution!" As if in a spontaneous act of indignation, some ten people rushed forward, grasping my arms, kicking my legs, pummeling me with their fists, and forcing my knees to the ground. To keep me down, two of them stood with their full weight on my calves. All the time they stretched my arms high behind my back and jerked my head backward.

The jet plane posture was so unnatural and so painful that some involuntary rush of adrenaline made me shake off my attackers. I even managed to rise to my feet, but this act of apparent defiance only triggered further blows. In the midst of the beating, I somehow saw out of the corner of my eye one person raising a wooden club. It was Fan Guang, the study leader who had been sent along to supervise our ill-fated peach-picking expedition, now promoted to the status of duty prisoner because of his loyal service to the police. I knew instinctively that I had to fend off a blow to my head, and I held up my left arm to shield my face before Fan's spade handle crashed down. At that moment I felt no pain, but I could see the jagged edge of a bone protruding sharply against my jacket sleeve. My left hand dangled limply from my wrist. Blood streamed along my fingers and spattered on the ground.

Everyone gasped. I could see shock on the faces of the nearest prisoners, and even the police seemed scared. Struggle meetings were supposed to punish, but never to draw blood, and an unspoken rule prohibited the use of tools as weapons. Suddenly a group of my squadmates, instructed to sit up front to observe my humiliation at close hand, jumped to their feet. On their faces I saw outrage at the viciousness of my beating. Captain Wang stepped quickly down from the platform to prevent a fight. "Stop! Stop!" he yelled, waving his arms in the air and motioning for a duty prisoner to come and set fire to my books. That accomplished, he dismissed the audience immediately and ordered me led away.

At the clinic the doctor sutured my wound, then nudged the bone back into alignment and immobilized my arm with wooden splints. I stayed in the barracks for a week without reporting for labor, taking pills to prevent infection. On the seventh day they ordered me to the fields despite my sling. I could manage only light labor, so I spent the next four weeks pulling weeds with my right hand. The doctor had set the break skillfully, and the injury healed.

"Fan Guang is only a small peanut," I told my friends after they reported their retaliation. They described how they had waited for a moment in the fields when they were not observed, then beaten the despised running dog soundly and thrown him into the muddy water of an irrigation ditch. The police captain on duty received a report that Fan had made trouble about his labor assignment.

I had many times caused trouble for Fan Guang during labor, assigning him the job of loading 150-pound sacks of grain onto a truck, for example, when I knew he lacked the physical strength to manage the task. "I obey you in study sessions. Out here you obey me," I would shout. We hated each other, but, hearing my friends' account that evening, I felt no satisfaction at their revenge, only weariness at the seemingly endless struggle. "Leave him alone," I urged. "Remember that revenge always comes around in a circle."

In the months that followed the struggle session, I paid no attention to the world outside. Being the target of such violence had numbed me, and I cared nothing about what happened at Qinghe Farm. Another year passed.

Then sometime late in the fall of 1969 I began to notice that the police were behaving strangely. Usually we labored each day until nearly sunset, but during one week in October they dismissed us early for several days in succession. Twice the captain in charge of our evening study session did not appear to make announcements, nor did he instruct us to hold our usual weekly meeting to criticize minor breaches of discipline within our squad, like someone's failure to fulfill the day's labor quota or some instance of petty theft. On three evenings the duty prisoners did not even call us for the final head count. So unusual were these departures from routine that I knew the Qinghe authorities faced some major problem, but I had no way to guess what distracted their attention.

The irregularities continued without explanation until early December, when one of our team captains called all one hundred fifty of us together in the yard for an important announcement. A captain we had never seen before read a list of names to divide us into two groups. He dismissed one to the dormitory and ordered my group of eighty to remain behind for further instructions. In a wooden voice he listed our names again, followed by the political label of forced job placement personnel. We would have three days to pack up our belongings and prepare to move, the captain stated. That was all. He dismissed us. In that instant, with no preparation or excitement, my reeducation-through-labor sentence was revoked.

I returned to my barracks feeling dazed, trying to absorb the news that suddenly, after more than nine years, I was no longer a prisoner. With Lu and Li, who had also been reclassified, I decided to walk through the open compound gates, past the security guards, just to see whether we could move around

freely. No one challenged us. We walked along the road beside
the police families' buildings and vegetable gardens and saw
that the camp personnel were also packing. We had no idea
what the changes meant, but we relished that first taste of freedom. As forced job placement personnel we would be captives
still, but we welcomed the larger bird cage.

On the third day after our reclassification, the new captain
called us together again to announce that those in our group
of forced job placement personnel who were residents of Beijing
and Shanghai would be relocated in Shanxi province for assignment to the Wangzhuang Coal Mine. The others, whose
homes were outside the major urban areas, would return to
their native provinces and remain under the supervision of the
local security authorities. I had no idea which destination was
preferable or what living conditions I would soon face as an ex-
prisoner in a coal mine.

Rumors flew all that afternoon, and information reached
us through the duty prisoners that all sections of Qinghe Farm
were being emptied. The entire staff of Beijing Public Security
Bureau personnel and their families were preparing to leave.
Not until the following morning did we receive an official explanation.

"According to the Communist Party's 'Number One Order,' " the company commander read in a solemn voice from
a sheaf of documents, "Qinghe Farm will be closed." I listened
almost in disbelief to the announcement that Lin Biao, Chairman Mao's closest comrade-in-arms and chosen successor, had
ordered the country to mobilize for war against the Soviet
Union. The nation was to prepare for a major attack at any time,
the company commander continued. Heightened security measures required that all prisoners be moved to the interior provinces, away from the coastal regions, the major urban areas,
and the principal railheads. We had to observe strict discipline
during this time of threat to our motherland.

I stood in line while the duty prisoners distributed a full
day's rations of wotou and salted turnips, then returned to the
barracks to finish packing and wait for the trucks that would
ferry us to Chadian station. I tried to make sense of the commander's announcement, but I had no idea whether China was
truly on the brink of war with the Soviet Union. It seemed

equally plausible that Lin Biao's directive had political motivations. Perhaps the sudden mobilization was part of the protracted power struggle among the highest leaders, or an effort to distract attention from the economic and political disarray that had resulted from three years of factional fighting in the Cultural Revolution. Without access to information or news, I couldn't begin to judge these developments.

On the nine-hour train ride to Shanxi, I tried again to absorb the changes in my own situation. As I watched the flat reaches of the Hebei plain give way to the barren mountain slopes of Shanxi province, I wanted to feel relief and excitement. Instead I felt confusion mixed with anxiety about what life as a resettlement prisoner would bring.

At the small railway station where we disembarked, I saw that no uniformed police awaited our arrival. Representatives from the Wangzhuang Coal Mine took charge of our arrangements and organized us into temporary companies. They wore the same black cotton padded jackets as the workers and peasants milling about the station, so I assumed they must be mine administrative personnel.

My initial impression of my new surroundings was of a uniform color of gray. As I walked the three kilometers to the Wangzhuang facility, I could see only gray brick buildings coated with coal dust climbing up the rugged gray hillsides. I overheard one of the Qinghe police transferred along with us grumbling already about the local conditions. Clearly he would have preferred to stay in the Beijing security district rather than being sent to this remote mountain setting. But like us, he had no choice in his work assignment.

Inside the Wangzhuang gates, I stared curiously at a cluster of workers who had just completed a shift underground. Looking for clues about the life I would lead, I stared at their stiff protective helmets of woven twigs, their knee-high rubber boots, and their patched jackets and pants, grimy with coal dust. Weary eyes peered out from blackened faces, and I tried to imagine myself as a coal miner. Then I reached my dormitory. Instead of glass, paper covered the windows, while coal soot filmed the kang and the floor. Life here would not be easy.

From the men inside sprawled on the kang, I learned that the coal mine, administered by a detachment commander, a

Party secretary, and a hierarchy of Public Security Bureau personnel, was organized into prison-style companies. The twelve hundred of us who had just arrived from Qinghe Farm would join eight hundred long-term resettlement prisoners, some of whom worked raising vegetables or making bricks or running the kitchen, but most of whom worked underground.

I asked the men about the food. Everyone ate in the regular workers' canteen, they told me, and I grew excited, despite the living conditions. That meant I really would receive a salary for my labor, I thought, and I would have money. I could choose my own food in the cafeteria, and I could eat meat.

That evening I told myself again and again that I was no longer a prisoner, that here the front gates remained open, that I could walk freely to the village when I had time off from labor. I began to think that maybe my knowledge of geology or engineering would at last prove of some use, and I fell asleep the first night actually looking forward to my new situation.

The mine security captains kept us busy for two days with administrative procedures pertaining to our transfer and our labor assignments. They mixed the newcomers into squads of experienced workers and then briefed us about the three daily labor shifts, about safety precautions, and about the mine's alarm system. On the second day I received assignment to a construction and repair squad. My task would be to inspect and replace the wooden posts that supported the mine tunnels. That afternoon the women workers in the supply company issued us new rubber boots, utility belts, protective helmets, and head-lamps. I felt transformed. After almost a decade of field labor, I was being treated like a skilled worker. Impressed by the brand-new, expensive equipment, I was almost eager to begin this new assignment.

On the third day, however, we mustered outside our barracks for a political meeting. Then all two thousand of us sat down cross-legged on the ground in the open yard. Before us stood the Party secretary. Rather than a welcome he issued a stern warning. "The situation of the newly arrived resettlement workers is not yet stable," he declared sharply. "They may be thinking about their homes and families, they may not feel adjusted to labor in the coal mine, they may even want to escape. Such attitudes will not be tolerated. All of you must be aware that you remain under the dictatorship of the proletariat and that you will continue your thought reform." At that point a squad of uniformed police guards entered the yard, usually a signal that someone would be arrested. A ripple of tension spread across the rows of ex-prisoners. The distinctions I had begun to draw between the life of a prisoner and a forced job placement worker suddenly seemed premature.

"Some people have been under investigation, and the police have come to make arrests," the Party secretary declared. As if on cue, the captain shouted out a name. Immediately several men in black padded jackets, those whom I had assumed at the railway station were civilian coal mine personnel, pulled the alleged culprit out of the crowd. I watched with horror the official procedures for arrest in Shanxi province. One of the black jackets, whom I then realized must be a security policeman in civilian clothes, thrust the victim's arms behind his back while another pulled from his pocket a length of rope and expertly lashed it around one of the frightened worker's wrists. Instantly he passed the rope toward the man's chest, under one shoulder, behind his neck, and under the second shoulder before tying a quick slip knot onto the second wrist. A third security guard then kneed the accused man in the stomach and forced his chin sharply backward. The guard holding the rope pulled it tight, forcing the bound hands upward toward the back of the neck. This trussing took only a few seconds.

Within a minute or two the victim had fallen on the ground unconscious. I watched his face turn from red to dark brown to almost black before all the color drained away, leaving a deathly white. The first black jacket released the tension on the rope and began to slap the bound prisoner on the arms to restore circulation. Then they left him on the ground and dragged out the next person. The whole process seemed meant to punish and intimidate, not to incapacitate or kill, I thought.

One by one, the police captain announced the names of five more men accused of such crimes as repeated theft and attempted escape. The black-jacketed guards swiftly strung up each victim, waited until he had slumped to the ground, and then revived him. The procedure reminded me of the slaughtering of chickens. Later one of the experienced ex-prisoners at the mine told me that even the toughest hoodlum could not withstand this treatment. If the rope remained taut for more than five minutes, the victim's arms would be permanently crippled. During my nine years in the camps, I had seen many beatings but never the cold efficiency of this rope torture. The meeting left me shaken. At that moment the mine's open gates seemed to offer a cruel mockery of freedom.

20

Resettlement

At the Wangzhuang Coal Mine, known internally as the Shanxi Number 4 Labor Reform Detachment, the twelve hundred of us transferred from Qinghe Farm in December 1969 remained trapped within China's extended penal system. We existed in a world apart, stigmatized by our forced job placement status and subject to continual discipline and control. Despite the increased measure of freedom given to us as resettled prisoners, we still had to fear arbitrary punishment from the security guards and confinement in the solitary cells that marked the mine not as a regular industrial facility but as a labor-reform camp. We still had to criticize our squadmates in compulsory evening study sessions and demonstrate a continuing effort to remold our thoughts. But more oppressive even than this surveillance and control was the final realization that our lives would never be our own.

With a permit issued by the security guards, we could pass through the gates to the village below on our days off. We could sit together at mealtimes, talk casually among ourselves, and even interact with the mine's sixty women workers. We could write letters, receive visitors, request an annual trip home, and apply for permission to marry. But without a work certificate or grain coupons, we could not leave. Like Ao Naisong before me, I understood with a crushing finality that my assignment to this labor-reform enterprise offered no possibility of termination, no chance of returning to normal society.

All of us newly released from reeducation-through-labor and relocated because of the alleged threat of war with the Soviet Union began our lives as coal miners on our fourth day in Shanxi province, apprenticed to the experienced ex-prisoners within our squads. From them we heard frightening accounts of frequent injuries and fatalities within the mine. I wondered whether we had been adequately prepared for our task. Here we needed specialized skills rather than the sheer physical strength used in digging irrigation ditches and leveling rice fields at Qinghe. Handling heavy machinery and explosives required expertise and precision. A careless move could cause a gas explosion, a runaway railway car, a flooded passageway, or a mine collapse. I hoped the other newcomers had also paid strict attention to the safety regulations.

Underground labor at the mine continued around the clock in three shifts. Each morning the workers on my construction team got up at four o'clock, swallowed two wotou and a bowl of soup in the canteen, lined up at the storage warehouse to receive our equipment, and then reported at four-thirty to the mine entrance. Not until midafternoon did we see daylight.

Often it took us an hour to reach the appointed labor site inside the mine, and then, with only our headlamps to guide us, we scuttled for eight hours through the small side tunnels in the darkness, bent over at the waist in order to carry heavy pine replacement posts deep into the earth. My team was responsible for checking the strength of the existing support beams to find any that had been weakened by dynamite blasts or by the ongoing chemical erosion that caused dangerous wood rot inside struts that looked outwardly solid. Working quickly to prevent a collapse, we would pry loose the old supports and hammer in the fresh posts.

Midway through the eight-hour shift underground, the captain called a break for food and water. The worker from our team in charge of provisions would deliver to each squad's work site a bucket of wotou and two cans of drinking water. Thirsty after our labor, we could spare no water to wash the soot from our hands before eating. We resumed work until two o'clock, then stopped to wait for the squad leader to check our labor quota. At two-thirty we climbed back up through the spur passageways to the main tunnel and emerged wearily into the afternoon daylight at about three-thirty.

Each afternoon after I had turned in my equipment, I waited to use the communal bathhouse that served the two thousand workers. The continual scarcity of water throughout mountainous Shanxi province meant that little was available for the comfort and hygiene of resettlement coal miners. I came to consider myself fortunate if the waist-deep bathing pool that held only twenty men at a time had been changed that same morning, and more fortunate still if I could wash among the five hundred miners on the first underground labor shift. After the second and third shifts, the water would turn dark and foul smelling. If it sat unchanged for two days, the conditions were terrible, but we had no other way to scrub off the coal dust.

After the evening meal we reported to our dormitories at seven o'clock for a two-hour study session. Typically we read selections from Chairman Mao's works as well as *Shanxi Daily* and *People's Daily*. Sometimes we criticized a squad member who had not fulfilled his labor quota or who had committed a minor infraction of discipline, most often petty theft or disturbing the peace.

The political atmosphere remained tense and threatening, largely because of the precariousness of Chairman Mao's control after three years of internal fighting in work units across the country. I didn't want to provide any opportunity for the activists in my squad to gain advantage by using me as a target, so I took care to talk only about commonplace topics, and I tried to interact with fellow workers who were former penal criminals and not intellectuals. Each day I met my labor quota, and each evening I read the newspaper and recited the required passages from Mao's works in study session.

Early in January we learned that the mine, like many other work units throughout the country, had been placed under military control. Beginning in 1968 Chairman Mao began calling up units of the army to take over the administration of major universities, factories, and propaganda organizations, like *People's Daily*, to put an end to internal factional fighting and reestablish social stability and industrial production. A People's

Liberation Army commander from the provincial capital of Taiyuan, whom we addressed as Army Representative Li, arrived
one morning with his young assistant to take charge at Wangzhuang, superseding the authority of the detachment commander and the Party secretary. Later I learned that Representative Li's main task, although never stated, was to discipline
any Public Security Bureau personnel who were not strictly
loyal to Chairman Mao and Lin Biao.

A few days after his arrival, Representative Li decided to
tighten workers' discipline within the mine. Every night a crowd
of male workers stood outside the women's dormitory, shouting
and whistling for the women to come out.

Like the men, most of these women had been arrested originally for penal crimes, not for political offenses. About one-
third of them were single. They lived by their wits and their
instincts. Every night quarrels broke out and sometimes open
fights as the men grabbed at the women, jockeying for their
favors. Most of the women, even some who had husbands and
families at home, took lovers and sex partners in the camp.

Representative Li announced that all the single women,
some of whom by then lived as virtual prostitutes, would be
sent as forced job placement personnel to the Shanxi Number
4 Prison on the outskirts of Taiyuan. There they would be assigned to factory work making garments or manufacturing toi-
letries like toothpaste. The new policy met immediate resistance. Many in the women's company enjoyed the sexual contact
with the male workers. They also feared that labor conditions
would be even harder in the prison than working in the supply
division at the mine, so they tried to find ways to remain behind.
Marriage to another resettlement worker was one way to gain
exemption from the decree.

I had always found the raucous nightly quarrels unpleasant
and had wanted nothing to do with the prison women, even
though I understood their resistance to the transfer. Soon after
Representative Li's decree, an older worker named Wang, one
of two other political prisoners in my squad, asked me to visit
his home the next Sunday at noon to eat dumplings. He had
been arrested in 1950 because of his work for the Nationalists
prior to Liberation. A gentle person with a broad open face, he
had graduated from middle school and worked at the mine.

Several years earlier he had married another ex-prisoner, and together they had restored one of the abandoned cave houses dug years before into the loess hillsides above the mine. These uninhabitable dwellings were assigned as living quarters to any ex-prisoners who could get permission to wed.

Wang had settled into a simple domestic routine. Each day he reported for labor followed by political study with the rest of us, but then at nine o'clock each evening he could escape. He could leave behind the smoke-filled, coal dust-covered room in the dormitory. He did not have to keep company with the fifteen men jostling for space on the lice-infested kang. He did not have to listen to their curses or their boasting, and he did not have to watch them spit with abandon on the concrete floor. For eight hours each night he could enjoy the rough comfort of his own home. Curious about such a life away from the mine, I accepted his invitation for lunch.

Wang's wife, a cheerful, intelligent woman of fifty, ladled steaming dumplings into my bowl, laced them with strong Shanxi vinegar, then asked me whether I was thinking about marriage. I assured her that I was not interested. She replied that I should think it over because if I were married, I could eat dumplings at home on Sundays and sleep comfortably in the winter months with my wife on a heated kang.

I told her I had long ago discarded the idea of marriage. Since my forced job placement status would never end and I could not change my job or my workplace, I refused to consider marrying and raising a family. I could not stand having my children forever branded as the offspring of a counterrevolutionary rightist. Nor did I have any wish to take an ex-prisoner as a wife, someone who had been driven to crime in her early life, or even a simple peasant woman from a nearby commune. The whole prospect repelled me, as did the alternative of finding a casual sex partner at the mine. I preferred to accept the loneliness of my single life.

Wang's wife listened to my reasons, but then persisted in her effort at persuasion. She knew someone older than I who had undergone a surgical sterilization so that there would be no possibility of an unwanted family, she explained. Not wanting to seem rude or ungrateful, I turned our conversation to other matters. Over the next few days, Wang pursued the topic of my finding a wife. "You wouldn't need to have any special feeling or even have sex," he urged me. "It's just a practical way to improve your life. If you are still thinking that someday you can return to your university, you are crazy! That time is over. You must be realistic."

Wang invited me a second time to his home for a meal. Seated on the kang was a neat, pleasant-looking woman named Shen Jiarui. She was a squad labor leader in the women's company, and she told me she was thirty-nine years old. I was then thirty-three. For some reason I deliberated only a few moments before making a sudden decision to marry. Why not, I thought. We are both human beings, we are both ex-prisoners, we share a similar fate. Neither of us owns any possessions, neither of us has any real freedom, so we will not blame or accuse or use each other. At that moment, simple parity seemed enough. Even in normal society, I thought, many couples meet only on their wedding day after a prearranged marriage. They never expect their union to provide love or happiness but rather convenience and economic support. Why should I ask for more?

We agreed to write letters of application to our company security captains requesting permission to marry. Believing that we were trying to circumvent the new policy reassigning the single women to the prison in Taiyuan, they refused to give us permission, but Shen said she would not give up. She had developed a special relationship with Representative Li, who liked her and often talked with her when he visited the warehouse. She told me she would appeal to the PLA commander. Also in January 1970 the political situation changed inside the mine. While I was waiting for Representative Li's response, my team captain suddenly called an evening meeting.

"Serious counterrevolutionaries" were continuing their plots to undermine the Party's control, he declared. A new "campaign to attack counterrevolutionaries" had begun, and we should pay strict attention to the "Six Articles." He referred to a Public Security Bureau document issued in 1968 that authorized serious punishment for anyone suspected of opposing the Cultural Revolution or the leadership of Chairman Mao at the height of the factional violence. When I heard this document mentioned again, I knew the political struggle would take on new intensity. I silently told myself to show even greater enthusiasm each day when I declared my loyalty and support for Chairman Mao and Lin Biao, his "closest comrade in arms."

Then the captain announced new disciplinary procedures. Beginning that day all workers would be confined to their teams. Married couples would live separately in their dormitories. We would labor each day and then report back to our own rooms. We were not to associate or talk with anyone outside our own team. Everyone felt apprehensive at these orders, not knowing what would follow. The atmosphere grew very tense. I wondered how I would be able to speak with Shen Jiarui. I had to know whether her request to Representative Li had been successful.

The next evening I spotted her in the cafeteria and walked quickly to stand beside her in line. "I got the approval," she said. Right away my squad leader ordered me to report to the team captain. In the office three captains listened to the squad leader's accusation that I had contacted someone outside my company. Then one of them threw a rope onto the floor.

"What were you doing?" barked the senior captain. "Don't you know the rules? You have broken discipline." Then he ordered the assistant captain, "Tie him up!"

I knew the rope treatment would be terrible for me. "Wait!" I said. "Let me tell you what we talked about."

"It doesn't matter," he shouted, grabbing my arm.

"She talked to Representative Li," I shouted. The captain hesitated. "He gave permission for us to marry."

They exchanged glances. They had to let me go and submit to Representative Li's orders, even though they hated being overruled. After that no one stopped me when I spoke to Shen in the cafeteria.

A few days later the captains grudgingly granted us one day off from work to register our marriage at the village commune headquarters, two hours away in the valley. On January 22, 1970, we signed our names on the legal certificate below the traditional characters meaning "double happiness." With that simple gesture I married someone I hardly knew. I felt very strange as we walked together back up the dirt road and across the hills. Representative Li had instructed that we be assigned one of the abandoned caves above the mine. Maybe later we would develop some feeling for each other, I thought. I resolved to try to build up a relationship with this quiet, resourceful woman.

For two months, while we stayed confined at night to our separate dormitories, Shen and I spent our free time between our labor shifts and our study classes digging out the cave to make it habitable. While we worked, we had some time alone. The entrance had entirely collapsed, and removing the hard-packed loess dirt was slow, heavy work. We used our mine pick-axes for excavating and a hand cart to remove the loosened earth. Finally we managed to carve out a door opening that measured nine feet high by ten feet wide and a living space that extended ten feet into the hillside. We left a square mound of soil at the front to serve as a kang and hollowed lengthwise passageways beneath it to allow the fire from the mud-brick cooking stove to warm our bed. By early March we had installed a stovepipe to vent the coal smoke, whitewashed the inside walls, and carried over from our separate dormitories some of our possessions. Each night I returned for study meetings and later slept with my squadmates on the kang.

Our political meetings each evening were longer and harsher than before as the squad leader urged us to uncover the class enemies and hidden counterrevolutionaries in our midst. Everyone worried about being accused of disobedience or disloyalty, and the opportunists among us found many chances to report on others as a way of gaining extra privileges during this movement to "clean the class ranks." In each squad personal antagonisms and resentments simmered. I might as well have never left the dog-eat-dog world of the prison camps. It was a relief each afternoon to leave the political tensions behind and work with Shen Jiarui on our cave.

One day while we rested, Shen said she wanted to tell me her story. Before her arrest she had been a librarian at the Railway Institute in Beijing where her husband, a scientist who had studied at an American university before Liberation, taught on the faculty. With him she raised four children, but he objected to the friendships she formed with foreign students and faculty at their college, and they quarreled. In 1962 they divorced, and the Party committee awarded him custody of the children. Two days later the Party assigned him a job in Shanghai, and the whole family moved away.

Shen lived temporarily with her father until she found work at the Foreign Languages Press. Later she formed a relationship with a co-worker who was a black American veteran, a former POW from the Korean War who had stayed on in China. Grateful for his promise to use his connections with the Kenyan embassy to take her out of China, she planned to marry him. She knew that such an interracial relationship would bring sharp disapproval from the Party authorities, but she hoped that his diplomatic connections would protect her.

Many times the Party leaders at her Institute criticized her, she explained, and she realized that when she went out to meet the American she was always followed. She refused to be intimidated. Then in 1965 she was arrested for having engaged in "illicit relations with foreigners," a serious crime tantamount to treason. Her fiancé, she told me, was deported to Kenya after she was taken to prison, and she never saw him again. I felt shocked to hear about Shen's experiences. When she finished, I said that I didn't want to ask her any questions, I didn't want to hear more about her previous life. Her past was her own.

Before we completed the work on our cave, Shen's oldest son, then nineteen, arrived unannounced one afternoon. Shen looked shocked. She had lost all contact with her children after being denied the right to see them eight years earlier. The boy had been assigned to work in the countryside in Inner Mongolia, he said, and was determined to find some way to transfer away from the harsh conditions in that remote area. From an uncle in Beijing, he had learned of his mother's assignment to the coal mine. That evening Shen Jiarui learned what had happened to her family since her arrest.

First her sons' father had been labeled a "bourgeois authority" in the early months of the Cultural Revolution, largely because of his American education, and confined to the university's makeshift prison under supervision of a rebel group. Wanting to qualify as Red Guards, the two oldest sons, then fifteen and thirteen, denounced their father for his counter-revolutionary crimes. They even joined a Red Guard team sent to smash the bourgeois possessions in their own home, which included a radio and a camera. Like many children left unattended during those years, the sons resorted to petty theft. In 1968, along with thousands of other youths, they were sent to labor in remote parts of the countryside, one to the steppes of Mongolia and the other to Heilongjiang, the province bordering Siberia. Before they left home, their father told them that their mother was an imperialist spy who had died in prison.

Family tragedy was commonplace during the Cultural Revolution, but this one suddenly became my responsibility. I was thirty-three, and I didn't know what relationship I could have to this young man of nineteen. Shen Jiarui and I had been married just slightly longer than a month when he moved into the partially finished cave. Some nights Shen got permission to stay with him. I reminded her of our previous agreement that children would not play any part in our marriage, but Shen insisted that I was now a stepfather and that she needed my help to find her other three children. The oldest boy arranged for temporary family leave and stayed in our cave for six weeks. In my free time I began to teach him English, math, and geography, and he learned quickly. From then on, he lived with us for five months of each year.

One morning in March, I reported as usual for labor at four-thirty to learn from a grim-faced police captain that Representative Li had ordered work halted for the entire day. When the captain summoned us for a battalionwide afternoon meeting, we noticed immediately that a military jeep had parked just inside the compound. We had no way to guess who would be the target of disciplinary action this time. Then a squad of uniformed police strode to the platform. Their captain shouted into the microphone, "Pull out the active counterrevolutionary Yang Baoyin!"

On command we raised our clenched fists and began to shout in response to the accusations of the activists scattered among us, "Down with counterrevolutionary Yang Baoyin!" "To resist reform is the way to death!" "Bend your head and admit your crime!" "Reform hard, become a new socialist person!" We followed up these slogans with the usual cries of "Long live the Cultural Revolution!" "Long live our Great Leader Chairman Mao Zedong!" As we shouted, three members of the mine's black-jacketed security police dragged forward a person bound tightly with a rope. He could neither walk nor raise his head, but on the platform one guard yanked back on his hair to show us his face.

The police captain shouted that Yang's crimes included stubbornness and resisting reform, then added something about his having attacked Chairman Mao Zedong. Static from the loud-speakers distorted the words, and I could hear only that the prisoner's sentence was immediate execution. As I walked back to the dormitory, I could see several security guards standing over a limp body on the dusty ground beside a dry creekbed. Two days later everyone whispered the details of the grisly scene. The executioner had shot the prisoner at close range, severing the head. He had then scooped out the brains and given them to one of the mine captains named Li, whose seventy-year-old father had eaten them for their medicinal qualities.

I tried to learn why Yang had received the death sentence. Rumors spread that he had been arrested originally for some kind of street crime and imprisoned for five years of reeducation through labor. After being reclassified as a forced job placement worker, Yang was sent to Wangzhuang. Half a year later he had requested leave to visit his home village, apparently to see a woman, but had failed to return after his travel permit expired. The mine security office notified the local police, who found Yang and brought him back. Failure to return was considered equivalent to escape, and the punishment for this disobedience was five weeks in solitary confinement.

I also heard that while Yang was in that cell, isolated and resentful, he had written on a cigarette pack the characters, "Down with Chairman Mao." People said that he had grown defiant after several weeks of incarceration. Whatever his intention, that subsequent offense sealed his fate. The PLA commander chose him as an example to instruct the rest of us about the consequences of counterrevolutionary insubordination. After that display of revolutionary-style justice, intended as a warning to the rest of us, the high tide of the political movement passed, and I moved with Shen Jiarui into our cave.

By the summer of 1970, Shen had succeeded in contacting her second son in Heilongjiang and establishing that her third child, a daughter, was happy with her father and stepmother and would continue living with them in Shanghai. When she learned that her youngest son was about to be sent to a foster home, I agreed to adopt him. Because we found we could not care for him in Shanxi, he moved in with my father and sister

and attended middle school in Shanghai. After all of these difficult arrangements had been made, we settled at last into a
simple domestic routine.

My only obligations, outside of my regular labor and political study, were providing our cooking fuel and replenishing
the water supply in the large ceramic cistern outside our door.
When I left the mine at the end of my shift, I always hoisted a
large chunk of coal onto my shoulder and climbed the twenty
minutes up the path to my cave. I rested briefly, then headed
back down the hill with my shoulder pole and two iron buckets
to fill at the communal faucet. I spent my remaining free time
building a small walled courtyard in front of our cave, making
use of the dirt we had excavated. I also helped Shen Jiarui plant
cabbages, tomatoes, and beans in our dooryard, and I built a
coop so that we could raise two chickens as a source of fresh
eggs.

As the months passed, a bond of mutual concern grew between us. The political movement that had thrown us together
had receded, and the tense period of searching out hidden class
enemies came to an end. The PLA commander had returned to
Taiyuan. For the first time since my arrest, I found some sense
of peace. After fifteen years of almost continual struggle and
fear, I believed I could partly let down my guard. The worst
threat for now seemed to be the petty antagonisms among the
workers.

My squadmates remained quick to criticize each other.
Often a small provocation became an opportunity for revenge.
Usually I avoided these petty squabbles, but one evening in study
class my own temper flared. I had worked the morning shift,
loading huge rocks into a mine cart and hauling the heavy loads
through the tunnels for more than eight hours. Accidentally my
cart had bumped into the cart of another squad member sometime that morning. The squad member, who already harbored
a grudge against me, claimed the incident was my fault. I replied
angrily that it was his fault. "Watch out," he snarled at me. "I'll
teach you a lesson at the first chance!" That evening when the
squad labor leader began talking about problems with the day's
production effort and issuing instructions for the next day's assignment, this squad member started protesting that I had in-
tentionally tried to block him from completing his labor quota

by knocking into his cart. At first he called on the leader to criticize me in front of the others for this mistake, but then as his anger grew, he reached out to pull me down from the kang, insisting that I had to report to the captain's office. Had he only accused me, I would have let the provocation pass, but when he grabbed me, I felt a direct physical challenge. I jumped up and hit him. He struck back, causing the squad leader to call the duty prisoners to restrain us. They tied both of us up and led us away to the row of confinement cells.

Solitary confinement at the mine was far less punishing than what I had known at Tuanhe Farm. Workers held for breaches of discipline were usually released after several hours, once they had confessed their wrongdoing. They received regular rations of wotou and water so that their strength would not be reduced or their labor productivity impaired. That evening I waited confidently for the security captain to come and criticize me so that I could confess my mistake and apologize for fighting. But after a couple of hours had passed, I realized I would have to spend the night in that small, windowless room, which contained no bed, not even a toilet bucket, and measured about six feet square.

In one corner I found an old copy of *People's Daily*, which I spread out on the tamped earth floor. I fell asleep. The next morning when the duty prisoner shouted for me to come out, I assumed that he would send me back to labor, but I had clashed with this man before, and he had apparently chosen this moment to take his revenge. "What have you done?" he shouted at me. "This time you have committed a big mistake. You have trampled on *People's Daily*, the mouthpiece of the Party. You have still not reformed yourself. You continue to oppose the revolution!" With those accusations he released my squadmate to return to labor and locked me again in the cell.

I felt shocked at this vindictive use of authority. My guard, who was a resettlement prisoner like me, had the power to suppress and humiliate me and also to keep me from reporting for work. At noontime the security captain arrived to ask what I had done. I admitted I had slept on the newspaper, but said that I hadn't meant to insult the Party, that it had been a mistake and I was sorry, and he told me to get out and go to work. By then I was four hours late, and I had to endure the labor leader's criticisms while struggling to meet my quota in half the usual time.

Not until January 1972, when our team captain suddenly ordered us into the yard for an important announcement from the central government, did I have to pay serious attention again to political affairs. That day the detachment commander strode to the platform and ordered us to listen seriously to his report. Then he read a brief announcement that Lin Biao, whom I knew as Chairman Mao's most trusted ally, had hatched an unsuccessful plot to overthrow the government and had died in a plane crash over Inner Mongolia. "A new stage in the class struggle has begun," the commander declared threateningly. "Some enemies want to use this opportunity to oppose the Communist Party. We must increase our vigilance."

Ordered back to the dormitory for a political discussion, I watched my squadmates' reactions. Many of them seemed unmoved by the news of this coup attempt by the country's second most powerful leader, but I feared that we, as ex-prisoners and the society's "bad elements," stood to suffer from the renewed attention to class struggle. Always we were the first targets of control by the organs of the people's dictatorship, the first to be used as examples of the dire fate that would befall any who refused to submit to the Party's authority. I guessed also that my squad leader had been instructed to watch my reactions with particular care. As one of the few intellectuals in the squad, I would be considered particularly dangerous at such an unstable time, capable of spreading counterrevolutionary ideas and inciting others to action. I had no idea what had really happened to cause Lin Biao's fall from favor, but I did know that whenever Chairman Mao felt his power threatened, a renewed effort at social control was launched.

I tried to make sense of the scanty information. The plane crash explanation seemed likely to have been contrived, a cover for some hidden conflict inside the government. I knew the Party leaders had been jockeying for power during the Cultural Revolution, and I wondered whether the sudden demise of Chairman Mao's closest ally signaled a weakening of his own authority and perhaps even the coming end of his power. Outwardly, as in previous political crises, I supported earnestly the most recent shift in the official line and denounced the evils of

Lin Biao as enthusiastically as I had for the past two years wished him a long, long life. But secretly I began to hope that the end of Chairman Mao's rule might lie not too far ahead.

The crisis seemed to pass. I remained watchful, but no one singled me out for special criticism. The newspapers published strident editorials about the need to root out supporters of Lin Biao and Confucius, now suddenly linked across the centuries as diehard revisionists obstructing the path to socialism, but inside the Wangzhuang mine we carried on with our labor without any special emphasis on political struggle. In the spring of 1972, I was even assigned a position of greater responsibility. The mine leaders decided to take advantage of my engineering background and transferred me from the construction crew to a technical squad. From then on my daily task was to measure the level of poisonous carbon monoxide that accumulated in the tunnels.

The new assignment had many advantages. Equipped with an expensive calibrating instrument imported from West Germany, I patrolled the tunnels to monitor the air quality. Later I wrote up reports recommending where and how to increase the circulation of oxygen inside the mine. Not only was I freed from heavy labor, but I had no daily quota to meet, and I could move about independent of the movements of the other workers. Sometimes I could even crawl into a niche in one of the side passages, turn off my headlamp, and fall asleep. The police technicians trusted my ability and relied on me to reduce the volume of their own work. Even though my future remained bleak, at least my labor was less burdensome than at any time in the past twelve years.

21

The Journey Back

During the Cultural Revolution local Public Security Bureau cadres approved requests from resettlement prisoners for annual home leaves selectively. Those labeled as counterrevolutionaries, especially if they lived in large cities where the fighting had directly threatened state control, were rarely allowed to travel. An ex–penal criminal from the nearby Shanxi countryside could usually visit his family without difficulty, but an ex–political prisoner like me was unlikely to receive permission to visit Shanghai. Even though I had saved enough money for the train fare in 1970, I hesitated about submitting a request. I knew that my travel certificate would be stamped by the Shanxi Number 4 Labor Reform facility, making it clear at each stage of my journey that I was not an ordinary citizen but a former labor-reform prisoner. I worried that I might be attacked in the streets or on the train as one of the "five kinds" of enemies or that my presence at home might bring shame to my family. Only in 1974 did I decide the political situation was stable enough so that I should apply.

I told the captain in charge of discipline, named Li, that I had been away from home for seventeen years, and that I had to go back to arrange for the burial of my stepmother's ashes. My family had already begun trying to purchase a small plot of land in Wuxi overlooking Lake Tai where she might rest forever near the place of her birth. Because of the guilt I felt at not being able to ease her burdens before her death, this seemed to me a special responsibility. It also provided a sufficient reason to request permission to visit my family. I still worried about the risks of travel during the "high tide" of the anti–Lin Biao, anti-Confucius movement, but when my application was approved, I prepared to leave. Captain Li instructed me to register at the local police station in Shanghai as soon as I arrived.

I didn't need to show my travel certificate to buy a local train ticket to Taiyuan, but at the provincial capital, I had to produce all my documents when I wanted to continue on to Shanghai the following morning. The railway agent hesitated, fired at me a list of questions about my crime and warned me about being obedient and returning on time, but eventually issued a ticket. I decided not even to consider finding a small hotel to spend the night, as I would have had to produce my papers and subject myself to questioning a second time. Instead I stretched out on a bench to sleep in the station. At midnight two railway police shook me awake to check my papers. I saw that they were detaining anyone without proper authorization to travel. They ordered me to report to the security office for questioning. "Where are you going?" the captain on duty demanded. "What is your crime? How long have you been undergoing reform?" I felt humiliated by such treatment, but after an hour they released me. Early the next morning I boarded the train.

From the Shanghai station I followed the familiar streets to my home. Much had changed. I had not written my family in advance of my visit. My number four sister, who worked as a middle-school teacher and lived at home with her daughter, opened the door at my knock. She seemed very nervous to see me. "Why did you come back?" she asked. "Is everything okay? Is there any problem? Did you get permission to leave? Show me your travel certificate." As her questions tumbled out, her voice rose almost to a shout. I could see she didn't know whether to believe me, and I realized that my sudden arrival caused her great fear. I had hoped for a very different welcome.

"Tell me where the neighborhood police station is, and I'll

go register," I replied coldly, handing her my papers. She seemed to relax as her eyes scanned the travel documents, but my youngest sister grabbed the papers from her hand and ran out the door. She had to report immediately to the police station, she called out. A few minutes later she returned with a stern-faced local security officer, who repeated many of the questions I had been asked at the railway station in Taiyuan. "Where have you come from? When will you return? How was your reform in the camps? How was your labor performance?" The process took about twenty minutes.

"Behave yourself," he warned me as he left. "You are not permitted to travel outside of the city limits without notifying us. You must return on time. Report to us before you leave!"

Late in the afternoon Father returned. He looked shocked to see me, as if I were a ghost. I didn't want my visit to upset him as he was still recovering from the effects of a mild stroke earlier that year. I noticed immediately that he could not use his left arm, and his speech came haltingly. My number four sister did most of the talking.

As we sat drinking tea, no one mentioned the family's problems. I asked casually about each of my brothers and sisters. My older brother and his wife worked in Nanjing, my number five sister lived in a dormitory at the radio factory where she worked as an engineer, my number seven brother remained in the far northwestern province of Xinjiang, where he had worked on a commune since 1964, and my youngest brother Wu Hong-ren, whom we still called Maodao, had suffered some mental problems. He was resting in a PLA recovery center, arranged by one of our cousins, in Suzhou.

My sister offered no details about anyone's past, and I didn't ask her to elaborate. So ingrained was the habit of silence, so intense the fear of criticism and punishment, that no one dared expose their personal problems. Besides, everyone had suffered, no one could help, and no one wanted to get involved in the difficulties of others, even if they were family members. I said nothing about my own ordeal, and no one asked what had happened since they last saw me during the summer vacation of 1957. Instead we spent the time chatting casually about our meals, the price of food in the shops, the weather, nothing more. The obvious tensions within the family made all of us uncomfortable, but I felt grateful just to be home. For years I had not expected ever to return to Shanghai.

I visited only one friend during my home leave, a former classmate from junior middle school whose father was British and who told me that his life had been very difficult, that the Red Guards had come several times to harass his parents and ransack his home. I said nothing about my own experiences, but I did confide the deep affection I still felt for Meihua. With his encouragement, I decided one afternoon to visit Meihua's sister, whose name was Meipin. I found that their once gracious two-story home with its lovely garden had become a retired workers' rest house, but someone there knew the address of the family's small flat nearby.

As I walked through a street market to reach the apartment building, I noticed a girl of perhaps sixteen following me and staring at me intently. "Come," she said, pulling at my hand. "Come with me. My mother is Meipin." I guessed that my school friend had notified Meipin that I would pay a visit, and the girl must have been sent outside to watch for a strange man in his late thirties. Later I learned that she recognized me from one of Meihua's photographs.

At the door Meipin greeted me warmly. Inside the room I could see Meihua sitting in a chair reading, but she didn't look up. "Don't talk too long," Meipin urged me as she left us alone. Then Meihua turned her face, but for several moments neither of us moved. I sat down across from her, but we still avoided each other's eyes. "I've just come back," I said to break the silence.

"How have you been?" she asked quietly.

I found it difficult to answer, so I returned her question.

"I suppose everything is fine with you," she said quickly. "How many children do you have?"

"Don't joke," I replied, conscious of the resentment in her words.

"Answer my question," she repeated.

"I'm not married, and I don't have any children," I said, forgetting in the nostalgia and pain of the moment the life that I shared with Shen Jiarui.

"How come?" she asked sharply. "Don't lie to me."

"How can you ask?" I said. "I'm still confined to the labor

camp, to a coal mine in Shanxi province. I cannot lie about that."

Meihua said nothing. On her face I saw shock and sudden understanding. "Now do you understand why I have never married?" I asked.

"How did you manage to come back?" she asked.

"I received permission for a visit home, but I will return tomorrow," I explained quietly. Then she cried. The tears streamed down her cheeks. Trying to control my own emotions, I stood up and touched her head to comfort her, but she brushed my hand away.

"Tell me about yourself," she said in a voice just above a whisper.

"I was arrested in 1960, and I've been in the camps until today," I said. "I don't want to talk about it. What about you?"

Meihua told me that in 1958 she had been assigned as a teacher to a training school for coal miners in the Northeast, that she had married a mining engineer in 1962, and that she had three daughters. She tried to smile. I stopped myself from asking why she had rejected me in 1957. "Maybe it's better this way," I said. "I don't know what would have happened to us if we had stayed together during these seventeen years."

Meipin called from the doorway that it was time for me to leave. "Half an hour is enough for you to talk," she said. "You two each have your responsibilities."

The next day I boarded the train for Taiyuan. I told Shen Jiarui nothing about my meeting with Meihua. Like hers, my past was my own.

The atmosphere grew more tense at Wangzhuang as 1974 passed. Every day we read newspaper editorials about the "antiright deviationist campaign," a fierce attack waged by Mao's wife, Jiang Qing, and her supporters to protect the ailing chairman's power. Directed against the thousands of cadres and intellectuals who had been persecuted during the Cultural Revolution and had recently begun returning to their jobs, it was in fact a campaign to crush Mao's rivals within the Party, Premier Zhou Enlai and Deng Xiaoping. I had not expected the power struggle to affect resettlement prisoners, but one afternoon in 1975 the team captain appeared in the dormitory during study session and announced that no one could leave the barracks, everyone had to remain inside. I went to bring my quilt down from my cave, required suddenly to live together with my squad. No one knew what had happened or why the mine authorities were exercising such tight control.

The next morning the captain came again to the barracks with a list of names. He called out several people from each squad, including me, told us each to bring a pen, and ordered us outside to sit in rows on the ground. Nearly a thousand sat together in my group, while the rest of the mine workers were ordered to another part of the yard. I looked at the faces around me, trying to guess the reason we had been set apart. All those near me, I realized, were educated and knew how to write, while those who were illiterate sat apart.

The captains in charge of the meeting passed each of us a sheet of paper and ordered us to write whatever words they read out. I felt frightened, because that day they carried guns. What followed was a list of perhaps sixty words, seemingly random, like "mao," "fan," "da," "zhong," and "xiao." They told us to finish and sign our names at the bottom, along with our company and squad number. From the selection of words and the inclusion of the characters for Deng Xiaoping's name, I could tell that someone must have written a "reactionary" letter or poster, perhaps critical of Mao Zedong and expressing support for Deng Xiaoping. The mine leaders were trying to identify the handwriting of the "diehard element" who had opposed the Chairman.

Several hours later the captains returned to the dormitory with a second list of names. Again my name was called. This time about 150 workers were herded into a smaller yard. The team captain stood before us. "You face a very dangerous situation," he warned. "Remember the Party's policy. If you confess, your treatment will be lenient; if you resist, you will be treated harshly. It's not too late to confess. Otherwise you are responsible for whatever happens! I will give you five minutes to think it over." No one spoke. "Okay," the captain resumed, "since you refuse to confess, we will discover the truth." He passed out a second sheet of paper, then warned us not to pretend because he already knew everything that had happened. No one should try to disguise his handwriting. If anyone deceived the Party, he would have to answer for that in addition to his original crime. Then the captain read out a long list of names and phrases, ending with "Deng Xiaoping."

The next morning we returned to labor, and I had no idea what had happened. Everyone was afraid to talk about the situation, fearful that we would be reported. We carefully acted as if nothing had occurred. Not until several months had passed did I learn that eleven people were arrested following that incident, accused of opposing the revolution because they supported Deng Xiaoping and opposed the growing power of Jiang Qing and the three Party cadres from Shanghai who with her schemed to succeed the ailing Chairman.

That political movement proved short-lived, but my life returned to normal only briefly. About a month later, in September 1975, I was standing beside one of the squad leaders deep in the mine, discussing the changes in carbon monoxide level, when I heard a shrill, squealing sound somewhere above me. I knew that the feeder tracks at my feet led 150 meters upward, on an angle of 35 degrees, to the main tunnel beyond. In the pitch blackness I could see sparks flying out from the rails. Instinctively I ducked behind a post. That was all I knew for three hours. Later I learned that a chain of three steel carts, each loaded with hundred-pound pine support posts, had been improperly coupled together and had broken loose, gathering speed as it hurtled out of control down the steep grade.

When I regained consciousness, I was in the main tunnel. The fresher air had revived me. I felt waves of intense pain throughout my body. I wanted to test how seriously I was injured and turned my head slightly. At my side I recognized the blurred shape of the squad leader, Qing Niannian, and spoke his name to see whether my mind would still function. He looked scared. Until that moment he had believed I was dead.

Four squad members rushed me out of the mine in a litter made from their clothing and set me down near the entrance. The team commander had already been notified of the accident resulting from the cave-in and had ordered a coffin. Bodies pulled from a collapsed tunnel were often severely mutilated and were disposed of quickly so as not to affect workers' morale. But in the sunlight outside the mine I opened my eyes again, this time speaking the team commander's name. Realizing he would not need the coffin, he ordered a medical worker to begin emergency care.

At the clinic the doctors feared I had suffered internal injuries. Wherever they touched me, I felt sharp pain, especially in the lower abdomen. The X-rays showed seven fractures, including two broken vertebrae and two breaks in my left shoulder. After twenty hours I could urinate, so they decided against surgery and left the bones to heal themselves. Shen Jiarui cared for me in the clinic, and after a week I could use my right hand to feed myself. During the second week a layer of skin peeled off my entire body. I never understood why. After three weeks I could stand, even though every movement was painful, and after four weeks I went home.

I rarely came out of my cave during the bitter winter months. Other ex-prisoners helped my wife by carrying the cooking coal and filling the cisterns. But one unseasonably warm day at the end of December, I did step outside to sit beside the chicken coop. The feeling of the sun on my face gave me a sudden sense of well-being. Listening to the clang of mine carts below, I marveled that I was still alive. I had met the king of hell, I thought, but he had not been ready for me. For the first time in fifteen years, I actually felt a surge of hope. So many times my life had been spared, I thought. There were still things that I could accomplish and enjoy. I began to look ahead again.

Two weeks later, on January 8, 1976, I learned the news of Zhou Enlai's death. Like people throughout the nation, I felt genuine sorrow at the loss of this man who, despite his support of Chairman Mao throughout the revolutionary period, had protected many from persecution and had stood as a symbol of integrity and compassion. I understood that the Premier had helped to justify and implement the most repressive policies of the preceding decades, but he had also provided a moderating influence within the Communist Party.

Shen Jiarui returned from her labor shift that day to report that all work in the coal mine would be canceled on January 10, and that workers, along with the security guards, their families, and children, would attend a memorial ceremony. Always before the resettlement personnel had been segregated for official meetings, but this time even the thirty staff members at

Wangzhuang who were not ex-prisoners but regular members of the local community would attend. I decided I had to go.

Venturing down to the mine for the first time since my accident, I moved slowly on my crutches. Inside the hall perhaps three thousand people sat in silence as somber funeral music played. A large photograph of the Premier stood on the platform draped in black bunting. Everyone wore a black armband and had pinned on a white paper flower. Shen Jiarui, along with the other members of the women's company, had worked overnight to provide these symbols of mourning. When the ceremony began with the solemn words, "We have lost a great revolutionary, a great leader, and our most respected Premier," I saw tears in many eyes. The detachment commander himself paused in his speech to wipe his cheeks. Everyone felt the loss, believing that without Zhou Enlai's intervention, the struggles of the previous decade would have resulted in even greater suffering.

After Zhou Enlai's passing I feared that political prisoners would face a greater risk in the transitional period that loomed ahead. People guessed that Chairman Mao, long ill with Parkinson's disease, also lay close to death, but no one could tell whether power would tilt to the conservative leaders or to the moderates when he was gone. At such politically uncertain moments I feared that old enemies, like us former counterrevolutionary rightists, might serve as scapegoats to show that opposition and dissent would not be tolerated. I worried that the five kinds of enemies might be attacked the way they had been at the start of the Cultural Revolution as the signal to begin a new political movement. With the succession to power unclear, everyone felt great tension and uncertainty.

I learned of Chairman Mao's death on September 10, 1976, when I stopped for my lunch break. The resettlement worker from our company who delivered the buckets of food seemed unnaturally quiet. Before he left, he pulled me aside. He had heard mournful music on the radio, he said, then whispered to me that something had happened, the Great Leader was gone away. He did not dare use the word "dead." I felt scared even to hear him mention something so serious when so many people over the years had been arrested and executed for suggesting that harm might come to the Chairman.

"Are you sure?" I asked.

"How could I say something like that if I were not sure?" he replied. "I heard it from the Central People's Broadcast." I asked when it had happened, but he told me the radio announcement had provided no details.

Restless after this momentous news, I completed my work assignment quickly and walked out of the mine entrance at noon, two hours before the end of my shift. The captain looked at me strangely but let me pass. I returned my belt and my headlamp. Everyone seemed unusually quiet. I heard no conversations, no quarreling. I could not ask if Chairman Mao was gone, as the question might imply that I was happy at the news. I waited anxiously until the next announcement from the loudspeaker.

When the word came, I joined in the chorus of outrage and grief, shouting "Long live Chairman Mao" and pretending along with everyone else that I did not believe such a thing could happen, that it couldn't be true, that our Great Leader couldn't be gone, that he would continue to have a long, long life. Again I guessed that the political instructors at the mine would pay special attention to the attitude of intellectuals during this dangerous period, watching for any sign of opposition. Whenever they asked my opinion about what had happened, I replied, "Right now is a very sad time. I don't want to talk about it." Of course, I hoped that Mao's passing would prove favorable, but I had to be especially careful not to reveal my thoughts. I kept my mouth shut and waited to see what would happen. Over the next several weeks after Jiang Qing and her supporters took power, I sensed a change in the attitude of the mine leaders. They seemed worried and distracted, and they grew lax about political study, instructing us to read the newspapers and then leaving us to nap or write letters or do some mending.

On October 7, I came out from the mine early to make a report on air circulation. I sat down to rest beside a dozen carpentry workers who were sawing posts and loading them onto carts. A former political prisoner leaned over to me and said with a laugh, knowing I came from Shanghai, "So you make up the Gang of Five." I didn't know what he meant. I had never heard the term "Gang of Four" used to describe

Jiang Qing's clique, and I thought he referred to the fact that rightists were one of the "five black categories."

"What are you talking about?" I asked and moved away. I always refused to speak in public about politics. Only later did I realize that he had heard on the radio that morning of the sudden arrest of the four from Shanghai, including Jiang Qing. Later that day I heard the radio announcement that "a new counterrevolutionary conspiracy has been defeated and the treacherous Gang of Four crushed."

After weeks of high tension during those rapid and unexpected political events, the newly appointed Party Chairman, Hua Guofeng, tried to restore calm and confidence. He also moved the Party away from the radical policies of the late Mao era, and within weeks we faced fewer restrictions at the mine. The captains in our company sometimes talked casually with us, treating us almost as equals. Even the security guards began to relax. We still recited Chairman Mao's quotations at study meetings, but we stopped waving the red book and were rarely instructed to sing Mao's words set to music, as we had been required to do almost since the start of the Cultural Revolution. Meanwhile, the *Shanxi Daily* ran frequent stories praising their native son, Hua Guofeng, and the local cadres at the commune headquarters talked proudly of the Party's new leader.

Early in 1978 the situation for political prisoners had improved significantly. A nationwide campaign to sweep away the followers of the Gang of Four had paved the way for a transfer of leadership at all levels of the Party, and I noticed that several of the "leftist" security guards disappeared from the mine, presumably punished for their loyalty to Jiang Qing during the last stage of the Cultural Revolution. Some of my teammates received letters from relatives advising them to wait patiently, as their situation would change. For once the Party's political retaliation did not target former prisoners, and the removal of the Gang's supporters had little impact on our lives.

Sometime in May Captain Li came to me with a special request. A graduate of the Beijing College of Politics and Law, he stood out from the other security personnel because of his education, and he had always treated me with unusual respect. That day he wanted to discuss his concern about the future of his two daughters, who were seven and nine years old. They had no chance for a good education in the local school, he explained, and he wanted to ask my help in teaching them math, physics, and English. I had always loved children, so I accepted, and every evening after I had eaten, I went to Li's office to meet his daughters instead of attending study session with my squad. This special bond with a mine official fed my growing confidence that I would soon be released.

In the spring of 1978, Deng Xiaoping began to regain his power, having twice been stripped of office at Chairman Mao's order during the Cultural Revolution. The news brought a dramatic change in atmosphere at the mine. The Party cadres and security personnel understood that the political balance had decisively shifted and that Mao's followers had lost all political influence. One day in June, Captain Li informed me of a new directive, an internal document not intended for public announcement, issued to "solve the problem" of the many thousands of political prisoners who remained in labor-reform camps and resettlement facilities. The order would be implemented in stages, he explained. Nationalist officials imprisoned at the time of Liberation or during the early counterrevolutionary campaigns of the 1950s would be released first. Rightists like me imprisoned after 1957 would also be released, but not immediately.

In late August I received an envelope in the mail postmarked Xinjiang. Inside was a letter from my Geology Institute classmate Wang, whom I had last seen at the Beiyuan Chemical Factory in 1960. I had no idea how Wang learned of my assignment to Shanxi. "We face a new situation," he wrote. "The Party's policy about rehabilitating counterrevolutionaries is not yet clear, but some of us will be released. I enclose a letter for you to give to the Public Security Bureau so that your name can be cleared. Eighteen years have passed, and I want to tell the truth." The second piece of paper stated: "On September 9, 1959, I went to the Engineering Geology Bureau in the Western Hills and stole fifty yuan from an engineer's bank account. Wu Hongda is innocent. I did not tell the truth at that time because he and I would have been accused as a counterrevolutionary clique. That would have been an even more serious charge against us. After eighteen years I tell the truth."

I didn't know what to do with Wang's letter. After several

days I told Captain Li's daughters to ask their father if I could
visit him at home the next day. I knew my request was highly
irregular, as an ex-prisoner could never approach a police captain privately. The next night, I handed him Wang's letter.
"Good, good," he said after reading it. "I will check your file.
I think I can do something." Later he told me he had good
news. He would attend an important meeting in Taiyuan for
members of the Shanxi Public Security Bureau over the National Day holiday to learn about a new policy for handling the
cases of counterrevolutionary rightists. He told me to do nothing about Wang's letter until his return.

On October 5, 1978, Captain Li gave me the information I
needed. "Forget the incident with Wang, forget the fifty yuan.
The document from the Communist Party Central Committee
states that the antirightist movement was necessary but was
overextended and that most cases will be corrected. The policy
for handling rightists will soon be implemented on the provincial level. Your case as a counterrevolutionary rightist will
be completely dismissed. Just wait." I wrote to Wang, warning
him not to mention the incident with the fifty yuan again.

One by one, after arrangements had been completed for
jobs and housing in their original work units, the resettlement
prisoners at Wangzhuang who had been sentenced as counterrevolutionaries received news of their release. I waited to leave.
The formal notification that my sentence would be corrected
came in early January 1979. My life began to change rapidly.
As an ordinary citizen I could eat meals in the cadres' cafeteria,
where the meat was leaner, the vegetables fresher, and the
prices lower. More importantly I no longer had to report to the
security captains. I was no longer a secondary citizen who could
be threatened and disciplined arbitrarily but equal in status to
the cadres. I felt proud to be considered once again a member
of the working class, almost as if I had been reborn, and I began
to make final arrangements to leave.

I asked Captain Li to contact my university to request that
the department of engineering geology take me back, and also
to check Shen Jiarui's file to see if there was any way she too
could be rehabilitated. I waited for news. One afternoon he
asked me to come to his home. He told me to look at the papers
he had placed on the table. Then he left me alone. I was amazed

that he had left Shen Jiarui's personnel file open for me to see. Inside I read the police record of her case and the details of her relationship with the American POW. I also noted that she had lied to me about her age and that she was actually nine and not six years older than I. For the first time I realized the extent of her involvement with foreigners in the early 1960s and the seriousness with which her crime was regarded. Hers was not a political mistake that could be erased from her record but a civil offense that would follow her permanently.

Captain Li and his wife wanted to help me, they assured me when they came back in, but I could see there was a problem. Then Li's wife began to speak. "I want to talk frankly," she began, explaining that she had been thinking about the circumstances of my personal life. "We don't want to revive the past," she continued, "or talk about who was wrong and who was right, but we believe you deserve to have a new beginning. So you must consider your future carefully. Shen Jiarui is perhaps not suitable for you. Her political situation is very different, and you must make a serious decision."

I thought carefully about the path ahead, but I could not leave behind the person with whom I had shared nine years of my life. I told Captain Li I would not accept an assignment to Wuhan without my wife, and a week later he arranged for me to teach English and math at the newly established Shanxi College of Economics and Finance, which needed faculty. There Shen agreed to work in the library there, so I accepted the position for one year. We prepared to leave.

On February 16, 1979, a small truck from the college parked near our cave, and a neighbor helped me to load the few possessions we had accumulated since our marriage. Very early the following morning Shen Jiarui and I climbed into the cab. As we wound along the dirt road skirting the hillside, I watched the sun rise above the rim of the mountains. I could still hear the echoing sound of coal cars clanging against each other when I reached the valley. I felt a brief sense of relief to be leaving the mine behind. Then my thoughts focused on the practical matters ahead and the new surroundings I would face later that day. At that moment I had no wish to remember the past. I wanted only to keep moving on.

We settled quickly into the teachers' dormitory at the

Shanxi College of Economics and Finance, which offered a two-year program in business and accounting. Everyone at the school knew that I had just been released from the Wangzhuang Coal Mine. While the students seemed to view me with special interest, even admiration, I felt the other faculty members' scrutiny. Who was this former prisoner suddenly accorded a college teaching position, their eyes seemed to query. The skeptical glances strengthened my determination. For the first three months of the new term, I concentrated all my attention on my work, studying the teaching materials, preparing for classes, and meeting with my students, whom I found highly motivated and hungry to learn.

It seemed that each of them had experienced some personal tragedy during the Cultural Revolution, and they visited me often in the evenings, eager to recount their stories and sometimes to seek advice about their studies, their family troubles, or their future goals. I began to realize the special esteem in which rightists were held by these young people, many of whom had reached their twenties before finding a chance to continue their interrupted education. Most of those I taught had attended middle school in the 1960s and had spent a decade adrift in the society. After the schools and colleges closed during the Cultural Revolution, they had joined the army, worked in neighborhood factories, or been "sent down" to remote parts of the countryside to labor among the peasants. Once college entrance exams were reestablished in 1977, they had studied feverishly, seeing this as their only chance to improve their lives.

In March Captain Li's older daughter came to stay with us so that she could attend school away from the coal mine. This was my way to repay my benefactor. I thought about her father's two faces. He was a professional Public Security Bureau cadre, but he had shown me his human side. He had used his authority, even breaking regulations and allowing me to read a personnel file in his home, to help me leave the coal mine. He had entrusted me with his daughter. But it was also he who had written the report that led to Yang Baoying's execution, and it was his father who had eaten the dead man's brains.

As the months passed, I grew very attached to Captain Li's daughter. I also found great pleasure in the ordinary activities of daily life, like shopping for food in the market, browsing in the bookstore, and listening to classical music on the small radio I bought as soon as I had saved some money. I felt contented, appreciated, and useful. Nothing disturbed this peaceful pattern until a visit from a student one evening reminded me that my past could not so easily be left behind. This young man named Hu, a Communist Party member to whom I had spoken openly about my years in labor reform, said awkwardly that he had come to offer me some advice.

"Teacher Wu," he began, "we students like you very much, but I've come to tell you that we're also very concerned about you. Your tail is longer than anyone else's, so you must always be careful to keep it tucked between your legs." I had heard this idiomatic saying commonly in the 1950s when I was a middle school student and people used similar words to describe the cautious and submissive behavior required of intellectuals after the Communists took power. I understood my student's message. He was warning me to be alert and not to be lulled or to feel overly confident. Even though I was free, I was not an ordinary person. I had a long record, and I could not assume that I would be left alone. I thanked him, reminding myself sharply not to let down my guard. Even though the Cultural Revolution had ended and intellectuals had been restored to positions of responsibility, the Communist Party might still find some reason in the future to suppress those who had resisted its authority in the past.

22

A Resting Place

I managed to visit Father twice after my release from the Wangzhuang Coal Mine, and I watched him grow frail. He asked me repeatedly to make inquiries about the works of English literature he had translated into Chinese, as his manuscripts had been seized during the Cultural Revolution. He wanted to leave behind something of lasting value, and I promised that I would try to see them published.

During the first of those trips home in 1979, with the fear of reprisals for any who dared disclose personal suffering lifted, he and my number four sister recalled the family's difficulties over the years of our separation. Only then did I learn that my stepmother had not died of a heart attack in 1960 but had committed suicide after she received my letter from the Beiyuan Chemical Factory telling of my arrest and imprisonment. I learned that Father had been labeled a rightist in 1958 to fill the quota at his middle school, and that in 1966 he had been forced to kneel down in a public struggle meeting while my fourth sister and my sister-in-law denounced him as a "stinking reactionary" and the Red Guards beat him with their belts. I learned that my youngest brother Maodao had tried to prove his "redness" and his deep love for Chairman Mao by joining a rebel group in 1967 at the small medical clinic where he worked in distant Guizhou province. Attacked because of his reactionary family background at a struggle meeting the next year, Maodao had suffered sharp blows to his head. He survived, but the damage to his brain had left him mentally disabled and subject to epileptic seizures. My father and sister cared for him at home.

In the aftermath of the Cultural Revolution, every family coped with its own suffering. Mine was no exception. I could do nothing except absorb the events of the past and try to help with the problems that persisted, to ease the resentments that lingered and offer advice about the medical needs of my father and brother. We all had to move on.

When I visited Shanghai again in the summer of 1980, the last time I saw Father alive, he told me about a letter he had written to my elder sister, who had moved from Hong Kong to San Francisco in 1969. Father had asked her to help me visit the United States, and she had written back that a friend of hers, a medical professor at the University of California, would come to see us. Maybe later some arrangement could be made for me to leave China.

Father believed that I could never live a peaceful life in my own country. The greatest mistake he had made, he told me, was his own decision to stay behind when the People's Liberation Army advanced toward Shanghai in 1949. He had been wrong to think he could continue to work hard for his country under communist rule. He had not known what would come, and he had caused his family much suffering. He did not want me to make the same mistake. As he spoke, I sensed his regret but also his pride that I had upheld the values he cherished. I also heard his concern. To keep me from further harm, he wanted me to leave.

Father had told me many times as a child never to give in to bullying but to pick myself up again if I fell down. I had not forgotten his stern questions after two older boys bloodied my nose in a schoolyard squabble: "Did you give in? Did you stand up again?" At that moment I had wanted sympathy and comfort, but Father had responded with firmness. The lesson had stayed with me, and I used those same words to try to bolster Ao Naisong's will to live in 1964.

Father understood my stubborn spirit and my strong will. He realized I would not change. As I listened to the conclusions he drew from his own experience, I remembered my student's words of caution in Shanxi. I realized both were right. I could not assume that because I had been released, because I was an ordinary citizen once more, I would not face problems in the future. The political campaigns that had struck again and again after 1949 had taught a bitter lesson. The Communist Party would tolerate only those who tucked their tails between their legs and bowed before its absolute authority. I could not do that. I began to think seriously about going abroad.

After that visit home I moved with Shen Jiarui in the late summer of 1980 to Wuhan, sending Captain Li's daughter back to her parents. I had completed my year of teaching at the Shanxi College of Economics and Finance and had been accepted as a lecturer at the Geoscience University. That autumn I received a letter from the medical professor inviting me to California as a visiting scholar. When my sister sent me an affidavit of financial support, I applied for a passport. I filled out many forms and submitted my request to the necessary Party offices, knowing that my chance for approval was slim. My application could be denied at any point in the bureaucratic process.

I also worked hard in the engineering geology department, determined to prove my academic ability and show those at the school who had known me before that I could join them again as a faculty member, even after nineteen years at hard labor. I had not fallen down permanently. I could stand up again.

In Wuhan I began to encounter my past. On my first day back at the university, I met Wang Jian, who had risen to become head of the university's personnel office. Neither of us could forget the meeting in 1957 at which he pronounced me a counterrevolutionary rightist and an enemy of the people, but that morning he spoke all the appropriate words of welcome and concern. "Everyone feels very sorry about what happened to you," he said, "but it was not only you who had difficulty. The Party and the whole country have had a disaster. Now it is over, now we can recover. We must forget all that. We must stand shoulder to shoulder and work together. You must let me know if there is anything you need." This was the standard language for Party officials to use with those who returned to their work units after being persecuted—we were all fellow sufferers.

I had already heard the same sentiment, with only slight variations, from many others, like Comrade Ma.

In February 1980, during the previous Spring Festival vacation, I had traveled from Shanxi to Beijing at my college's expense to buy textbooks for the expanding curriculum. One day I had telephoned Comrade Ma who, like Wang Jian, had been promoted for her faithful service. Now head of the Political Work Section of the Beijing Geology Bureau's Party committee, she seemed startled to hear my voice. I asked if I could pay her a visit.

"How are you?" she greeted me cautiously when I reached her office. "You look fine."

"You've put on weight," I answered, seeing before me not the zealous young woman I remembered but an impassive middle-aged cadre.

"It's my age," she said. "How are you doing?" I guessed she must have been about forty-five.

"I'm fine," I answered. "I'm here." I had nothing to say to her, no complaint, no reproach. I just wanted her to see that I had returned, that I had never given in. To watch me standing before her was enough to make her feel shamed.

She never apologized. "It's over, it's over," she repeated. "All that happened is in the past. The whole country has suffered, our Party has suffered. There have been terrible mistakes. I'm very happy you have come back. We can do something together in the future." Just the Party language.

Maybe very deeply in some corner of her heart, I thought, Ma can feel some genuine human emotion, but I expected she would still place the welfare of the Party before the welfare of any individual person, and that she would not admit even in 1980 that the country's suffering had been caused by the Party's leadership. In 1957 she had been young and trusting. She had believed everything the Party did was right. Now her face looked lined and her bluntly cut hair showed streaks of grey. As I looked around that room, I felt a brief moment of triumph. You can destroy many people, I told her silently, but you cannot destroy them all. I felt that hers was the life that had ended, while mine was just starting again.

On that trip back to Beijing, I also traced a former squadmate from Tuanhe Farm named Liu, one of the activists who in 1968 at Qinghe had written reports about my reactionary thoughts at the time I tried to conceal my foreign novels. Liu's report on my love for *Les Miserables* had earned him two days rest from labor, but it had also contributed to the struggle meeting's fury that ended with Fan Guang smashing a spade handle down on my forearm. I never mentioned that incident.

Instead I asked Liu about Ao Naisong's disappearance. Their group had been transferred as resettlement prisoners to Qinghe Farm in 1966, Liu told me, and just a few weeks later, Ao had spent all his savings to buy quantities of porkhead meat, peanuts, biscuits, and sorghum wine. He invited his friends to join him for a special lunch and before they parted gave away his possessions, his fountain pen to one friend, his small English dictionary to another, and his bicycle to Liu. "We didn't understand Ao's generosity, but we all took a nap after lunch," Liu recalled. "By the time we woke up, Ao was gone." Back in the dormitory, they found his lute still hanging on the wall, but Ao was missing. Several days later Liu and another squadmate noticed a rope tied around a tree trunk near their labor site. They pulled on the line and at the other end found Ao's body with a rock tied around his waist.

A rightist like me, Liu had been given a post as senior interpreter at Xinhua News Agency after his release in 1979. He lived in a comfortable apartment, he was about to remarry, and he clearly wanted not to remember his own actions in the past, not to talk at all about political issues. Instead he wanted me to admire his goldfish tank, which gave him great pleasure. Liu had found a peaceful life, I thought, but somehow he reminded me of those goldfish, swimming mindlessly around and around inside their tank.

On that trip to Beijing I also found my friend Wu, the water controller who had sent the woman to me in 1965 with a package of precious meat. Wu told me his wife had been sick on the day they planned the family visit to Tuanhe Farm, and that her sister had offered to go in her place. Wu had later divorced his peasant wife and remarried, but he knew the sister's name and address, far away on the eastern edge of the city. The next day I left by bus to find the woman whose face had stayed in my thoughts for fifteen years. The trip took two hours.

Some neighbors directed me to a newly built house of mud

bricks, not yet whitewashed. Chickens pecked in the yard. A short, round-faced woman with a kerchief covering her hair stepped out of the door. Her eyes were very clear, and I saw the small scar below one brow. "Do you remember me?" I asked. "At Tuanhe Farm you helped me, you brought me some meat, do you remember?"

She nodded, invited me inside, and grabbed a cloth to wipe the dust from the seat of a wooden chair. I noticed a stale smell and saw clothes scattered on the tamped earth floor beside a bucket of dirty laundry water. She poured me a cup of hot water, apologizing for not being able to offer tea. For half an hour I listened to her tell about the hardships she faced. She was recently divorced, her husband had drunk heavily and sometimes beaten her, she had two children, she still worked in the fields and had to feed the pigs and chickens. Her words tumbled out. I felt depressed to realize the difficulties she faced living her ordinary life. She asked if I would move back to Beijing. She seemed to hope I might somehow solve her problems.

"I wanted to come to thank you," I said. "Your visit was so important to me, and I always remembered your kindness. Let me know if I can do anything for you." That day I had twenty-five yuan in my pocket, and when she turned away, I slipped the money under a plate on her table. I had no other way to help. Then I said I must go. I looked back once and saw her still standing at the corner of the house. The distance grew between us, and I knew I would not see her again. I had repaid my debt as best I could. I had my own life to lead, my own problems to solve.

That fall in Wuhan, shortly after the start of my work at the engineering geology department, a telegram arrived from my sister. Father was dead. I reached Shanghai on September 12, 1980, and took a bus to the morgue. The hospital workers removed Father's icy body from the refrigerator unit so that I could say good-bye. I ran my hands from his face to his toes. My sister wept beside me, but I had seen too much death. I had no tears.

His death had come suddenly. One evening he had complained of severe abdominal pain. Knowing the end was near, he left me a parting message. "Tell Number Three to get back my translations," he whispered to his brother's grandson, then living with him in Shanghai. "And tell him he cannot stay here. This is not the place for him." By midnight Father was gone.

At home I helped my sister make final arrangements for Father's cremation. I also met with two cadres from his middle school who came to discuss the details of his final retirement pay as well as the statement they would make, representing his work unit, at his memorial service. They showed me the remarks they had prepared. I read quickly the official language.

I had not seen my older brother since our meeting in the Beiyuan Chemical Factory's visiting room in 1960. Twenty years had passed. Drawn together again for our father's funeral, we never mentioned that outburst but spoke casually and politely. As the eldest, my brother should have made a statement at the memorial service on behalf of our family, but he felt uncomfortable writing the words of leave-taking and asked me to draft something for him to read.

"Our father has already gone," I wrote. "In his life he suffered ever since the early 1950s. He was persecuted in 1952, 1958, and 1966. Each time he was innocent. After he was rehabilitated in 1960, he lost his wife, and he was cut off from his son. In 1966 he lost all his remaining property. Even today the situation of his property is not clear. For our family all this is a tragedy."

"You can't say this," my brother yelled when he read my words. "Are you crazy?"

"No, this is the last time we can say something for our father," I replied firmly. "If we don't tell the truth now, we will have no other chance."

"I understand that what you write is true," my brother replied, trying to reason with me, "but don't ask for more trouble."

"All we've had is trouble, so what's the difference?" I said.

"Now I understand why you became a rightist," he said, his tone changed.

Then I too became sharp. "We're not talking about my situation, we're talking about the memorial service," I said. "If you agree with my statement, read it. If you don't agree, write it by yourself. You are the representative of the family." He took the paper and walked out, then returned and told me to read it myself.

The middle school cadres came again, wanting to check our family's statement before the service. They had to make sure our remarks were acceptable. I watched the Party secretary's face cloud as she read what I had written. "This is not satisfactory," she declared sharply. "The past is the past. We know your father very well, and he was a good man. The Cultural Revolution was very bitter, but you must think about his whole life, about our motherland, and about our great Party."

"This is our family's opinion," I stated. "If you find I have said something untrue, please tell me."

"I'm not saying that it is wrong or right," the secretary answered placatingly, "but we want the memorial service to proceed smoothly and also to suit the current situation."

When I insisted that the statement expressed our family's opinion, she left, then returned with another person a short while later. "We disagree with your decision to make such a statement," she declared. "If you insist on this kind of speech, we cannot hold the memorial service."

"Cancel the service if you want," I replied, "but this is our opinion. These are our last words to express our feelings about our father." At that point my brother drew me aside and rebuked me for jeopardizing the memorial service when the family members and my father's friends had been invited. I backed down. I agreed to rewrite my statement, and the Party committee members looked relieved.

The next morning in the formal meeting room at the crematorium, the Party secretary read her statement. Then came my turn. I stepped forward, pulled the revised speech from my jacket pocket, and felt my hand drop to my side. I couldn't read those words. My voice choked with emotion as I spoke out exactly what I had written the first time. Beside me, my brother pulled on my jacket, but I brushed away his hand. Everyone stared, but no one could stop me. Then the service was over. Father's friends shook my hand. One said, "You spoke well, you spoke well." I knew everyone realized that I had spoken the truth.

Back at home my brother asked to talk to me, his face tense with anger. "Now I realize what kind of person you are," he began, "and I want to raise two questions. First, do you know how much damage has been caused to our family by your becoming a rightist? Second, out of so many students at your university, why did you become a rightist, and why out of those who became rightists were you one of the few to be arrested?"

I felt my face flush with anger. "First," I said, "I certainly realize the hurt I have caused my family, but I am innocent, and I am the person hurt most of all. Second, I don't know why other students did not become rightists, but I want to ask you, do you think even as a rightist I deserved this persecution?" My brother didn't answer, and we didn't speak again.

I thought many times after that about his words. I knew my brother was not a bad person, I knew he too disliked the Communist Party, but after his trouble in 1955 he had surrendered. He became accommodating and pragmatic. Even though he had suffered a few times, more often he had succeeded. He had a good job, he was trusted by the government, he had two children, he could enjoy his family life, while I had lost twenty years and had several times come close to death. Maybe people have to be pragmatic, I thought. Maybe he is cleverer than I. Maybe his is the better way. But another voice inside me called out: Someone has to stand up.

A year later, in October 1981, I received another urgent telegram from my sister telling me to come home immediately. My youngest brother was dead. She was very upset when I arrived after two days on the train from Wuhan. She explained that Maodao had been increasingly strong-willed and often refused to stay at home. He had told my sister repeatedly that he wanted to marry and have a family, that he didn't want to spend his life as an invalid. He had left the house two weeks before and not come back. My sister had reported his disappearance to the local police, and they had located him in a hospital in Beijing. They told her to wait for further news. The next time they came, they informed her Maodao was dead. They had not allowed her to see the body, and she had waited for me to come.

I knew immediately something was wrong, even before two policemen from Beijing arrived to explain their findings in the case. "Your brother was very weak. We tried to save him. We took him to the hospital in Beijing and then to the Number Nine People's Hospital in Shanghai. There was nothing more we could do. We are very sorry. We will take care of all the arrangements. Please trust the government and do not take your loss too hard." They still would not tell us where we could find Maodao's body, even when we insisted that his family had the right to say good-bye.

I cycled immediately to the Number Nine People's Hospital and found that my brother's name did not appear in the registration book. I refused to leave. Finally a nurse showed me a separate book listing those dead on arrival. There, crossed out with a red line, I found the name Wu Hongren. During the following week I pressed the police for an explanation. At last they allowed us to see the body, and immediately I noticed bruises on the arms and legs. From then on I knew for certain my brother had not died from illness. I could not let the official explanation pass, and I refused to sign a release for them to proceed with the cremation. Step by step, despite many evasions and lies, I uncovered Maodao's story.

My brother had taken a train to Beijing to apply at the Great Hall of the People for reinstatement of his medical worker's registration. In their effort to clean up the streets of the capital before the October 1 National Day holiday, the police arrested him as a vagrant. Held in jail, he refused to eat and then spent three days in a police hospital in Beijing before being loaded onto a boxcar with more than one hundred other prisoners for return to Shanghai. On the train the guards beat him.

Having learned that much, I agreed to release the body for cremation. I could do nothing more to help Maodao, and I believed the two policemen dispatched to handle the case in Shanghai could not answer my final question about the actual cause of my brother's death. They didn't know, and it was not they whom I wished to hold accountable. I would have to go to Beijing to press my inquiry.

Ten family members gathered at the cremation hall to pay their last respects to Maodao. From behind a curtain, a worker wheeled a cart draped with a paper sign that read "Wu Hongren Memorial Ceremony." Our brother was dressed in new clothes, and his face showed the signs of makeup. "Go ahead," I told him silently as I held his cold hand. "Don't come back. You are fortunate to leave this world behind. You have finished your life, and your suffering is over. Go be with our parents. They will care for you now. Everything will be peaceful ahead." Funeral music played, but this time there were no speeches. No words seemed better than any words. A worker pushed the body back through the curtain. My heart remained hard, and no tears came.

Outside I asked one of the Beijing policemen to give me the claim check so I could return to pick up my brother's ashbox. I knew he was lying when he said he didn't have it and I should just come back in three days to ask for the ashes. This was his way of exercising power and exacting revenge.

"This was our brother," I shouted. "How dare you keep the claim check for his ashes?" The family and the Shanghai police representatives surrounded me, trying to calm me down. I regained my control, then spat out, "Take it with you. I will not give up. Wait for me in Beijing." There was nothing more I could do in Shanghai, so I returned to Wuhan where my teaching responsibilities continued.

Throughout that year I wrote several letters to the Beijing Public Security Bureau asking for the claim check for my brother's ashes, but I received no reply. I could not ask for leave again and had to wait for summer vacation to travel to Beijing. Ten months passed before I could pursue any further the actual cause of my brother's death. During that interval much happened in my own life.

The Party leaders at my university continued to deny my request for a passport. I had done important work in setting up the new engineering hydrology laboratory, they said, and I was badly needed by my colleagues and my students. They hoped I would think more about my university's development and less about my personal wishes. They felt sure I would agree to postpone my request to travel abroad.

I had no choice. I knew their polite language was a way of letting me know I still was not trusted and was not being accorded the privilege of travel. Concerned that my sister's affidavit of financial support would expire and that I would lose my only chance to go to the United States, I disregarded their polite appeal and asked again for approval. One day the Party secretary called me in. The university had agreed to my request, he said, but I would not be able to leave until I had solved my family problem. I asked what he was talking about. He said my wife objected to my going abroad.

I had talked about this decision many times with Shen Jiarui. At first she had disagreed, saying she feared I would not come back and she would have no future. "Listen," I had told her. "I have a big tail, they can catch me again any time. We must grab this chance. I will go first and find some way to send for you." Later she agreed to support me. I could not believe she would betray me to the Party secretary.

At home I told Shen Jiarui angrily that I had intended to stay with my marriage, that I had refused the chance to divorce her in 1979, that I had found a way to take her out of the camp and had insisted on a job for her together with me in Wuhan. The one thing I could not tolerate was for her to stand with the Communist Party in the effort to prevent my freedom. For me this was the most terrible thing. We quarreled and moved into separate rooms.

Later that year I decided to request a divorce. The tensions between us already made daily life difficult. Then I learned that her youngest son, whom I had adopted in 1970, had sold to some foreigners three of the paintings left me by my father. The previous summer I had visited a large warehouse in Shanghai filled with the loot carted away by Red Guards during the Cultural Revolution and had managed to identify just a few of Father's possessions. I had left seven paintings in a shop to be remounted and had given the receipts to Shen Jiarui's son, who offered to retrieve them after I returned to Wuhan. Instead he used them as a source of easy cash. For me that was the last straw. I wanted nothing more to do with my wife or her son. My marriage was over.

When classes ended in July 1982, I traveled to Beijing to pursue my brother's case. I began at the lowest level with a policeman at the front desk of the Public Security Bureau and carefully explained my request for Maodao's ashes. He told me to return for an interview in two days. When I refused to wait that long, he threatened not to consider the case at all. Without asking for permission, I walked down the hallway until I found an office with a sign that read "Beijing Public Security Bureau Party Committee." Very angry by then, I knocked.

More talk, more delay, more evasion followed, but the Party cadre knew I had evidence of police abuse and wanted to settle the case. "We must criticize ourselves," he said. "We confess we did some things that are wrong. Your family still does not have your brother's ashes. That is not right. We accept your criticism of our part in this matter and will try to make improvement. Our two policemen, not knowing the policy, failed to give you the claim check for the ashbox. We have not had time to notify you. We are very sorry about this." I left with the claim check in my hand.

From Beijing I returned to Shanghai to collect my brother's ashes. I knew the time had come to fulfill my last responsibility to my departed family members. With a cousin's help I had arranged to purchase a small burial plot in Wuxi on a hillside overlooking Lake Tai. There my stepmother, my father, and my brother could rest peacefully. I bought a ticket on a local train from Shanghai to Wuxi and took with me three ashboxes, as well as the stele engraved with my mother's name. My father had buried her in a grave beneath a marble monument in 1945, but the Red Guards had ransacked that cemetery in 1966, toppling her gravestone in their frenzied sweeping away of the "four olds." I could do nothing to reclaim her body. The small ivory stele, hidden away in our attic, was all that remained.

I watched the two cemetery workers finish preparing a hole, then paid them and asked them to leave. For more than an hour I sat alone in that beautiful place as the sun set over Lake Tai. With Maodao's death my family's suffering was over. At the same time my marriage had ended and my chance to travel abroad seemed lost. I had no sense of where I was going, but the heavy burden of all those problems had lifted from my shoulders. The things that have happened are past, I thought, and whatever will come still lies ahead. I felt peaceful. Somehow I believed my life would improve. I would move ahead.

Epilogue

I left China in 1985 after waiting more than four years for a passport. I barely scraped together enough money for my air ticket by selling my possessions and borrowing from friends. I arrived in San Francisco with forty dollars in my pocket. During my first weeks in the United States, I worked day and night, even sleeping on the desk in my university office so that I could stay awake to work the late shift in a Berkeley doughnut shop. My older sister could not help me financially, and I wanted to rent an apartment and get established quickly.

A year before I had wed a young graduate of the Geoscience University. In Wuhan she had visited me many times in the evenings, and after my divorce, as we talked and walked together, our understanding grew. Despite twenty-six years' difference in our ages, we fell in love. We planned that she would follow me to the United States as soon as I could get settled and arrange for her financial sponsorship. Half a year later she arrived, only to tell me she had fallen in love with someone else. By then she called herself Diana. I let her go, wanting her to be happy.

That first year I read a number of books about China written in English. I found that none of the histories or memoirs included any contemporary detail about the labor-reform camps, even though that experience had affected many thousands of my countrymen during the past forty years. I began to consider writing about my own past and trying also to document the organizational structure of the Chinese prison system. At the University of California, Santa Cruz, in 1986, I gave a talk to students and faculty, recounting for the first time in public many of the events in my personal life. Before that sympathetic audience the tears rolled down my cheeks. For the first time I wept.

In 1988 I became an associate of Stanford University's Hoover Institute and a year later completed the research for a documentary study of China's reeducation-through-labor system. In 1992 I set up the nonprofit Laogai Foundation, and I also told the full story of my life to Carolyn Wakeman.

Meanwhile in 1991 I married a woman from Taiwan named Ching-lee. For the first time I found deep personal happiness, but just four months after our wedding I arranged to travel back to China with a CBS camera crew. I believed people in the West did not grasp the critical role of the labor camp system in supporting and perpetuating Communist Party rule, and I wanted to record on film the conditions within the vast network of China's secret prison facilities. I wanted to provide visual images to show the world the camps into which I and so many others had disappeared. Outside China much was known about Nazi concentration camps and about the Soviet gulag, but almost no information was available about the carefully developed system of forced labor that had kept millions of Chinese citizens incarcerated in sometimes brutal and dehumanizing conditions, frequently without sentence or trial.

Returning to China with this objective meant risking my own rearrest and reimprisonment. Despite the danger, my wife Ching-lee insisted on accompanying me. We both recognized that the Chinese government would act harshly toward anyone trying to expose its labor-reform system and its sale of prison labor products to international buyers. Before I left California I made out a will.

As a precaution David Gelber from CBS News and Orville Schell, the American writer and China scholar, interviewed me on camera in April 1991 outside an old fort at the entrance to San Francisco Bay with the Golden Gate Bridge in the background. I felt as if we were preparing a final bit of evidence in case anything unexpected should happen during my journey. Perhaps I would once again disappear.

During that interview I explained my reasons for returning to China. Even though I had wanted to forget the suffering of the past after arriving in the United States and had wanted to heal the wounds in my heart, the nineteen years of sorrow would not stop returning to my mind. I could not forget what I had experienced or those who still suffered inside the camps. If I didn't undertake this task, I asked, who would?

I arrived in Tianjin after a flight from Hong Kong on June 9, 1991, and registered my visa with the Chinese Customs Office. At the crowded railway station the next morning, I hired a passenger van, scrutinizing carefully the faces of several different drivers to try to discover one who was unlikely to be an agent of the Public Security Bureau. I told the driver we were going to visit a friend who worked as a security guard at the Qinghe Farm. Fortunately he asked no questions.

At the Yonghe Bridge over the Yongding River, the driver offered some explanation to an armed police guard, who let us pass. In front of us stretched Qinghe's western district, which I had not seen since 1969. Ten minutes farther down the road, we passed a twenty-foot brick wall topped with electrified wires. Its iron gates stood tightly closed. Above them I saw a sign announcing the Beijing Qinghe Shrimp Farm. During the winter of 1961–62, I had spent four months close to starvation inside those walls in the area I knew then as Section 585.

I asked the driver to stop so that my wife could urinate. When he objected that this was not a good spot, I insisted her need was urgent, and he stopped the van near the gates. We walked along a narrow path, following the curve of the wall. Ching-lee carried a videocamera hidden inside her shoulder bag, its lens protruding through a small hole, so that she could photograph the surroundings. In a few moments we reached the graveyard I had known as section 586. The reeds grew as tall as my head and whistled in the wind. The past rushed before me, but I had no time to reflect. I heard footsteps behind us.

"Hurry! Finish shooting the camera," I urged Ching-lee, "and squat down in the ditch." A security guard wearing a straw hat shouted at us.

"What are you doing? You can't stop here." I told him my wife had to urinate. "Leave immediately," he ordered us.

"Talk to him," Ching-lee insisted, "so I can film more."

"How much do those pigs weigh?" I asked the guard, pointing to the fields. "They look as if they weigh two hundred pounds. What do you feed them?"

"Who are you? Where are you from?" he challenged.

"We are from Shanghai on our way to Chadian to visit a friend who works in the farm headquarters," I answered to give Ching-lee time to videotape. The guard let us pass, and we climbed back into the van.

As we drove, I could see hundreds of prisoners on the north side of the road, digging a long expanse of irrigation ditch. Most of them worked without shirts in the summer heat. The labor conditions seemed not to have changed since 1969. Soon we passed other prisoners working in vineyards, in rice fields, and repairing roads. All the while Ching-lee pointed the concealed camera out of the window.

"Thank you very much," I said to the driver when we had returned safely to a village on the outskirts of Tianjin. I asked him to drop us at a small restaurant and paid his fee, then watched him drive away. We returned by bus to the city and caught an evening train to Beijing.

On June 13 Ching-lee and I rented bicycles and rode out to the Tuanhe Farm southwest of the capital. The traveling bag containing the small videocamera sat in her bicycle basket. Taking a side path onto the farm property, we stopped while I pretended to fix her bicycle. Ching-lee pressed the button on my camera and began to film. Suddenly two other bicycles appeared. One blocked the path ahead of me while the other rammed purposely into my bike from behind to knock me to the ground. A security policeman twisted my arms against my back.

When I insisted I was a visitor from the United States, he released his grip, telling me that this was a forbidden area and that I would have to pay a fine. I argued that I had lost my way and that I had seen no sign prohibiting entrance. Then I stuffed a wad of money into his hand. He seemed satisfied, and we climbed onto our bicycles and pedaled away.

Two days later, warned by an American friend who served as our contact that he was being followed, we left Beijing immediately by train for Shanxi province. At the railway station in Taiyuan, I hired a taxi, hoping to visit three labor-reform coal mines where I could find ex-prisoners who had worked with me fifteen years before. I knew my contacts would not ask questions and would provide whatever assistance I asked. By then I needed to learn whether the Public Security Bureau had discovered my activities, so I decided to stop first at the mine where I was well known. If I was not arrested there, I could gamble that for the moment my objectives had not been detected.

At the Wangzhuang Coal Mine, Ching-lee and I went immediately to visit the detachment commander, named Liu Sheng, who as head of the mine's production section in 1975 had waited at the tunnel entrance for me to emerge after a serious cave-in. That day he had expected to see a corpse, but had found me still alive. Liu Sheng greeted me warmly, pleased to establish contact with a former resettlement prisoner who had returned from the United States. He offered us tea and asked us many questions about life in California—what kind of house we lived in, whether I could drive a car, how much money I earned. Later he invited us to stay overnight in his room, but I refused politely, while Ching-lee used the cover of our visit to record with the videocamera the surroundings where I had labored for nine years.

The next day, June 19, we reached the Yinying Coal Mine, which I knew by its internal name as the Shanxi Number 2 Labor Reform Detachment. There I found two workers I knew well who had been transferred from Wangzhuang in 1978, and I asked them to take me up to the hills near a mine entrance. Ching-lee climbed behind me along the rough path, photographing the dormitories and the watchtowers below as well as our guides. I knew I could trust my old friends, but I feared at each step that we would be discovered.

The next morning one of them went with us by bus to the Guzhuang Coal Mine, also called the Shanxi Number 13 Labor Reform Detachment, which was twenty kilometers away. He told us to wait in an empty dormitory room while he found some workers whom we could interview on camera. For more than three hours, I asked these men questions about their past, their life at the mine, their labor, their salary, their visiting rights, their current political status, trying to learn how much the situation of resettlement workers had changed since my release in 1979.

Late in the afternoon I told my friend to arrange for me to enter the mine itself. He warned me that the risk of detection underground was too great, then reluctantly brought me a helmet, some boots, and a toolbag for my camera. We waited for darkness. At nine o'clock I entered the tunnel, blackened my face with coal dust, and climbed onto a motorized cart that one of the workers, a labor monitor, would drive. I tried to film in the dim light inside the mine. An hour later I returned to the dormitory and thanked my guide for taking such a risk. Ching-lee and I reached Taiyuan the next day and flew to Shanghai.

There I adopted the identity of a business representative for an American company. Ching-lee posed as my secretary. We visited the Shanghai Laodong Machinery Factory, the Shanghai Laodong Steel Pipe Factory, and the Huadong Electric Welding Factory. Our goal was to obtain an export contract for forced labor products and official brochures describing the prison labor enterprises, and also to film the surroundings where forced labor products were manufactured. I had hoped to pass the completed videotapes to another American contact. When that person proved unwilling to carry out the films for me, I again feared discovery and immediately changed course, hiring a taxi to Hangzhou. There I had a friend who had been released from the Wangzhuang Coal Mine in 1979.

My former squadmate asked no questions when I appeared suddenly at his home. I wanted him to take one of Ching-lee's suitcases through customs at the Hangzhou airport and check it as unaccompanied cargo on the flight to Hong Kong. I had wrapped the videotapes in some clothing inside the suitcase and had also hidden duplicates somewhere inside China as a precaution. I gave my friend some money in an envelope and my wife's airline ticket, asking him to meet her after checking the luggage and pass her the ticket two hours before the plane's departure. He took a considerable risk, but the plan worked smoothly. Ching-lee concealed eight other rolls of film and some of the written materials from the labor-reform enterprises inside her shoes and her underwear, and we flew to Hong Kong separately.

On July 24 I returned to China alone, preparing to travel with the CBS News crew. I made some arrangements by telephone and fax to inform the Shanghai Laodong Machinery Factory that I would be returning in ten days prepared to sign a contract. Then I left by myself for Qinghai province far to the northwest, site of the largest concentration of labor-reform camps in China. Orville Schell tried to persuade me by telephone not to undertake this journey, knowing that no one could protect me in remote Qinghai if my clandestine activities inside the camps were discovered. I felt grateful for his concern, but again I knew that no one else could obtain information about this remote and secret area. If I didn't go, who would?

An ex-prisoner named Zhou met me in Xining, the capital of Qinghai province. After serving an eight-year sentence for counterrevolutionary crimes from 1956 to 1964, he had remained for twenty-seven years as a resettlement worker. He showed me a number of factories along Nanshan Street that looked on the outside like ordinary state-owned enterprises but that in fact were labor-reform facilities. "One-third of the population of Qinghai province," Zhou told me, "consists of resettlement prisoners and their families." Their labor had been used, he told me, to reclaim wasteland, construct roads, open up mines, and build dams, not just prior to 1979 but throughout the 1980s.

At the Qinghai Hide and Garment Factory, whose internal name was the Qinghai Number 2 Labor Reform Detachment, I presented the business card of an American company manager. The detachment leaders offered to sell me 200,000 square feet of lambskins for $1.49 per square foot. They told me proudly that they had their own Hong Kong sales agents and that they had exported their products to Japan and Australia. After I visited the factory's workshops, I asked a manager named Wan about the skills of his workers and whether he could guarantee the quality of his products. He escorted me to the company's display room and allowed me to take photographs of their medals and awards, some sample orders from foreign countries, and an export license. I even managed to point my lens quickly at the one item he told me not to photograph, a banner hanging on the rear wall commending the factory as an "advanced collective for suppressing rebellion and preventing chaos" and dated October 1989, four months after the June 1989 democracy movement had been stopped by the army's tanks and guns in Tiananmen Square.

At last, I thought, I can show the world evidence of the two functions of the labor-reform camps. Politically they suppress dissidents to reinforce the system of dictatorship, while economically they exploit prisoners to earn foreign exchange for the Chinese communist regime.

Back at the hotel I asked Zhou to get me a Public Security guard's uniform. "Don't ask questions," I told him. "I'm going out to hire a taxi. Tomorrow I'll visit the labor-reform camps in the Chaidamu Basin." I planned to cover about two thousand kilometers on my six-day journey, visiting six to eight labor-reform camps on both banks of the Qinghai Lake.

My first stop was Tanggemu Farm, the headquarters of the Qinghai Number 13 Labor Reform Detachment. In this remote region there were no tourists, no outsiders, and no regular residents. I had decided to adopt the identity of a Public Security Bureau correspondent so that I could walk around carrying a videocamera. I asked the driver to stop at Tanggemu. Then I walked for about two hours, trying to see how close I could get to the prison buildings. I picked my way across the barren terrain, then somehow stepped into a twelve-foot-deep gully. I knew immediately that my left shoulder was dislocated, but I managed to climb out and return to the car for help.

The driver wanted me to go back to Xining immediately for medical care, but I refused to leave empty-handed. I persuaded the driver to twist and pull my arm until he had snapped the shoulder bone back into place. Then I borrowed his belt and strapped my arm firmly against my waist. I set out on the road with my camera bag again, wishing I had not thrown away my bottle of Advil. I had feared that my foreign medicine would identify me as an American if I were ever searched. Near the entrance gates I managed to blend in with a crowd of security guards and prisoners leaving for their work sites in the fields and to run the videocamera using only my right arm.

Because of my accident I had to cut short my travel in Qinghai. Back in Shanghai the first thing I did was to telephone Ching-lee in America. She was relieved to hear my voice after five days without contact. Then I bought some medicine for pain relief and took a bath.

After my return from Qinghai, I waited with the CBS reporters on August 12, 1991, in a suite at Shanghai's Portman Hotel, where the delegation from the Shanghai Laodong Machinery Factory would meet us to sign a contract. The cameraman, posing as my company's executive secretary, had hidden three different cameras inside the room so that he could shoot from different angles. The negotiations proceeded smoothly and, joined by Ed Bradley, the host of the CBS program "60 Minutes" who posed as the president of our company, we signed an agreement to purchase $88,000 worth of goods.

On September 15, 1991, CBS aired the "60 Minutes" program about my return to China, documenting the extent of the labor-reform system and the government's sale of forced-labor products. A cover story on the Chinese gulag appeared the same day in the international edition of *Newsweek* magazine. On September 19, China's Foreign Ministry spokesman Wu Jianmin released a statement. "CBS and *Newsweek* magazine have severely distorted the facts. They are notorious for vilifying China. This results from their ideological prejudice and their extreme hatred of the Chinese socialist system, which has been chosen by the Chinese people. The author has mistaken black for white and confused right with wrong." For me it was another small triumph.

*   *   *

At different times during my years as a prisoner, the thought had returned that someday I would tell people what happened behind the walls of China's labor-reform camps. Partly for that reason I practiced the complicated strategies of elephant chess in my mind and took care to store facts, speeches, and scenes in my memory. When other inmates beat me severely at the Cultural Revolution struggle meeting, I reached up to shield my head from injury. After my squadmates pried me loose from the stones and timbers of a coal mine collapse, my first impulse was to test my ability to think and speak. I had learned not to care if they hurt my body, but I had to keep my mind intact so that I could remember.

My travels in 1991, when I returned to China to film the conditions within the labor camps, fulfilled part of a consuming mission. Even though I had found safety in the United States, I had never found rest. Always I recalled the faces I had left behind. Always I worried that while I had escaped, the labor-reform system continued to operate, day by day, year by year, largely unnoticed, unchallenged, and therefore unchanged. I felt urgently the responsibility not just to disclose but to publicize the truth about the Communist Party's mechanisms of control, whatever the risk to me, whatever the discomfort of telling my story. Each time I revisited my past, I hoped it would be the last time, but I had decided that my experiences belonged not only to me and not only to China's history. They belonged to humanity.

Index